Donald H. Sheridan
Southwestern Community College

Basic
Communication
Skills

Charles E. Merrill Publishing Company
A Bell & Howell Company
Columbus, Ohio

THE MERRILL SERIES IN CAREER PROGRAMS

LIBRARY
University of Texas
At San Antonio

International Standard Book Number: 0–675–09238–8

Library of Congress Catalog Card Number: 72–143450

2 3 4 5 6 7 8—76 75 74 73 72 71
Printed in the United States of America

THE MERRILL SERIES
IN CAREER
PROGRAMS

In recent years our nation has literally rediscovered education. Concurrently, many nations are considering educational programs in revolutionary terms. They now realize that education is the responsible link between social needs and social improvement. While traditionally Americans have been committed to the ideal of the optimal development of each individual, there is increased public appreciation and support of the values and benefits of education in general, and vocational and technical education in particular. With occupational education's demonstrated capacity to contribute to economic growth and national well being, it is only natural that it has been given increased prominence and importance in this educational climate.

With the increased recognition that the true resources of a nation are its human resources, occupational education programs are considered a form of investment in human capital—an investment which provides comparatively high returns to both the individual and society.

The Merrill Series in Career Programs is designed to provide a broad range of educational materials to assist members of the profession in providing effective and efficient programs of occupational education which contribute to an individual's becoming both a contributing economic producer and a responsible member of society.

The series and its sub-series do not have a singular position or philosophy concerning the problems and alternatives in providing the broad range of offerings needed to prepare the nation's work force. Rather, authors are encouraged to develop and support independent positions and alternative strategies. A wide range of educational and occupational experiences and perspectives have been brought to bear through the Merrill Series in Career Programs National Editorial Board. These experiences, coupled with those of the authors, assure useful publications. I believe that this title, along with others in the series, will provide major assistance in further developing and extending viable educational programs to assist youth and adults in preparing for and furthering their careers.

Robert E. Taylor
Editorial Director
Series in Career Programs

PREFACE

Many instructors have been forced to try to adapt textbooks directed toward the liberal arts student to meet the needs of vocational and technical students in a terminal program. This misapplication of material is an injustice, since it fails to recognize the differences in the types of students using the material and in the future utilization of this material, as well as in the basic skills themselves.

It is the expressed purpose of this book to challenge these career students with many of the ideas and concepts used in the academic areas, *plus* materials of a more specialized nature—allowing only for the difference in the application of the same learned skills.

This book, *Basic Communication Skills,* is an end product of experiences in teaching students in career programs. The division of the book into five parts provides a logical sequence for the discussion of the communication process. Part I explains the stimulus-response basis of communication, with a series of visual stimuli intended to evoke emotional responses. The basic theories of communication and the use of words to convey accurately the speaker's meaning are the subjects of the second part. The third part is concerned with written communication, including discussions of sentences, paragraphs, outlining, and basic grammar rules. Part IV outlines the procedures of oral communication of all types. The book concludes with selected readings, which are specifically intended to help career programs students become aware of representative materials published in their own professional journals.

Throughout the text, after each major topic, sample exercises are provided for practice and reinforcement of the principles being discussed.

I am indebted to Dr. Robert E. Taylor, Judy Nichols and Lynne Wakefield for their helpful criticism, advice and assistance in the preparation of this text. Also, a special thanks to Rus and a small task force called "The Group."

Donald H. Sheridan

CONTENTS

Part I   **A Response Must Have a Stimulus**   **1**

Part II   **Understanding Ourselves through Communication**   **33**

Chapter 1   Words and Meaning   35

The Real World and the World of Words, 35;
Connotation and Denotation, 38; *Exercises*, 40

Chapter 2   Language, Thought and Behavior   43

Perception and Observation, 43; *Exercises*, 47;
Inference and Assumption, 47; *Exercises*, 51;
Distortion, 52; *Exercises*, 61; *Judgment or Fact?*
63; *Exercises*, 65; *Propaganda and Advertising*, 66;
Exercises, 72

Part III   **Shaping the Written Response**   **73**

Chapter 1   The Topic Sentence and the
Controlling Idea   75

Exercises, 79

Chapter 2   Paragraph Development   81

Details, 81; *Exercises*, 83; *Comparison and
Contrast*, 84; *Exercises*, 86; *Illustration*, 87;
Exercises, 88; *Reasons*, 89; *Exercises*, 90;
Chronological Order, 92; *Cause and Effect*, 93;
Exercises, 94

Chapter 3   Outlining Procedures   95

Topic Outline vs. Sentence Outline, 98;
Exercises, 100

Chapter 4   Rewriting and Proofreading
Exercises   103

Part IV   **Shaping the Oral Response**   **111**

*The Impromptu Speech—or—"C'mon in, the
water's fine."*, 114; *Some Self-Starters for
Impromptu Speeches*, 117

Chapter 1   Some Speech Mechanics   119

Notes, 119; *Rehearsals*, 121; *Introductions*, 122;
Conclusions, 124; *The Importance of Bodily
Actions*, 126; *Exercises*, 128

Chapter 2   The Speech to Inform   131

Introduction to the Informative Speech, 131; *Body
of the Informative Speech*, 132; *The Conclusion of
the Informative Speech*, 134; *Sample Evaluation
Sheet for the Informative Speech*, 136

Chapter 3   The Speech to Persuade   137

Some Elements of Persuasion, 138; *Three Forms of
Persuasive Speaking*, 143; *Exercises*, 145; *Sample
Evaluation Sheet for the Persuasive Speech*, 146

Chapter 4   Group Discussions   147

Elements of Effective Discussions, 149; *Group
Problem-Solving Discussions: A Case Study*, 150;
Exercises, 158; *Sample Evaluation Sheet for the
Group Discussion*, 159

Part V   Selected Readings   161

Auto Biography, Richard Armour, 163
A Boyhood In Ras Tanura, William Tracy, 168
The Hawks, Alan Devoe, 176
Ready or Not, Here Comes Jumbo, *Time*
     Magazine, 179
The Problem Passenger, Chaytor D. Mason, 189
The Civilized Engineer, Samuel C. Florman, 196
The City, Genevieve Ray, 204
The Billion-Dollar Disease, Charles Straub, 210
What Is Happening to Our Great Lakes?
     Andrew Robertson, 220
Must Technology and Humanity Conflict?
     Joseph Wood Krutch, 227
Is the Peace Corps Dead? Walter P. Blass, 234
Industrial Arts and the Space Age, Harold E.
     Mehrens, Jr., 241
Inaugural Address, January 20, 1961,
     John F. Kennedy, 245
The Valley of Tomorrow, U.S. Department of
     Agriculture, 249
Less Peace Corps, More James Bond, John
     Rothchild, 259
The Usefulness of Scientists, Howard Reiss and
     Jack Balderston, 265
The Sons of Martha, Richard McKenna, 277

Index   295

PART I

A Response Must Have A Stimulus

A RESPONSE MUST HAVE A STIMULUS

Never before the Twentieth Century has the importance of the individual been so evident. This is the age in which everyone has something to say and a means of reaching an audience. This is the age of sweeping social programs, educational opportunities and equal rights, on the one hand, and starvation, the cold war, the hot wars, racial strife and social upheaval on the other.

Our biggest problem still lies in the fact that the ordinary citizen, with all his desire to be heard, lacks the adequate tools with which to communicate and doubts his own importance as an individual. We owe it to ourselves to reverse this trend. Farmers, mechanics, draftsmen, nurses—citizens all, skilled in their individual trades—must now become skilled communicators and take an active part in the affairs of their career organizations, communities, and nation.

Why not leap into life, fully and with relish, as a farm boy leaps into the swimming hole? If you must first test its temperature with your big toe, then life is not for you and you might as well just drop out of the human race. The world needs individuals with strong stomachs and an appetite for living.

The age of timid silence is behind you. It is your obligation to have something to say, the ability to say it, and an awareness of your own importance as an individual. If you don't think one person has, or can have, much effect on his fellow men, I need only refer you to the history books, for they are full of such examples. What one man can't accomplish by himself can often be accomplished by many dedicated individuals working together in a common cause.

For those who say, "There's nothing to say" or, "I can't think of anything to say," I would ask them to repeat those words to the families of those men who have died in the many dirty wars on this globe; the millions of people in the world who wish *they* had the opportunity to speak *their* minds; to the multitudes in this country who are still fighting for the rights guaranteed them in their own Constitution; or to any man who has ever tried to understand the meaning of life and the role of man.

We respond readily and with obvious enthusiasm when our favorite team wins the World Series or the Super Bowl. We respond with obvious disgust when the service at our favorite restaurant is lousy, or when our coffee is cold or our beer is warm. The process is really quite the same whenever we respond; only the stimulus is different. Our every response is governed by our past experiences (what we have been led to expect) and by our individual frame of reference.

The following series of photographs and ideas are designed to act as self-starters to stimulate some sort of written and/or oral response. The photographs are the photographers' answers to the writers' compositions. The key to their communication and impact is that they *show* what loneliness is; what anger is; what happiness is.

A good piece of communication—oral, written, or graphic— creates a mood. The subject matter is obvious, the image is sharp, and the composition is interesting. All the parts are related to the whole and the message is universal.

But notice that, as in all communication, what is left out is just as important as that which is included. In other words, negation is just as important as creation. Say only what you have to say to make your point clear, and then stop. Anything beyond this belabors the issue.

In responding to these photographs, try to put into words what the photographer captured with his lens. It makes no difference whether your response is written or oral, only that it is brief and to the point. You should draw upon your own experiences in formulating a response, and take care to organize that response.

If you feel that your response can best be communicated in a single sentence, then respond in that way. (Your sentence could well serve as a topic sentence for a later written assignment or as an introduction for a speech.)

The important thing here is that you do, in fact, RESPOND.

Photo courtesy of *Chicago Today*

LONELINESS IS . . .

DESPAIR CAN BE . . .

BEING OLD AND ALONE IS . . .

WHEN THE WORLD HAS PASSED YOU BY AND
NO ONE REMEMBERS . . .

A MAN DOES NOT HAVE TO DIE TO
EXPERIENCE DEATH . . .

Respond to this man—
Respond to his plight—
Respond!

Photo courtesy of *Chicago Today*

CHILDHOOD IS . . .

LITTLE BOYS ARE . . .

WHEN I WAS A SMALL BOY . . .

FUN IS . . .

Boys are made out of bottle caps,
        baseball trading cards,
        frogs, snakes, gym shoes, and peanut butter . . .

CITIES ARE . . .

CROWDS ARE . . .

PEOPLE ARE . . .

FACES IN A CROWD CAN BE . . .

PEOPLE CAN MOVE LIKE TIDES
AND YOU CAN BE . . .

WHEN I'M IN A CROWD I . . .

A CROWD IS A MOB WHEN . . .

WHEN SOMEONE CARES ENOUGH . . .

A HELPING HAND IS . . .

COMPASSION IS . . .

WHEN A MAN REACHES THE
BREAKING POINT HE . . .

GIVING UP CAN BE . . .

WHEN I CAN'T COPE WITH THE
WORLD AROUND ME I . . .

SORROW IS . . .

Photo courtesy of *Chicago Today*

ANGER IS . . .

DETERMINATION CAN BE MEASURED BY . . .

COURAGE IS . . .

IT TAKES GUTS TO . . .

GETTING "FIRED UP" IS LIKE . . .

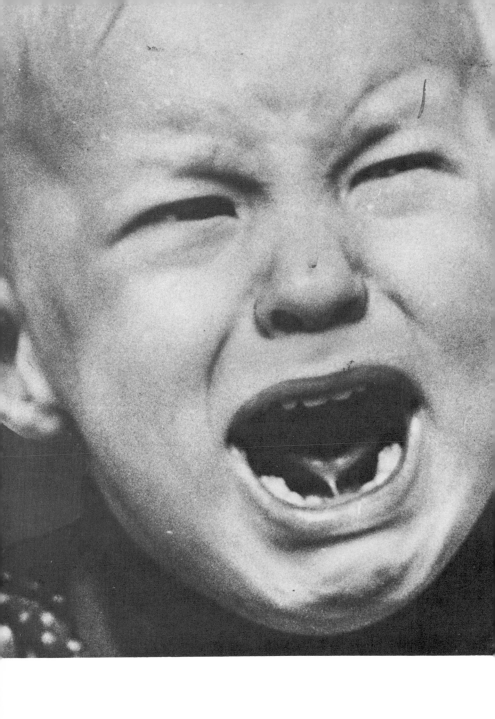

FEAR IS . . .

FEELINGS CAN BE HURT BY . . .

PAIN CAN COME IN MANY FORMS . . .

TEARS TASTE LIKE . . .

OFTEN WHAT SEEMS FRIGHTENING
CAN BE . . .

FRUSTRATION CAN BE . . .

SOMETIMES I GET MY OWN
SIGNALS CROSSED . . .

ALMOST SUCCEEDING IS LIKE . . .

THE BEST LAID PLANS OFTEN . . .

SHARING RESPONSIBILITIES CAN
SOMETIMES LEAD TO . . .

WHEN I GOOF UP I FEEL LIKE . . .

"PROGRESS" HAS TURNED OUR
ATMOSPHERE INTO . . .

POLLUTION CAN BE BEST DESCRIBED BY . . .

THE GREATEST DANGER COMES, NOT FROM
A LACK OF PROGRESS, BUT . . .

THE AIR WE BREATHE AND THE WATER
WE DRINK ARE . . .

FRESH AIR SMELLS LIKE . . .

POLLUTION SMOTHERS MAN AND
ANIMAL ALIKE . . .

Reprinted with permission from the *Chicago Daily News*
Photo by: John Jaqua

BEING A NONCONFORMIST OFTEN MEANS . . .

GETTING AWAY FROM IT ALL IS . . .

WHEN I FEEL THE WIND IN MY FACE . . .

FREEDOM IS . . .

MOVEMENT IS . . .

EXCITEMENT IS . . .

DANGER IS . . .

DOING YOUR OWN THING IS IMPORTANT
BECAUSE . . .

Chicago Tribune Photo

WINNING IS . . .

LOSING CAN BE . . .

WHEN I WORK HARD TO ACCOMPLISH
A GOAL I FEEL . . .

TENSION IS . . .

LEADERSHIP IS . . .

WHEN EVERYBODY WANTS TO GET
INTO THE ACTION . . .

SPORTSMANSHIP . . .

Chicago Tribune Photo

CHANGES CAN BE DISASTROUS . . .
                    HEALTHY . . .
                    DIFFICULT TO ACCEPT . . .
                    DESTRUCTIVE . . .

OUR SYSTEM IS . . .

DISSENT CAN BE . . .

MOBS ARE . . .

   LAW IS . . .

      THE **REAL** THREAT IS . . .

FREE SPEECH AND RESPONSIBILITY ARE . . .

THE SILENT MAJORITY IS . . .

ORDINARY PEOPLE LIKE YOU AND ME ARE . . .

WHO ARE THE REAL HEROES?

FATHERS ARE . . .

HUSBANDS ARE . . .

BROTHERS ARE . . .

MEN ARE . . .

PATRIOTISM CAN BE MANY THINGS
TO MANY PEOPLE, BUT TO ME IT . . .

ADDITIONAL RESPONSE STIMULUS

There has been an atomic attack and you find yourself in a fallout shelter with ten other people. The shelter was designed to accommodate six. You have been elected leader of the group and it is up to you to decide who is to leave and who is to remain. You have no idea how extensive the attack has been, or what fate may await the people who must leave. Make your decisions as logically as possible and be ready to defend them.

. . . Mary, the psychology professor, is a few years older than the rest of the group. The others respect her and recognize her grasp of the situation and her ability to take command. She is rather cold and impersonal, but has helped to quiet the group's nervousness and settled an argument between Don and Hazel. Even though no one seems close to her, you feel she would a valuable organizer.

. . . Don is a gay romantic. His smile, his guitar music, and his sense of humor have helped improve everyone's mood. He gets along well with everyone—too well with some of the girls. He has already offended Hazel with his rude gestures, and some of the girls have noticed his flirting eyes roving about as he sings.

. . . Hazel is studying nutrition and dietetics. She is a very sexy, attractive girl. One of the first things she did was to appraise the food supply. Her training has given her practical knowledge of how to ration food to avoid waste. She is also an imaginative cook who can prepare even canned foods appealingly. She is efficient to the point of being domineering and bossy.

. . . Alberta is a brilliant girl who has been given a graduate assistantship to do research on radiation. She has been pampered all her life and is horrified at the thought of wearing the same clothes for a month, being unable to take a bath or wash her hair, and sleeping in the same room with many other people. Her scientific knowledge would be a definite asset; her whims and attitude would be a liability.

. . . Joe is a Negro football player, the center on the college team. He is highly respected by everyone. Joe is the only one who was able to lift the heavy metal plate that had to be placed over the shelter door. At one point, when Chet took it upon himself to set the oxygen tank valve, Jack flew at him, shoved him out of the way, and reset the valve properly. A fight might have ensued had Joe not parted the two men.

. . . Laura is a literature major, has read extensively and writes well herself. Already she has entertained and diverted the group by retelling one of the books she has recently read.

. . . Nancy, Chet's wife, has a pleasant personality. However, she has been the most nervous and upset of the group. Her temperamental mood is partly due to the fact that she is expecting a baby in the very near future.

. . . Chet, Nancy's husband, is a medical student. He has had two years of medical study, three summers in a camp as a medical director, and close association with his father, who is a doctor. You realize he would be a great aid. However, he refuses to stay unless his wife also stays.

. . . Paul is a young minister. His calmness, optimism, and faith are an inspiration to the entire group. He helped quiet Nancy's tearful outburst. At that time he revealed that he has learned to remain calm, of necessity, because he is a diabetic. He would require a special diet. Excessive excitement causes him to faint.

. . . Jack is a mechanic and has a great deal of practical know-how to recommend him. Although lacking in formal education, he has had experience with air filtration systems, air purifiers, and oxygen supply. However, he has already been reprimanded by Hazel for snitching a Hershey bar from the limited food supply. Despite his technical know-how, he fails to grasp the necessity for self-control as far as the food and water supply is concerned.

PART II

Understanding Ourselves Through Communication

CHAPTER 1:   WORDS AND MEANING

The Real World and the World of Words

> Humpty Dumpty said . . . : "There's glory for you."
> "I don't know what you mean by glory," Alice said.
> Humpty Dumpty smiled contemptuously. "Of course you
> don't—till I tell you. I meant, 'there's a nice knock-down argu-
> ment for you'."
> "But 'glory' doesn't mean a 'nice knock-down argument',"
> Alice objected.
> "When *I* use a word," Humpty Dumpty said in a rather
> scornful tone, "it means just what I choose it to mean—
> neither more nor less." (Lewis Carroll, *Through the Looking
> Glass*)

In this amusing way Lewis Carroll reminds us that any connection
between the real world and the world of words is purely arbitrary.
Most of the problems of communication between individuals arise
from a failure to recognize this arbitrary relationship. S. I. Haya-
kawa focuses attention on this problem when he explains the relationship between words and reality by substituting the terms *maps*
and *territories*. He claims that words describe reality, just as a map
describes a territory. He goes on to point out that "the word is not
the thing" any more than the map is the territory. Words, therefore, are like maps, and although false maps (words) cannot change
reality, they can change our interpretation of reality.

We use words to describe things, people, feelings, attitudes,
theories, philosophies, and so on. We can choose many different
words to describe the same thing—and this is where trouble often
starts!

35

Suppose the foreman says that the shop steward made an *unfortunate* decision. The union members in the shop assume he means that the steward made a *wrong* decision. It is quite obvious to them that the foreman is being *unfair* by *criticizing* the steward. The foreman counters by saying that it would be best if the men would just *forget the whole matter.*

Now, "forget it" is something you might say to someone when you get fed up with their inability to see and accept your point of view. It is often the same as saying, "I can't get through to you. You're either too *stupid* or too *stubborn* to see the truth." Yet the foreman may simply have been expressing his desire to escape from an unexpected conflict. The whole problem here was the failure by both sides to correctly interpret the relationship between the words and the reality.

Man has advanced through the use of language but, by the same token, the complexity of human language has created many of his problems. There would be less misunderstanding if each object and feeling had but a single word to describe it. This is not the case, and I suspect that we are rather glad it isn't. However, recognition and acceptance of this verbal communication problem is the first step in overcoming it.

Each object, person, or idea can be described by many different words, and each word might well trigger a unique response from every person to whom it is directed. This process is easy to understand if we can accept the idea of the human mind's being much like a computer. Information can be fed into a computer and stored there for future reference. The human mind works the same way. The mind is a storehouse of information and attitudes which are "stockpiled" there as the result of all past experiences.

Much of the information stored in the human mind may never be used; the conscious mind may not even be aware of the existence of some of the information kept in the dark recesses of the subconscious, but nevertheless it is there. When your hear the word *Siberia* what comes into your mind? Salt mines? Bitter cold? Desolation? Chances are quite good that you have never actually been to Siberia, but past experiences—what you have read and heard and seen in pictures—have been stored in your "computer." The word *Siberia* is fed into that computer and it responds with a mental image of the place called Siberia which is distinctly your own, and may be quite unlike that of another person.

What kind of territory is described by the following map?

A new girl is moving in next door to you and her name is *Zelda Grutzmacher*. The name is fed into your computer and, if your "computer" has been programmed like those of most young men, the reply is likely to be something like this: "Ugh! With a name like that, she must be a loser." Zelda might actually look a great deal like Raquel Welch, in which case the map wouldn't represent the territory and your computer would blow a fuse. No matter what the girl's name may be, it won't change her looks!

Irving J. Lee, in his article, "The Work of Words," seemed to sum up the problem when he wrote:

> Our adjustment (and ultimately, survival) is correlated with our expectations, that is, our ability to predict happenings accurately. This is a way of saying that the correctness of our expectations depends upon the similarity of structure of the language used and the happenings represented. If the statements, by means of which we are oriented, are not adequate representations it will be difficult to prepare for what is to be met in the world of direct experience.

Man's common failure to recognize the arbitrary relationship between the word and the object (that the word is not the thing) is made clear at one point in the novel *Bread and Wine* by Ignazio Silone. There is a scene in the book involving some men playing a card game called *settemezzo*. In this game the King of Diamonds is the key card and their particular King of Diamonds is worn out from handling and is easily recognizable. One of the players suggests substituting the Three of Spades for the King. A heated discussion erupts because one of the players claims such a substitution would be impossible. He flatly states: "The King of Diamonds is always the King of Diamonds. He may be filthy, torn, or have holes in him, but he's still the King of Diamonds. . . . In the same way the Pope is the Pope. Why? Because he is. . . ."

We also make the mistake of thinking that words can give us certain guarantees. We assume that a fine-sounding word guarantees quality. You think not? If you were to drive into a strange town while on a trip and, stopping for lunch, you noticed there were but two restaurants in town, which one would you select: *Mom's Place* or *Ptomaine Corners*? Chances are, you would select *Mom's Place* simply because the name seems to give you certain guarantees—home cooking, large portions, friendly atmosphere. Take your pick. Would the alternative be the heartburn special served at *Ptomaine Corners*? Changing the names of these diners would not change the quality of food served. On the other hand, the names do lead us to expect certain things (we first describe, then see). We think that *Mom's Place* ought to be run by "Mom" herself. So the old lady slinging hash becomes "Mom." Yet the truth of the matter may be that the only real mom is the one who is mashing the spuds in the kitchen of *Ptomaine Corners.*

Connotation and Denotation

This brings us to the definitions of connotation and denotation. The sharpest *denotation* would be the thing itself, the object. Since we are speaking of language, we must apply denotation to the world of words and infer that denotation is the factual language we use to describe something. Denotation is best exemplified by the dictionary definition. (Man: *homo sapiens.*) It is connotative language that we are most interested in because it is the language we most often use. *Connotation* is suggestive and indicates our personal attitudes. (Man: predictable, dependable, beast, fink, cruel, kind, thoughtful, selfish, stinker, bastard, wonderful, creative, self-centered, destructive, compassionate, sneaky, tender, loving.) All of these words might be used to describe the same man, depending on who is describing him. The thing to remember is that the man will remain the same no matter what we call him. The words simply suggest the attitudes of the speaker.

In these troubled times our attitudes seem to be more polarized than ever before. The troubles in Southeast Asia, inflation, campus disturbances, drugs, racial strife, pollution and a host of other domestic and international problems have forced most of our population into opposing camps. People are either hawks or doves; pro-establishment or anti-establishment; conservatives or liberals; hippies or squares, etc. These polarized attitudes will be reflected in the words we use to describe reality.

The word *automobile* is a rather neutral word. That is, it does not necessarily trigger a positive or negative response. (It does sometimes trigger a response, of course, depending on the "computer" into which it is fed.) We can stimulate a positive or favorable response by substituting the word *limosine*. We can stimulate a negative or unfavorable response by substituting the word *junker*. All these words refer to the same thing—the same reality.

The following pairs of words mean roughly the same thing, but they have different connotations:

Favorable	Unfavorable
cautious	cowardly
thrifty	tight
practical	unimaginative
trusting	gullible
idealist	prude
sanitary engineer	garbage man
persuade	brainwash
withdraw	retreat
inexpensive	cheap

We all know that beer is beer and not something else. But when the advertising agency comes up with the slogan "The Champagne of Bottled Beer," they know and hope that the consumer will associate their product, beer, with champagne. Certain cigarette advertisements depict a cowboy as smoking the advertiser's brand. The cowboy has always been a masculine symbol in this country, and they imply that to be as masculine as a cowboy, you should smoke that brand.

Simple, precise language often seems to lack the color and excitement we desire, so we tend to color it a bit and, in the process, often distort reality.

In the following statements the blank spaces are for the purpose of inserting words to indicate attitude. Note that the words to be inserted can be interchanged because they lack concreteness, or precision.

Example: Blackwell power mowers are _____ and there is no lawn job too _____ for the Blackwell. (*rugged, tough*)

Example: Our new parts manager is very _____. When it comes to the automotive business he is as _____ as anyone. We couldn't ask for anyone more _____. (*thorough, knowledgeable, competent*)

Example: I have this _____ blind date for you. She's a _____ blond with a _____ personality. You ought to have a _____ time. (*great, beautiful, delightful, fascinating*)

After the date you might wish that he had used the following terms to describe the blind date he lined up for you: ugly, stupid, *horrible, boring.* All of these words are examples of abstract terms. What one person may view as beautiful, another may term ugly. When your friend says he has a beautiful girl lined up for you, he means that in *his* opinion, she is beautiful. As you hear him, you imagine *your* ideal of beauty. When in fact she doesn't turn out to be a Bardot, you are disappointed. Someone else might have inserted the words *wild, sexy, swinging* and *groovy.*

If the foreman mentioned earlier would have taken the time to explain what he meant by the word *unfortunate,* or if someone had asked for a clarification, or if, instead of telling the men to "forget it," he had taken the time to discuss their differences, the problem could have been prevented. There were obviously several opportunities on both sides to keep that incident from exploding into a breakdown of communication, but each man was so preoccupied with his own point of view that he failed to see the other man's.

Of course we must color our concrete language with abstractions and examples to bring our personal meaning more sharply into focus. But the key to the use of abstract language must always be communication. If its use can clarify the ideas being expressed, by all means, use it. If its use will cloud the meaning or create confusion, forget it. The fatal illness in communication is to let the words get in the way of what you are trying to say.

Exercises

---

1. Explain the differences in connotation between the following pairs of words:

   break, smash
   hurt, injure
   dirty, filthy
   dispose of, throw away
   old, elderly
   television, boob-tube
   cluttered, messy
   happy, elated
   pretty, attractive
   pig, swine
   car, automobile

fiddle, violin
cigar, stogie
woman, broad
cheat, swindle

2. The following are examples of neutral words. For each neutral word list two synonyms, one of which triggers a favorable connotation, while the other causes an unfavorable connotation.

FAVORABLE	NEUTRAL	UNFAVORABLE
thoroughbred	horse	nag
	teacher	
	write	
	kill	
	lawyer	
	car	
	house	
	food	
	boy	
	meat	
	liquor	
	preacher	
	boxer	

3. What do the following words connote and why?

liberal
chastity
conformity
intolerance
capitalism
patriot
socialism
atheist
blue-collar
hippy
conservative
demonstrator
grass
consumer

4. The following words apply to the same person, yet our mental image of this person will differ depending on the word used to refer to this person. Why?

William, Willie, Will, Bill, Billy

5. What are your different responses to the following words used
   to describe the same person?

   teen-ager
   adolescent
   youth
   young man
   juvenile
   guy
   fella
   brat

6. Select ten of the most distasteful words in your opinion and do
   the best you can in substituting words that change the connotations from unfavorable to favorable.

   Example: *slob* is changed to *unkempt*
                Nazi is changed to *nationalist*

   Also select ten pleasing terms and give those unfavorable connotations through substitution.

   Example: *patriot* becomes a *fanatic*
                Medicare is changed to *socialized medicine*

CHAPTER 2:   LANGUAGE, THOUGHT
AND BEHAVIOR

Perception and Observation

Every individual has a certain responsibility for what he says, just as he has a responsibility to uphold the system that allows him to express his ideas freely. Understanding the thought process that precedes statement may be the first step in closing the communications gap that separates many of the individuals in our society today.

Our formal thinking and the statements resulting from this thought are founded in our observations of past experiences. Individual experiences so shape our observations that two people rarely observe the same thing in the same way. Someone once said, "We are prone to see what lies behind our eyes rather than what appears before them." In other words, we see only what we know.

Two men look under the hood of a car. The first man, a mechanic, sees a 327 V-8 with four barrels. The second man, an accountant, sees only a mass of metal and a greasy tangle of wires. The mechanic sees logical relationships between every part of that engine. He is in his own element and feels competent to handle any problem that might arise. At the same time, the accountant feels only confusion and helplessness.

However, if the two men were faced with the task of evaluating the service department's financial statement, it would be the mechanic who would feel confused. It would be difficult for him to make sense out of the maze of figures and lines. The terms themselves, *accounts receivable, accounts payable, liabilities* and *assets,* might seem familiar—just as the word *carburetor* might seem

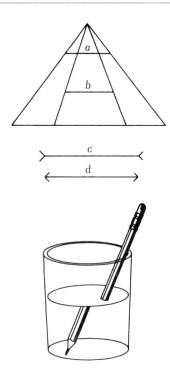

Is *a* longer than *b*? Is *c* longer than *d*? Are there really
two pieces to the pencil standing in the glass of water?

familiar to the accountant—but they would not describe any reality for him. "We see what we know."

An accident takes place between two automobiles, one driven
by an elderly man, the other by a teenage boy. A crowd gathers. If
you were to arrive on the scene and ask "What happened?" the
answer to your question will probably differ depending upon the
individual to whom you directed it. An elderly person in the crowd
might answer something like this:

> *Some young punk just ran into that man over there. I think
> the kid was drag-racing with another car. Someone said he
> thought he saw a six-pack on the floor of the kid's car. The
> highways aren't safe anymore with all these young hoodlums
> running around. Why I can remember . . .*

Ask the same question of a young man in the crowd and you
may get this reply:

> *Some old farmer was out sight-seeing when he should have
> been paying attention to the highway. He was probably look-*

ing at his neighbor's cornfield or something. When people reach his age, they ought to have their licenses taken away. These Sunday drivers cause more accidents by poking along than those people who are driving at the speed limit. They ought to stick to driving their tractors.

As Walter Lippmann says, "We define first, then see."

Different people observing the same scene will notice different things. What they observe, or rather what they choose (consciously or unconsciously) to observe, will depend on their interests.

A married couple meets a mutual female acquaintance on the street. The married woman notices that the other woman is wearing the same outfit she was wearing the last time they met. She also sees that the other woman's hands are red and rough, and that there is a run in her stockings. The man, on the other hand, notes that the woman's figure is just as nice as it has always been. He also observes that her skirt is short enough to show her shapely legs.

This is not to say that the man didn't "see" the run in the stockings, or that his wife didn't "see" the shapely legs, but they didn't consciously register these observations; they didn't "notice" them. It may be that later, upon reflection, the husband will realize there was something—something he can't put into words—which made the woman seem less attractive than his memory of her. You see, the rough hands and the run in the stocking registered, but not consciously. This leads us to the next point.

There are two parts to every observation. There is that part which is visually and consciously registered, and that part which is filed mentally or unconsciously.

A tool-and-die maker uses a certain brand of hand cleaner to get the grease and grime from his hands before leaving the shop. His hands and arms break out in a rash. The next time he uses the cleaner, his hands and arms are again covered with a rash. He observes consciously that when he uses that particular brand of cleaner, he gets a rash. He changes to another brand of cleaner and assumes that the problem is solved. But the same thing happens. At this point, an observation that had been filed unconsciously in his mind comes forward. He remembers that he had switched lubricants on the same day he tried the first hand cleaner. He changes the lubricant and the problem is solved. This link between our visual and mental observations is often referred to as intuition.

A man arrives home after work and settles down in his favorite chair to read the newspaper. He has the uneasy feeling that something is different, but he can't put his finger on it. He has the same feeling all evening. Later, as he is preparing for bed, his wife mentions that he failed to notice her new hairdo. This example indicates a facet of observation: individuals often see the familiar things as they always were, even after changes have taken place. The changes are registered, but often unconsciously. The feeling this man had, this "intuition," was his mind's attempt to draw a relationship between the visual observation and the mental observation.

Most observations will take on one of two different forms: (1) those things we expect to see, the observations deliberately sought; and (2) the unexpected, spontaneous observations. In making a valid judgment of a situation or event, the observer must notice the obvious, but must also notice the obscure and evaluate his findings based on the relationship of the two.

There are many obvious reasons for the stock market to sustain a downward slide. An investor might observe these reasons and either sell short, figuring that a small loss is better than a great loss, or hold out in the belief that the market is in a constant state of flux, and will bounce back. A clever investor will observe those obscure symptoms that usually *precede* a drop in the market and sell out *before* the market begins the slide. This same clever investor will re-invest at the first obscure signs of a bull market, thus making a killing at the top and the bottom.

The first investor observed the obvious—lower reported corporate earnings, tight money policies, etc.—and reacted to those factors without further reflection. The more observant investor looked beyond the obvious and noted there were an unusual number of large block transactions reported to the Securities and Exchange Commission. This unusually active dumping of large holdings into the market, plus some cutbacks in corporate production, led him to expect the market to go down. He was able to make his move before the slide began on the basis of his thorough observations.

Detectives receive extensive training in the development of observation, and they know that the difference between apprehending a criminal and letting him escape often lies in the ability to observe the facts—both the obvious and the obscure. On occasion, the most important piece of evidence is the piece that was originally overlooked because it seemed commonplace.

Obviously no one can observe everything, but a good observer will approach a situation or a problem with a receptive mind. It takes an active mind to draw relationships between seemingly unrelated evidence.

Exercises

1. As a class exercise, briefly observe the photograph on page 26. Now close your books and discuss the photograph. Have someone in the class list the various observations made by members of the class. When you feel you have extensively discussed your observations, open your books and check the photograph with your list of observations. What is missing from the list of observations? Does the list include anything not shown in the picture? If so, what might account for the additional observations?

2. Sketch the outside of your classroom door and check your sketch with the real thing. How observant have you been?

3. Briefly describe the interior of a machine shop, a milking parlor, and a dentist's office. Compare your descriptions with those of the other members of the class. Check the differences in descriptions of the dentist's office between someone who has recently been to the dentist and someone who has never been to the dentist. Check the farm descriptions written by ag students with those presented by business or drafting students. Besides familiarity, what accounts for the differences?

Inference and Assumption

An inference is a conclusion arrived at by examining evidence; a statement about the unknown based upon the known. "The sun will rise tomorrow morning" is an example of an inference. It is a statement about the unknown based on the known—the sun has come up every morning so far.

Most people would accept that statement as true, even though it is based on assumption. An assumption is a premise that most people will accept automatically as true. Since most people would accept the fact that the sun rises every morning, they would accept your conclusion "The sun will rise tomorrow morning."

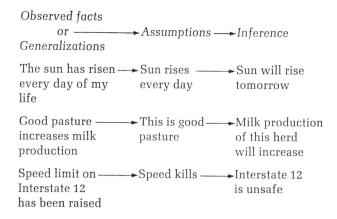

This entire process is based on human nature. It is not necessarily logical. It depends on conclusions drawn from evidence, the validity of commonly accepted assumptions, and the ability to accurately assess the value of observed facts and generalizations.

Since inferences go beyond the observable and deal in probabilities, it is important to take care in evaluating the evidence accurately. When we say that Harry has a bad temper because he has red hair, we are assuming that red hair and temper are somehow related. This assumption is based on the faulty generalization that "people with red hair have bad tempers," (or, in all *probability*, someone with red hair will have a bad temper).

There are many assumptions about human nature, some of which go back hundreds of years. Some of these assumptions gained popularity through literature: "You can't trust a hungry man;" "He who hesitates is lost." There are so many assumptions about human nature that it would be impossible to list them all, but here are a few.

Fishermen are liars.
Women are gossips.

Poor people are stupid.
Fat people are jolly.
Old people are conservatives.
Young people are liberals.
Blonds have more fun.
Unemployed people are lazy.

There are many faulty assumptions related to race and national origin as well.

Frenchmen are good lovers.
Scots are tight.
Negroes love watermelon.
Chinese are clever.
Germans love to march.
Russians have little regard for human life.
Englishmen are stuffy.
Irishmen have quick tempers.

The danger does not lie in the fact that we use inferences based on assumptions. The danger lies in the implicition of cause-and-effect relationships and in the bases of our assumptions. Too often the assumptions upon which we base our inferences have been drawn from unreliable sources or hearsay, or result from the misinterpretation of reality.

A friend once remarked that the first thing you should do when stopped by a policeman for a moving violation is take out your wallet and turn to the "green stuff." The inference was: You can bribe a policeman. My friend assumed that policemen are dishonest. When asked upon what observable facts he had made his assumption he answered: "Everybody knows that policemen are crooked. Besides, I had a friend once who told me. . . ." You have no doubt heard this kind of story before. The most distasteful thing is not that a friend of a friend once bribed a policeman, but that the story puts a blot on all the honest policemen who try to uphold the respect for our civil laws. There are assumptions made concerning almost every group of people, whether that group has as its basis race, religion, nationality, or occupation. Most faulty assumptions stem from a lack of familiarity with the facts.

Here is a random sampling from a recent questionnaire concerning occupational groups.

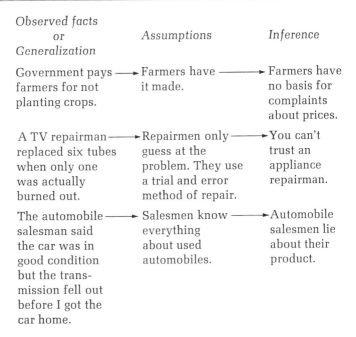

Observed facts or Generalization	Assumptions	Inference
Government pays farmers for not planting crops.	Farmers have it made.	Farmers have no basis for complaints about prices.
A TV repairman replaced six tubes when only one was actually burned out.	Repairmen only guess at the problem. They use a trial and error method of repair.	You can't trust an appliance repairman.
The automobile salesman said the car was in good condition but the transmission fell out before I got the car home.	Salesmen know everything about used automobiles.	Automobile salesmen lie about their product.

You can go a long way in dispelling this kind of thinking by taking the time to evaluate your original observations and generalizations. Verification of the observed facts or generalizations and the assumptions stemming from them would go a long way in evaluating the validity of the conclusion.

For instance: Do all farmers receive Soil Bank payments? What percentage of total farm income comes from Soil Bank payments? Under what circumstances are the Soil Bank payments made? What other factors determine a farmer's income? Who made the observations? Is the source of information reliable? The same kinds of questions might be asked to test the validity of the other inferences cited in the examples above.

In all three of the previous examples, the people who made the inferences did so by exercising three steps: observation, assumption, and conclusion. Not a single person took a fourth step—verification. It is like reading a book without a final chapter, or seeing a play without a final scene—the conclusion is based on speculation. The loose ends are just that, loose ends. Verification is like the final chapter or the final scene; it ties up the loose ends.

Very often this process is reversed; that is, the observer will back-track from an inference, through the assumption, to the observed fact.

> Farmers have → in fact → they have → because → Government
> no basis for   it made   pays them
> complaints   for not
> about prices   planting
>   certain
>   crops.

The use of connectives such as *because, since,* and *so,* and verbs like *ought, should,* and *must* often signals this kind of thought process. This is just one example of how many words in our language can act as signs for what lies ahead, the same way highway signs indicate certain things to motorists.

Exercises

1. Write a brief essay describing your personality as others might describe it. What assumptions are they most likely to make? Why?

2. What assumptions might be drawn from the following observations?

    A. A student looks over his shoulder during a test.
    B. A car is parked along the side of the highway and the trunk of the car is open.
    C. A woman's scream is heard from within a house.
    D. An ambulance is parked in front of a house.
    E. A mechanic looking under the hood of your car shakes his head.
    F. An automobile salesman and a customer seem to be having a heated discussion.
    G. The phone in the next apartment keeps ringing, but no one answers it.
    H. A draftsman picks up the blueprints from his desk and throws them away.

3. There is a common assumption that there is too much violence on television. On what is this assumption based? Can a case be constructed for the opposing viewpoint? On what is this new assumption based?

4. What are some of the more common assumptions held by young people with regard to middle-aged people?

5. What does the older generation assume about youth?

6. What do Americans usually assume about foreigners? On what generalizations are these assumptions based?

7. What does management assume about labor? Labor about management?

8. Most fables are examples of the observe-assume-infer process. Examine a few well-known fables in an effort to further understand this process.

Distortion

So far we have spent time on the steps in our thinking process that precede the conclusions we draw. We have noted the importance of observation, generalization, assumption, and inference. Few people will question the importance of careful examination of all evidence before reaching a conclusion. There are times, however, when the evidence is distorted. It is necessary to recognize distortion if we are to place any value on our conclusions.

We are all tempted to distort the facts from time to time in order to support our own viewpoint, but the purpose here is to present you with the tools that will equip you to recognize distortion.

One of the most common forms of distortion is the use, or rather misuse, of statistics. Americans seem to thrive on statistics; they have become as common (and as American) as apple pie, baseball, and hoola-hoops. Americans talk about and read about average incomes, average housewives, average third-basemen, earned-run averages, batting averages, average-sized families, average working men, average mileage, stock market averages, the average amount of time it will take to do this or that, crime rates, death rates, accident rates, birth rates, the number of rats a city has, the number of cows a state has, and thousands of other statistics which annually fill several almanacs and uncountable files.

One of the most obvious forms of distortion comes from the term *average*. In some cases we like to think of ourselves as above average; in other cases, below average. Many people find, disappointingly, that they are "only average." However, before we can evaluate evidence based on the term *average*, we must know what *kind* of average is referred to. There are four different methods of arriving at *average*. These methods can be used to prove almost anything.

Arithmetical average is determined by adding all the figures and dividing by the total number of figures. (100, 80, 78, 60, 50: Total = 368 divided by 5 = 73.6.)

Simple mean average is merely the mid-point between the extremes. (100, 80, 78, 60, 50: Mid-point between the extremes, 100 and 50, is 75.)

Median average is the middle number in the series. (100, 80, 78, 60, 50: Middle number is 78.)

Mode average is the figure which appears most frequently. (In this case there is no mode.)

An earlier statement said that the different methods of determining average can be used to prove or support almost anything. Let's take a look at this claim in action.

A small company, Littlepage Offset Printing Company, has decided to try a new system of promotion based on the assumption that it is better to promote from within the organization. The experiment is the result of a morale problem within the company. Some members of top-level management were opposed to the new system, but agreed that a few men might be used as a test group. Nine men were selected as management prospects and were sent to a management training program at a nearby college.

After eighteen weeks the course was completed. The men were evaluated according to their class work, tests, potential, and attitude. The following grades were submitted to the Vice-President in charge of Personnel.

Trainee	Grade
Brown	100
Smith	95
Jones	90

Trainee	Grade
White	85
Jackson	80
Green	75
Morgan	70
Hanks	70
Billings	0
9 men	665

You will notice that eight out of the nine men originally selected passed the course. The zero represents Billings, who dropped out after the first week. Three men did exceptionally well; the next two men did not do quite as well, but still justified their selection to the test group; the last three men did not do nearly as well, but nevertheless they passed.

The Vice-President could now join those members of management who were opposed to the program from the start by stating that the experiment indicated that the company would have to go outside their organization to fill management positions. By using the simple mean average (the mid-point between the extremes) he could state flatly: "These men were selected because they seemed to show the most promise. I'm afraid, gentlemen, that's all they showed us—promise. When the chips were down, the best they could come up with was a 50 percent average."

By using the median average (the middle number in the series) he could side with the originators of the plan. "The group came through with an 80 percent average, well above passing. I think this indicates real promise."

He might choose to hedge by using the arithmetical average (totaling and dividing). In this case the arithmetical average is 73.88 percent. The mode average (the most frequent number in the series) is 70 percent.

Note that the highest average, using any of the four types, is only 80 percent; yet five of the men had 80 percent or above. Interesting also is the fact that if the 0 percent of the man who did not attend the course was dropped out of the computation, the arithmetical average would rise from 73.88 percent to a handsome 83.1 percent. The simple mean average would skyrocket from 50 percent to an excellent 85 percent.

Whenever you see the word *average* used to support an opinion or a conclusion, a little light ought to go on indicating that perhaps a closer investigation should be considered before you accept that average as meaningful.

Another powerful and clever way of distorting the truth is through graphs. Charts and graphs can be most helpful in depicting reality visually and should not be overlooked as an effective method of presenting evidence, but human nature often allows us to be deceived by our preconception of the truth. For example: Automobile sales at the Shadey Brothers Automobile Agency have risen steadily but undramatically in the last ten years. The owners have attributed the increase in sales to the fact that the people in the community trust the integrity and business practices of the Shadey Brothers (an unfounded assumption since they are the only automobile dealership in the community). The Shadey Brothers plan a stepped-up advertising program in an effort to increase new car sales.

In their full-page ads, they want to demonstrate graphically the steady rise in new car sales over the past ten years. They are considering the use of the accompanying sales chart, which hangs on the wall of their agency office.

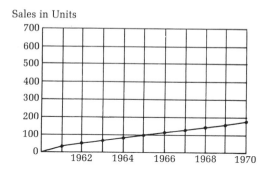

Sales in Units

But somehow the chart fails to depict a headlong charge by the public to gobble up the new cars offered at the Shadey Brothers Agency. After toying with the chart and adding some advertising copy, the Shadey Brothers have come up with the accompanying graph to be used in their full-page advertisements.

The same material is presented in both illustrations. By changing the legend on the graph, they have created the visual impression that new car sales at Shadey Brothers are going clear out of sight. Instead of listing new car sales in units of 100's (as on the original chart), they are charting the sales in units of 20's. Now

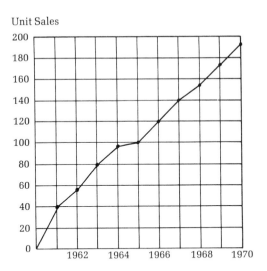

Unit Sales

the curve rises at five times the original rate. The accompanying copy goes something like this: "There can be no doubt that honest dealings, top trade-in dollars, courteous customer treatment, and excellent service are always reflected in volume sales."
Polls can also be misleading, as the following example shows.

Thesis: In a recent poll, 75 percent of the mature college students agreed with our present policy in Southeast Asia.

Supporting statistics:
    Number of students polled: 90
      Men: 48
      Women: 42

      Disagree: 49   (31 men, 18 women)
      Agree: 41   (17 men, 24 women)

It is obvious from the statistics that a clear majority of those students polled *did not* agree with our foreign policy in Southeast Asia. How then could the results of the poll show that 75 percent agreed?
    The answer is quite simple. Notice the qualifier, "mature college students." There were four married students in the group polled. These four, on the basis of age and marital status, fit the qualifications of "maturity." Of these (three men and one woman),

three voted *Agree* and one voted *Disagree*. They represent the 75 percent referred to in the results of the poll. Clearly the 75 percent does not represent the group. The statistics are of little value in reflecting the truth.

It is also possible to influence the outcome of a poll by the very way in which the question is phrased. In a personal evaluation of a set of statistics gathered by poll or questionnaire, it is a good policy to check the actual format of the question to determine whether or not it is designed to foster favorable or unfavorable response.

The following pair of questions are structured to influence the answers.

> Do you favor continuing aid to our European Allies?

> Are you opposed to sending more American dollars to support the Europeans?

Very often a question phrased in a positive manner will receive a supportive reply; likewise, a question worded in a negative way will receive a negative response. The phrasing of the question will perhaps have little effect on those individuals who have strong feelings either pro or con, but may well influence those people who are riding the fence or those who have little information regarding the topic.

Sometimes the statistics used are obviously designed to impress only the foolish.

> There are approximately 200 million people in the United States, and most of them eat bread. A smart man will invest in a franchise with the *Bun and Biscuit House*.

> Ten thousand men used our soap and reported less body odor with regular bathing.

It is also possible to distort the truth by omitting parts of the total truth. Notice that by cutting a portion of the accompanying picture, the remaining portion conveys an entirely different message.

Distortion by omission can be misleading also, as the following example shows:

> A man who had purchased an automobile on credit noticed immediately afterwards that there was a defective

seal in the transmission. He returned to the agency several times in an attempt to exercise the warranty. On each occasion he was snubbed by the service manager. He then tried to see the sales manager, but was referred to the service manager. After several more attempts to have the car repaired, he commented, "If I can't get this car serviced, I'm not going to make any payments." One of the mechanics heard the statement and mentioned it to the service manager. However, what he repeated was a somewhat abridged version: "If I don't get service now, I don't pay."

The service manager, who was annoyed with the customer anyway, went directly to the sales manager and told him he ought to be more selective in okaying customer credit, because he just heard some crank say, "I'll be damned if I'm going to make any payments."

Is there any meaningful relationship between what the customer originally said and what he was reported to have said? What has been omitted? Even professional journalists sometimes distort their reports:

A U.S. Senator recently said: "If, in the future, we cannot coexist with Communist China and our relations deteriorate into a shooting war, we must, because of their overwhelming advantage in manpower, rely on our atomic arsenal in order to destroy them." In order to create a sensational story, an anxious newsman printed the following version of the Senator's statement: ". . . we cannot coexist with Communist China and . . . must . . . rely on our atomic arsenal in order to destroy them."

The reporter's use of the ellipsis (. . .) indicates to the reader that something has been omitted, but how many readers will ask exactly what has been deleted? Another example will show how easily distortion can affect your life.

Tim Murphy had worked at the Wheel and Hub Company for several months and soon had worked his way up to top man in the production line in the balancing department. He "made rate" regularly and enjoyed the benefits of several hours of overtime every week. Murphy was somewhat loud and gruff, but everyone on the line accepted him as a good co-worker. That is, almost everyone. Frank, the foreman, never did appreciate Tim's temperament, nor did he appreciate Tim's ability to make top money so quickly.

Soon, Tim was making more money than he had ever made before. The more money Tim made, the more money he and his wife spent. They bought many things on time and came to depend on Tim's rate and overtime to make ends meet.

Then one week Tim's daughter broke her glasses and needed a new pair in order to remain in school, his wife bought a new sofa, and his automobile insurance was due. That particular week Tim was working harder than ever before and was counting on his rate and overtime to bail him out of his financial problems. However, nothing seemed to work out. One of the men on the line was sick that week and the whole line slowed down so Tim failed to make top money. Then on Saturday his balancing equipment started acting up. The more the equipment balked, the madder Tim became. Soon he was swearing at the machinery and slinging oil rags around and had just reached the outer limits of human patience when Frank came along and said, "What'sa matter, shanty, the work getting to ya?"

Tim turned around and gave Frank a knuckle sandwich. Frank went straight to the plant manager and complained about Tim. He said that Tim was a hot-tempered Irish so-and-so, a trouble-maker. "I made a joking remark, all in fun; and he popped me."

Tim was fired.

Tim was fired not really because of what was said, but because of what was not said. By omitting certain facts, Frank had distorted the truth to the extent that what the plant manager was told had little to do with the actual circumstance.

Omitted were the facts that Murphy was a hard worker who drove himself to the limit; he counted on making top rate; he counted on overtime pay; and Frank and Murphy were involved in a personality conflict. The comment that triggered the punch was not, as Frank would have the plant manager believe, "a joking remark," but a clear reference to national origin, a slur on Tim's masculinity—*work getting to ya*—the wrong things to say to a proud, hard-working man.

This example of distortion by omission leads to the next step in distortion. Whenever some part of the truth is omitted, the remaining portions take on a greater significance. By eliminating all those parts of Frank and Tim's argument, the remaining facts received increased emphasis. All that is left is Tim's temper and violence. He becomes a picture of a man who cannot get along with his superiors; he becomes a trouble-maker.

Omission of facts and sharpening of the remaining facts often becomes the basis for stereotyping. When we refer to the typical Irishman or typical Negro or typical football player, we are guilty of stereotyping. A stereotype is a fixed or conventional picture of an ethnic group, profession, political group, etc.

A brief look at some of the common stereotypes will point out that stereotyping is a direct result of omission and sharpening.

A young man with long hair, dyed shirt and sandals is often classified as a hippie. A common stereotype of the hippie is a person who has withdrawn from society; a person who is basically lazy; a person with radical views concerning law and justice; a person who rejects the accepted behavior patterns of our society. The fact that this particular young man may be a hard-working, sincere drama student preparing for a role in which he portrays a hippie is completely ignored. It is quite possible that he may be picked up by the police and questioned about a recent bombing; or, denied service in a local restaurant, entirely on the basis of his appearance and because the people around him have already stereotyped him and placed him in the category "hippie."

A stereotype presents a very narrow view founded on fear, ignorance, and bias; when it is viewed as proof it ought to be very carefully evaluated. Stereotypes are generalizations inferred from faulty assumptions.

Distortion has been presented here as part of human behavior. This material does not presume to eliminate distortion, but only to draw your attention to its existence. You will be a better communicator if you can familiarize yourself with as many of the aspects of communication as possible.

Exercises

---

1. Find at least one example of distorted facts based on statistics. Bring this to class and be prepared to point out how the distortion was achieved.

2. Locate a graph that appears to be distorted. What has led you to believe that distortion exists? If, in fact, distortion does not exist, can you restructure the graph to create distortion?

3. Read some of the more popular polls. Do you feel they honestly portray the truth? Why? Is the question phrased in such

a way as to influence the answers? How might the question be changed to affect the outcome of the poll?

4. Find some examples of the use of averages in support of some generalizations. What kinds of averages do these appear to be?

5. Conduct a poll of your own among your friends and neighbors. On one half of the people use a question designed to influence the response in one way; on the other half use the same question *reworded* to influence the answer in the opposite way. Compare the results of your polls.

6. Each of the following terms refers to a particular group of people. How might each group be described through the use of stereotype?

old maids	Southerners
librarians	New Englanders
Negroes	miners
laborers	people on welfare

7. Find some newspapers containing articles in which you feel important facts have been omitted and other facts sharpened. Be prepared to defend your findings in a class discussion.

8. Can stereotypes be used t describe something other than human beings? Can stereo ypes apply to animals? Buildings? See how many non-human steretoypes you can uncover.

9. Write a brief paragraph describing a national or racial group (not an individual) without the use of a single element of stereotype. Discuss the difficulties you have with this assignment. Why?

10. Write another paragraph about a different group using *only* stereotype material. However, eliminate all direct and concrete reference to the group itself by using proper names and national origin. On what facts has your paragraph been based?

Judgment or Fact?

When a person makes a judgment it shows his approval or disapproval of a person, place, thing, or idea. Since judgments concern personal values, they are dependent upon the prejudices of the judge. Facts, in contrast, are statements which can be proven true or false; they can be verified.

Everyone ought to develop a practice of careful evaluation and honest investigation in reading and writing. This analysis will help you detect those statements which do not need verification or are unverifiable. "Ice is cold" and "Fire is hot" are examples of statements acceptable without verification. These facts and others like them are examples of common knowledge. Most people already know that fire is hot and need no "proof;" but if necessary, it could be demonstrated.

Obviously we cannot personally verify all the facts. According to the 1960 U.S. Government Census, New York State had the largest population of the fifty states. It would be impossible for an individual personally to make a recount to verify this. We must rely on the accuracy and reliability of our sources for facts outside the realm of personal verification. In this case the Bureau of the Census is known to be as impartial and competent a source as can be found for population statistics.

Some statistics can and should be verified before you act on them.

> Hancock County is growing in population at the rate of 10 percent per year, but health and educational facilities are expanding at a rate of only 2 percent per year.

Before you vote for increased city and county taxes, you would want verification of these figures. It might be shown that the current facilities are functioning at only 50 percent capacity, in which case the increase in population would not immediately overburden the existing facilities.

Judgments are part of the total communication picture and often they are quite sound and well founded in facts. Few people would advocate abolition of judgments, but there is a need for a greater awareness to distinguish the "good" judgments from the "poor" judgments.

Sandy Koufax was one of the greatest pitchers ever to play in the Major Leagues.

This statement can be considered a "good" judgment. The facts upon which the statement is based are verifiable.

1. Won 165 games
2. Struck out 2396 batters in 2325 innings
3. Pitched four no-hit games

(Notice also that "one of the greatest" allows room for other pitchers to be classed in a similar group of "greats." This qualifying statement would go far in stimulating greater acceptance of the judgment.)

Now try this statement on for size:

"Bill Virdon was a great outfielder in the Major Leagues."

1. Won the Rookie of the Year award in 1955
2. Played for many years in the Majors
3. Was considered a fine defensive fielder
4. Had good speed

The second statement is based primarily on personal preference. The fact that Virdon won the Rookie of the Year award in 1955 does lend some amount of credibility to the original statement, but it does not give Virdon free entrance into the Hall of Fame.

"Playing for many years in the majors" likewise does not constitute greatness. Many ballplayers have knocked around the majors for over a decade as utility players and have been used to plug a gap here or there, and as pinch runners and pinch batters.

Good defensive ability is a necessity for playing major league baseball. While it is true that some men have made the majors without this ability I think we can assume that most ballplayers are handy with a glove. Most people however would agree that hitting is also an integral part of the game.

The same thing can be said about speed. Most ballplayers have "good" speed. Yet some players with only minimal speed can be good runners and base stealers. What exactly is meant by "good" speed?

Compare the two statements with respect to verifiable facts. Try always to separate those judgments which are based on personal preference and not verifiable from those which are supported by evidence and logical thinking.

Exercises

---

1. Check the following statements and determine which of them are based on fact, on judgment, or on inference. (Some may be based on a combination.) Support your conclusions.

   A. I saw Bill drinking a malt at the drugstore.
   B. I could tell by the sound of the engine that the engine needed a ring job.
   C. There is absolutely no need for new gun legislation.
   D. Farmers can eventually receive more money for their products through a withholding tactic.
   E. Consumer prices are increasing, so farmers must be getting more money for their livestock and cash crops.
   F. According to the farmer's almanac, we should have a mild winter.
   G. Marty is a good carpenter.
   H. The vault at the bank ought to be full of cash.
   I. I saw Anne and Mary talking at the Horse Club meeting, and I know they were discussing Mary's chances of beating me in the upcoming barrel races.
   J. The fact that truck drivers' wages are continuing to rise proves that the Teamsters' Union is doing its job.

2. Bring two examples of judgments with which you can agree and two examples with which you disagree. Explain the causes for your agreement and disagreement.

3. The following are all judgments. What facts or evidence may be used to support these judgments?

   A. Everyone should have a formal education.
   B. People should drive defensively.

C. If you want to get ahead, learn a trade.
D. The country's population is shifting to the West coast and to the states of Florida and Texas, because people want to settle in a good climate.
E. Budweiser is the best beer on the market today.
F. It is safer to fly on a commercial airplane than it is to drive your own automobile.
G. Baseball is the most popular sport in the country.
H. If you want higher wages, form a union.
I. We need the protection afforded by a defensive missile system.
J. Factories have a depressing effect on the people who work in them.

Propaganda and Advertising

Most of the material thus far in this chapter has dealt with the formation and transfer of ideas between individuals. We have spent some time trying to understand the relationship between the world of things and the world of words, between the definition of a word and the emotional response the word evokes. We have discussed the importance of accurate observation and perception, and some of the things which influence us in this action. We have seen the need for critical analysis to distinguish between fact, inference, and judgment, particularly where personal opinions are involved. We have been exposed to some of the methods of distortion.

Another entire area of communications is based on the same principles used in personal communication, but is aimed at influencing great numbers of people. The techniques of propaganda and advertising are employed to influence the behavior of the masses. Propaganda and advertising are used to stimulate us to believe in something; to actively support someone, something, an idea perhaps; to buy a product, a service; to behave in a predictable manner according to a specific stimulus.

Although the term *propaganda* has recently fallen before the forces crying "foul play" and claiming that it is nothing more than a system of deception and distortion, a close look at propaganda will indicate that it is simply a form of spreading information to indoctrinate an audience according to a plan. The word *indoctrinate* is also suspect, but it means simply *to instruct*.

Propaganda can take on many different forms and wear many faces. A public relations campaign sponsored by a state government in order to *stimulate* more tourism, *attract* new businesses and industry, and *increase* investment within the state is a form of propaganda. It is designed to propagate the idea that the state has a great deal to offer. The campaign is also designed to *instruct* the public as to the advantages of this state over the other forty-nine states. The campaign is further designed *to influence behavior*—move here, buy here, settle here, invest here, play here, visit here.

Much of the public suspicion regarding the term *propaganda* comes from its connection with political motives and movements: "Beware of Communist propaganda." Communist propaganda warns the world of the dangers of capitalism. It brands the democratic nations as aggressors, labeling the United States a decadent nation of war mongers. By and large this propaganda is designed for indoctrination within Communist nations. It is a form of training whereby the Communist Party can keep its people in check by using the United States and other democratic powers as symbols of the threat to the survival of the Communist system.

This example demonstrates what can happen through *association*. The American public has heard *propaganda* used so often in connection with Communism that the word has become almost synonymous with Communism. Association can be defined as a propaganda device by means of which the propagandist attempts to establish a connection between some object, person, or cause which the people fear or hate, and the idea he presents in connection with this fear. He hopes the audience (reading or listening) will transfer their attitudes to the object he is presenting.

In the case of the public relations bulletin prepared by the state, the aim is for the audience to associate employment, profit opportunities, good living conditions, etc., with that particular state.

Many large companies use this technique in their advertising.

"International Ball Bearing and Wire Company is dedicated to the American Way of Life."

In evaluating this propaganda technique as to its truthfulness and value, the reader must ask: Is there really a connection; is there sufficient proof to establish the connection? Does this connection make International's product any more desirable? What is the motive behind the company's statement?

Another propaganda device which is closely related to association is *identification*. This technique is most often used by an individual in order to receive broader acceptance in the group he is trying to influence. The more they accept him, the greater will be the possibility of their accepting his ideas. A manager addressing a group of employees may remind them that he once worked within the ranks. A politician campaigning before an American Legion group may remind his audience that he is also a veteran and can thus better understand their concerns.

Winston Churchill used this technique when he spoke to the Congress of the United States on December 26, 1941.

"The fact that my American forebears have for so many generations played their part in the life of the United States and that here I am, an Englishman, welcomed in your midst makes this experience one of the most moving and thrilling in my life, which is already long and has not been entirely uneventful. I wish indeed that my mother, whose memory I cherish across the veil of years, could have been here to see me. By the way, I cannot help reflecting that if my father had been American and my mother British, instead of the other way around, I might have got here on my own. In that case this would not have been the first time you would have heard my voice. In that case I would not have needed an invitation, but if I had it is hardly likely that it would have been unanimous. So perhaps things are better as they are. I may confess, however, that I do not feel quite like a fish out of water in a legislative assembly where English is spoken. I am a child of the House of Commons. I was brought up in my father's house to believe in Democracy. . . . I have steered confidently towards the Gettysburg ideal of government of the people, by the people, for the people."

Identification is used to gain the trust and acceptance of the audience. You might want to review Churchill's comments in an attempt to spotlight the key phrases that would lead to identification. Remember that, despite the success or failure of the speaker or writer to gain audience acceptance, the ideas themselves will have to stand or fall on their own merits.

The propaganda technique called *bandwagon* is commonly associated with political campaigns and is aimed at creating the impression that "if you want to be on the winning side, you'd better get behind Snodgrass before it's too late." Since no one wants to be on the losing side, this can be very effective. The idea is to create the impression that there is a popular movement gaining momentum from growing popular support and acceptance.

It would be a mistake to limit the bandwagon approach to politics, because it is used frequently in advertising:

> All your competitors are switching to computerized machine operations. If you want your company to keep up with the trends . . .

It is a technique quite common in everyday life as well.

> What do you mean, you don't think you'll bowl with the boys this year, all the other fellows will be bowling. You'll be the only one . . .

> Why can't I go to the beach? All the other kids will be going . . .

The bandwagon technique is an obvious attempt to influence a person's behavior through an emotional appeal rather than through logical persuasion based on evidence and good judgment. It is rooted in the premise that the crowd can do your thinking for you, and thus negates the value of personal opinion.

Bifurcation is a method used more and more by the propagandist these days. Hate, fear, and mistrust foster the division of people and nations into camps based on opposing points of view. Bifurcation can be devastating because it is based on the premise that there are only two sides to any problem; everything is either black or white—never gray.

> You are either for our involvement in the Middle East, or you are against it.

> You can be for federal aid to the parochial schools, or against such aid.

You either raise our wages, or we strike. There is no other alternative.

How ridiculous to say something like this. A wise person can always recognize that bifurcation indicates the extremes, and there is much room between the extremes for dozens of alternate points of view. It is certainly possible to be in favor of some federal help for parochial schools without being overwhelmingly in favor of Uncle Sam's picking up the entire tab. This technique would be less dangerous if individuals would recognize the possibility of taking a stand somewhere between the extremes.

Another deceptive device is the use of the *testimonial* in gaining acceptance of a product or idea. In this technique the propagandist or advertising executive uses some authority as an aid to selling an idea or a product. The problem is that the authority is very often not an authority at all, but merely a well-known personality or public figure.

Charley Fingers, the famous shortstop for the Oil City Slickers, uses *Glop* for his hair. How about you?

Roger Rugged, famous movie star, says his investment in Arid Acres was the best he ever made. If you are looking for a fine investment, don't you think you should do as Roger Rugged did?

Larry Leaky knows the value of a battery that won't let you down. Says Larry, "I can't afford a battery I can't depend on. The new Dynamite Battery is a sure-starter." Take it from Larry, fellas.

"One hundred doctors claimed that the ingredients in Neutralite were instrumental in relieving upset stomach."

While all the products mentioned may be excellent and the ideas expressed well grounded in fact, the obvious questions would be:

Is Charley Fingers an expert in grooming?

Is Roger Rugged a good financial advisor?

Is Larry Leaky an automotive expert?

Did the one hundred doctors mean to imply that Neutralite was better than other products? Do other products offer the same results? Under what conditions did the doctors come by their observations? Who paid for the experiments or tests?

The use of *favorable generalities* (glittering generalities) relies on words that trigger favorable response, words that imply positive attitudes. The propagandist who uses this technique hopes that the audience will overlook the fact that he supports his point of view with abstractions. He hopes that they will be convinced by the appeal itself and overlook the lack of evidence. These generalities are usually loaded with emotional content. If a person claims he is for "human rights," each person in the audience can apply his own stand on human rights and then equate that with the propagandist's views on the same subject.

> If you want job security and a solid future consider a position with the Barrett Company.

Job security and a solid future are things everyone is interested in, but just what do they mean? How are these things defined by the Barrett Company?

> As a candidate for the Senate, I want you all to know that I am for human rights. I have an unwavering desire to see the best possible life for all our citizens. I plan to work hard to provide equal opportunity for everyone. My position will be to vote only for positive legislation that will continue to allow for the growth of the American Way of Life.

These sound like honorable goals, if we only knew what they really mean. Once again, fine-sounding words do not guarantee a favorable outcome. As a matter of fact, words can't guarantee us anything. We must look beyond the words to the facts that back them up, for we cannot let our reason be lulled to sleep by our emotions.

The use of *invectives*, commonly referred to as *name-calling*, is an attempt to deceive the public through strong verbal denunciation. Here again, words with strong emotional overtones are often used in place of concrete evidence. And whereas positive connotation was sought in the use of glittering generalities, invective relies on those words and phrases that stimulate negative response.

> Are we going to stand by while the corrupt, crime-infested unions destroy everything we've worked so hard to achieve?
>
> Mr. Jones is self-centered and egotistical and has no business being the plant foreman. He has nothing but contempt for his

co-workers and will take advantage of them every chance he gets. He will exploit us all if he gets the chance.

We can't allow these cheap, inferior products to be imported from abroad. Every time we purchase a foreign product we are putting an American out of work, denying some young person a college education, and taking the food out of some poor American's mouth. These selfish, self-seeking foreigners have been milking this country dry for too many years, and it must stop if we are to survive.

Where is the evidence in the preceding examples? They are loaded with sheer emotional impact, but they lack concrete support.

Propaganda devices will be present as long as there are different points of view. Propaganda itself presents no threat to the educated and analytical individual, the person who takes a critical look at all the facts before making a decision. The only thing the propagandist fears is truth, and the person who takes the time to ferret it out.

Exercises

---

1. Look through some newspapers, magazines, and trade journals, and find two examples of each of the propaganda techniques discussed in this chapter. (These may be excerpts from advertisements, editorials, or news.)

2. Select a topic of current interest and establish a point of view regarding the topic. Write a brief paragraph supporting your point of view and using one of the propaganda techniques. Then write a paragraph using another of the techniques, and so on, until you have written a paragraph for each of the devices. (Use the same topic in each of the examples.)

3. Select what you feel is the most dangerous example of propaganda that you have encountered in your readings. Explain why it is so dangerous. What are its major appeals? What does it presuppose about human nature? What does it expect the reader to do? What facts does it present? Are the facts distorted?

PART III

Shaping the Written Response

CHAPTER 1:   THE TOPIC SENTENCE AND THE CONTROLLING IDEA

For effective communication ideas must be well organized. Paragraphs, like blueprints or schematics, must tell a clear and concise story. In reading blueprints, a tradesman refers to the legend for guidance. In reading a paragraph, we expect the topic sentence and the controlling idea to perform this same function. The topic sentence should tell the subject of the paragraph; the controlling idea tells the writer's attitude toward this subject matter.

If the legend is faulty, a builder may have a very hard time following a given set of plans. The finished product may differ greatly from the draftsman's original concept. Both the draftsman and the builder have a mental picture of the finished product and its purpose; but, as the result of poor communication, their concepts may be quite different.

The paragraph is the verbal counterpart of the blueprint. Like a blueprint, a paragraph can be artistic, creative, bold. Whether it relies on simplicity or innovation, the key is that it *does* communicate. How well it communicates depends on the writer's preparation of his material.

The following paragraph is an excerpt from a student's paper.

(Topic sentence) *Henry Ford developed an inexpensive standardized automobile that transformed America into a nation on wheels.* Henry Ford's childhood days were spent on a Michigan farm. Even at an early age, he was full of ideas that cried for development. His desperate need for funds drove him into automobile racing and the eventual formation of the Ford Motor Company. The company had many struggles and reversals. One of the biggest struggles the company had came as the result of Ford's controversial labor policy. But Ford did not restrict himself to the automobile industry. He once ran for the Senate in Michigan. He also developed a radio homing beacon for use in the developing aircraft industry. He was also the chief proponent of what is called the "vertical trust"—the controlling of materials from their raw state to final production. Yes, the life of this great man was as legendary as his accomplishments.

Let's take the time now to analyze this paragraph, keeping in mind the comparison between this paragraph and a blueprint. The overall topic is Henry Ford. The specific paragraph, according to the topic sentence, is about one aspect of Henry Ford and his work. While all of the material is related to the life and work of Henry Ford, and thus fits the general subject, almost none of the material included fits the *controlling idea* as stated in the topic sentence: the development of *"an inexpensive standardized automobile that transformed America."* Each of the following subjects, all from that one paragraph, might well be included in a complete biography of Henry Ford.

1. Boyhood days on a Michigan farm
2. Automobile racing
3. Formation of The Ford Motor Company
4. The union shop
5. Political activities
6. Contributions to aviation
7. Industrial innovations

If they are to be used in a single paragraph, the topic sentence should deal with the whole picture. Perhaps "The automobile magnate, Henry Ford, had a rich and diversified life." However, this material is so broad and comprehensive it would be better treated in a longer work.

Can you detect some similarities between the Henry Ford paragraph and the following example?

An architect is asked to design and lay out a home workshop for a client. The architect submits a blueprint for a basement workshop, but also includes a detailed floor plan of the entire home, including bedrooms, baths, family room, garage, off-street parking, landscaping, etc.

While all of these are part of the home and the homeowner's concerns, they had relatively little to do with the original request. In other words, they were related to the overall topic (home design), but had little to do with the controlling idea (home workshop).

The following ingredients, all from the blueprint, might be included in a project that called for the complete design of a home geared to fit the needs of a modern family, with above average income and plenty of leisure time.

1. Basic living quarters (living room, bedrooms, kitchen, bathrooms, etc.)
2. Leisure living and recreation, hobby area, etc.
3. Garage and parking
4. Traffic flow
5. Landscaping

The architect was asked for a paragraph, but wrote a book instead.

A writer should limit the material to be covered in a single paragraph. The *controlling idea* aids in this limitation. Include only those materials that support the controlling idea—no more, or less. The reader's attention should be focused on this one idea through examples.

A topic sentence contains the topic (idea) that the paragraph is to develop. That "idea" is all important. The paragraph will revolve around that idea: the idea *controls* the direction of the paragraph. The paragraph "proves" the idea with supportive materials and examples. Using this approach should help you to exclude material that does not develop your central idea.

Let us assume your English teacher has assigned a theme limited to 500 words. You have been asked to write about some aspect of outdoor recreation opportunities in the United States. You select the following topic sentence and controlling idea: "Outdoor recreation for the sportsman is *limitless* in the United States."

Here is a partial list of the supportive materials you might use:

1. Hunting big game animals
2. Hunting waterfowl
3. Hunting small game and vermin
4. Fresh water fishing
5. Salt water fishing
6. Water skiing
7. Sailing
8. Snowmobiling
9. Baseball
10. Golf
11. Tennis
12. Hiking and mountain climbing

But the assignment was for 500 words. You have enough materials and ideas for several *books*. Everything on the list seems related, like the thousand parts of an automobile. None, however, seem to have a direct relationship, like that of a drive shaft and a rear axle. If you re-examine the paragraph topic you can easily get to the heart of the problem. The controlling idea is expressed in the word *limitless*, which also describes your supporting materials.

You should also reconsider the general topic. Your first list of supportive materials included many kinds of outdoor recreation. Why not select *one* with which you have some keen interest and special knowledge? For in reality, each of the entries in that original list is at *least* a subject for a comprehensive paper.

If we substituted "fresh water fishing" for "Outdoor recreation" in our original topic sentence, we might end up with a topic sentence like this:

"Fresh water fishing opportunities are limitless in the United States."

Although the topic has now been narrowed considerably, it is still book-length. Why not limit that topic to a single type of fresh water fish? Why not further limit your subject to a single geographic area that *has* limitless opportunities for taking that fish? Something like this:

Walleye fishing in Northern Wisconsin is both exciting and inexpensive.

Now the topic sentence fits the assignment and contains a twofold controlling idea which can be thoroughly supported in 500 words. Only that material which supports *exciting* and *inexpensive* will be included in the final paper.

You also have the added benefit of a natural division into two major supporting paragraphs. One paragraph can support the excitement of the sport, while the other deals with its minimal costs.

The list of supportive materials now looks something like this:

1. Walleyes are a large type of fresh water game fish.
2. Walleyes taken in the cold waters of Northern Wisconsin put up good fights.
3. Taking this fish on light tackle is a real challenge.
4. Northern Wisconsin abounds in well-stocked lakes.
5. Lakes are readily accessible.
6. Resident and non-resident licenses are inexpensive.
7. Lodgings are abundant and reasonable.

Now that we have fixed both your attention and the reader's on the controlling idea, the 500-word limit seems easily within reach.

Before you can master paragraph unity, you must first master the concept of controlling idea. This principle applies to oral communication as well. In the following examples of topic sentences the controlling ideas are in boldface type. Notice that the controlling idea need not be limited to a single word, but can be two words, a phrase, or even a clause.

1. It takes both **skill** and **patience** to build a model airplane.
2. Mountain climbing takes a great deal of **courage.**
3. Trouble in the Middle East **poses a threat to World peace.**
4. Jack is a **great football player** and an **excellent student.**
5. **Making the playoffs** was the team's greatest desire.

Exercises

---

1. Copy the following topic sentences and underline the word or words that constitute the controlling idea.

   A. Every boy should have a dog.
   B. Coho salmon fishing in Lake Michigan has become a popular sport.
   C. Airplane hijacking poses a real problem to airlines and airline passengers.
   D. The United Nations has made a notable contribution to world peace.
   E. The ability to react quickly is a necessary part of defensive driving.
   F. Of the various contact sports, I like hockey best.
   G. The United States is an industrial giant.
   H. The automobile industry must take an active part in controlling air pollution.
   I. Crime is a real threat to the internal peace of our country.
   J. Charley Caldwell is the best plant manager we have ever had.

2. In publications related to your own vocational interests find examples of topic sentences with clearly stated controlling ideas. Bring these examples to class for use in a class discussion.

3. Write three topic sentences with controlling ideas. Underline the controlling ideas. Write several supporting statements for each topic sentence. (You might want to save copies for use later in the chapter on outlining procedures.)

4. Read the following list of sentences and phrases. Although they are generally related, several are more closely related and could be assembled in a single paragraph. Select those sentences and phrases and ideas that belong together. Re-arrange these selected materials in a paragraph under a *topic sentence and a controlling idea which you will supply.*

   A. Dozens of companies manufacture snowmobiles.
   B. Ice boating and ice skating are two popular winter sports.
   C. The Minnesota Vikings play football right on into the coldest weather.
   D. A snowmobile is quite simple to operate.
   E. Competition between manufacturers will drive the cost of snowmobiles lower as the popularity of snowmobiling rises.
   F. People of almost any age can enjoy . . .
   G. Golf courses, open fields, and country roads . . .
   H. Snow need not be deep . . .
   I. Although their popularity is greater in the North, even areas with relatively mild winters have taken to the craze.
   J. The techniques are basically the same, summer or winter.
   K. More and more people are enjoying leisure time activities.
   L. Automobile racing is popular in Florida.

CHAPTER 2: PARAGRAPH DEVELOPMENT

The relationship between the individual sentences in the paragraph and the controlling idea is an important part of developing the written response. However, it is only a part; and just as there is a relationship between the sentences and the controlling idea, there must also be a clear relationship between each of the sentences. Just as roof rafters and ceiling joists support the roof of a building, they also support each other. It takes all of the members of a team, each doing his own part as well as working together in a team effort, to insure success. And just as a football team may change their tactics to fit the individual game situation, so the writer uses different tactics under different situations. In one game a team may rely on its ground game and ball control. In another game the team may go to a wide-open passing attack. In another game it may stress defense. All of these game plans have something in common—a logical design for victory.

So it is in communication. There must be a logical connection between each of your statements. The nature of your material will determine the organization and development of the paragraph.

Details

One of the most common ways to develop ideas is through the use of details. By describing a process step-by-step or picturing the intricacies of a scene, a writer can communicate information.

What kind of paragraph might rely on detail for its development? Paragraphs stressing the proper preparation of a cornfield for planting; demonstrating the completion of an income tax return; pointing out the proper way to tune an engine; stating the effect of the rising cost of living on consumer purchases.

REMEMBER THE RELATIONSHIP OF THE PARTS TO THE WHOLE

When you tell a friend about an automobile that is fully equipped, chances are you include all those items which you feel are necessary to fit your ideal of a fully equipped automobile. You might say that the car you had in mind has power steering, power brakes, factory air conditioning, electric seats, electric windows, rear window defroster, turn signals, stereo system with rear-seat speakers, and leather interior. You have used details to support your term *fully equipped.* You have selected only those details which support your concept and bring it more sharply into focus.

In the following paragraphs from *Moby-Dick,* notice how Herman Melville relies on detail to create a vivid picture of whaling in the nineteenth century.

> Of all the wondrous devices and dexterities, the sleights of hand and countless subtleties, to which the veteran whaleman is so often forced, none exceed that fine maneuver with the lance called *pitchpoling.* Small sword, or broad sword, in all its exercises boasts nothing like it. It is only indispensable with an inveterate running whale; its grand fact and feature is the wonderful distance to which the long lance is accurately darted from a violently rocking, jerking boat, under extreme headway. Steel and wood included, the entire spear is some ten or twelve feet in length; the staff is much slighter than that of the harpoon, and also of a lighter material—pine. It is furnished with a small rope called a warp, of considerable length, by which it can be hauled back to the hand after darting. . . .
>
> Look now at Stubb; a man who from his humorous, deliberate coolness and equanimity in the direst emergencies, was especially qualified to excel in pitchpoling. Look at him; he stands upright in the tossed bow of the flying boat; wrapt in fleecy foam, the towing whale is forty feet ahead. Handling the long lance lightly, glancing twice or thrice along its length to see if it be exactly straight, Stubb whistlingly gathers up

the coil of the warp in one hand, so as to secure its free end in his grasp, leaving the rest unobstructed. Then holding the lance full before his waistbands middle, he levels it at the whale; when, covering him with it, he steadily depresses the butt-end in his hand, thereby elevating the point till the weapon stands fairly balanced upon his palm, fifteen feet in the air. He minds you somewhat of a juggler, balancing a long staff on his chin. Next moment with a rapid, nameless impulse, in a superb lofty arch the bright steel spans the foaming distance, and quivers in the life spot of the whale. Instead of sparkling water, he now spouts red blood.

"That drove the spigot out of him!" cries Stubb. "'Tis July's immortal Fourth; all fountains must run wine to-day!"

. . . Again and again to such gamesome talk, the dexterous dart is repeated, the spear returning to its master like a greyhound held in skillful leash. The agonized whale goes into his flurry; the towline is slackened, and the pitchpoler dropping astern, folds his hands, and mutely watches the monster die.

Exercises

Write a paragraph using detail for the support of your controlling idea. Confine your paragraph to a maximum of 200 words. Use one of the following topic sentences.

1. The Kansas City Chiefs professional football team is loaded with talent in the defensive line.

2. America is rich in scenic wonders.

3. A custom car is a unique piece of automotive equipment.

4. A beautiful table setting makes food more appetizing.

5. A well-managed filling station has a variety of facilities for the motorist.

6. A good first-aid course should include all the basic emergency procedures.

7. Several steps are necessary to successfully adjust a carburetor.

8. Many basic minerals are necessary for soil to adequately support plant life.

9. Our area of the state abounds in small game animals.

10. _____ offers the winter sports enthusiast unlimited recreational opportunities.

Comparison and Contrast

Comparison and contrast are effective and popular means of paragraph development. *Comparison* points out the similarities that exist between two or more persons, places, things, or concepts. *Contrast* draws our attention to the differences between two or more persons, places, things, or concepts.

Use of comparison and contrast for development or analysis depends on the ability to see basic relationships in the world around us. We can easily point out the similarities that exist among all the sedans produced by the "Big Three" automobile manufacturers. Within the middle price range we can find the same basic package of accessories, the same safety equipment, and a close proximity in luxury items. In other words, we can compare them feature for feature, and come up with some striking similarities. By the same token, we can take a look at their entries in the sports car field and find some real contrasts—for example, the contrast between the *Maverick* and the *Challenger*.

This method can be applied to almost anything. We can compare the American people to their Canadian neighbors and come up with hundreds of similarities. The better we can come to know them and understand, the more ways we can liken them to ourselves. We watch many of the same television shows, drive the same makes of automobiles, dress in similar clothing, have professional teams in the same leagues, believe in the free enterprise system, usually support each other in international affairs, and have the same basic aspirations about issues such as world peace, pollution control, and education.

This method is very often the key to success in such fields as advertising and marketing. A model home is constructed to fit the needs of the average family. The salesman can compare the features of his model with the needs commonly requested by the new-home buyers.

Even in dating, we often look for a companion who shares some things in common—someone who likes the same music perhaps, or reads the same books, or likes pizza.

Comparison and contrast as methods of development or analysis are used in connection with other means of development, rather than alone. The salesman who compares the features of his model home may well cite examples of how his particular home solved the problems of Mr. and Mrs. Smith and their four children. Chances are he will use some illustration to prove his point. He will probably use reason and rely on logic to make his sale. (These techniques will be explained later in this chapter.)

If we were to compare New York City and Miami, Florida, we would surely find many similarities. Both are East coast seaports with large transient populations. However, more understanding comes from contrasting the two cities. Miami's reputation relies on excellent climate, and much of its attraction is in the area of outdoor recreation. New York, on the other hand, is famous as a great cultural center offering theatres, museums, art galleries, ballet, and opera. Miami has room to spread; the city is spreading rapidly outward from its center. But New York has nowhere to go but up, and so it continues to move vertically.

Look at it this way: Using comparison and contrast together is like traveling down a joint highway. For a time, both U. S. 66 and Missouri 40 run together. They pass through the same towns, pass the same sights, and share the same traffic regulations. After a time, the two highways branch out and go their separate ways. Now U. S. 66 becomes unique. It has its own speed limits; it bypasses many small towns and has its own sights and topography. Whereas U. S. 66 bypasses the towns and allows the motorist to make better time, Missouri 40 allows the traveler the opportunity to take a more leisurely trip and take advantage of the personality of the countryside and the small towns along the route. After diverging, the two routes are quite different.

Comparison and contrast: twins reared under the same conditions, possessing some similar qualities, yet as opposite as the two poles of a magnet. Comparison and contrast: twin cities, like Minneapolis and Saint Paul or Dallas and Fort Worth, alike in many respects yet basically different.

Comparison and contrast can be used under vastly different circumstances. "Compare and contrast the poetic qualities of e. e. cummings and John Donne" is a question you might be asked in a literature class. However, as a manager of a hardware store you might be asked this question by a confused customer: "Compare the advantages and disadvantages of a circular sander and a belt sander." Or "What is the difference between water-base and oil-base paint?" A lumberman has no doubt been asked this question many times: "What is the difference between indoor and outdoor plywood?" Because comparison and contrast lend themselves so readily to combination with other techniques of development, they are very popular.

Exercises

---

1. Write a brief comparison between two well-known products in your vocational area. Be prepared to give a brief oral presentation of the same material. In the oral presentation you may ask the class to role-play, and you can set a situation in which this kind of presentation would be called for: sales meetings, product seminar, Chamber of Commerce meeting, in-service training session, etc.

2. Write a paragraph contrasting an expensive product with a competing product selling for considerably less money. Remember, the aim here is to key on the differences between the two products. (Again, it will be to your benefit to select a product from your area of vocational interest.)

3. Compare *and* contrast one of the following:

   A. The two major political parties in the U.S.
   B. Purchasing a home and renting a home.
   C. Buying on time and paying cash.
   D. Trading for a new automobile every year or keeping the old one until it no longer works.

E. The qualities of hard wood and soft wood.
F. Detergent oil and non-detergent oil.
G. Buying clothes and making your own.
H. Registered nurses and practical nurses.
I. Secretaries and clerks.
J. Two daily newspapers.

Illustration

While a picture may be worth a thousand words, it is often necessary for the writer to use the words in place of the photograph. When we speak of *illustration* we mean that the writer supplies a narrative example that supports the controlling idea.

If more than one example is used, it is best to put the most important one last, which gives the illustration more dramatic impact on the reader. The writing will have a rising curve of importance which will add to the reader's anticipation—he will want to read on; he will have a sense of discovery and growing awareness.

> America is truly the land of opportunity. Marty Justen was an illegitimate child, born in the small coal town of Lucas, Iowa. He lived with foster parents until he was seventeen years old. He then falsified his age, joined the army and received training as a large earth-moving equipment operator. The tremendous versatility of the equipment fascinated Justen and he continued to work with the equipment after his tour of duty with the army. He saved enough money to make a down payment on a small caterpillar tractor of his own. He kept busy seven days a week. Grading jobs, small paving contracts—no job was too small. The bigger jobs were contracted out to the outfits with the equipment to handle them. Soon he made a down payment on a larger "cat" and then a back-fill.

Before long he was handling the landscape and fill jobs for subdivisions and shopping center developments. Several years ago, Marty Justen began buying and developing his own land. He formed a diversified corporation involved in sales and distribution of large earth moving equipment, the acquisition and development of recreational lands, shopping centers and home building, and mineral exploration. From a penniless, unwanted child to a corporate wizard at the controls of a multi-million dollar conglomerate—there can be no doubt that the United States is still the land of opportunity.

All the facts work together to provide a complete illustration. Each fact is a separate part of the story, but the parts make up the whole. The entire story is the illustration that supports the controlling idea, *"America is the land of opportunity."* Notice too, that each part of the illustration is more important and spectacular than the preceding part. In building to a climax, we have used the same technique that the fiction writer uses to achieve the desired effect.

Exercises

Write a paragraph of illustration using one of the topic sentences listed below (200 word maximum).

1. The instinct to survive is one of man's most powerful instincts.

2. Heroes are ordinary people who react courageously under dangerous circumstances.

3. The dog is truly man's best friend.

4. Some people go to rags and ruin almost overnight.

5. When the chips are down, desire can often overcome a lack of skill.

6. Gold has caused men to do many strange things.

7. _____ was the one event that had the greatest influence on my life.

8. Most people will go to extremes to fulfill the need to belong.

9. A cat has an exceptional sense of balance.

10. Clothes don't always make the man.

Reasons

Whenever you state an opinion you are apt to be ready to back that opinion with reasons (i. e., justifications), supported by facts (details). Are you going to invest in that new business in town? If so, why? If not, why not? You may want to reply to a recent editorial in your home town newspaper. You may be asked why the community should support the college's vocational programs, or why tax dollars should go to fight the pollution of our natural resources, or why a traffic light is needed at the corner of Main and Spruce streets.

Both a written and an oral reply to these questions can be developed by reasoning and supported by fact. Your reasons should be arrived at only after careful consideration and clear thinking. Your attitude ought to be summed up in a topic sentence through the controlling idea.

Whenever we use reasons and reasoning, we are making value judgments; and though we use logical thought processes, we should be aware that we are "interpreting" evidence and facts. The interpretation provides the difference between development by reasons and development by details.

> I am opposed to cigarette smoking because it is dangerous to my health. There is overwhelming evidence to support my point of view. The American Cancer Society offers what I consider to be substantial evidence that smoking can cause lung cancer, heart disease and a number of other illnesses.

Here I have offered reasons which support the controlling idea for my point of view. However, each sentence expresses an opinion based on tests and statistics. Let's flip the coin and see what happens.

I continue to smoke cigarettes because there is little proof to indicate that cigarette smoking is harmful to my health. Many doctors and researchers commissioned by the tobacco industry have carried out extensive tests and claim they haven't turned up a single positive link between cigarette smoking and lung cancer. They have also concluded that excess body weight and inactivity are the chief causes of heart malfunctions.

Reasons, therefore, come from within your mind—they are opinions and judgments. *Why* you smoke or don't smoke is a position supported with *reasons*. *What* smoking is and *how* to smoke are questions that can be answered with details. A smoker needs certain materials, cigarettes, matches ashtrays; the smoker uses the matches to light his cigarettes; the cigarette smoke is inhaled into the lungs; the spent cigarettes are deposited into the ashtrays. These are all *details*, not reasons.

Exercises

Read the following two groups of sentences. Select a topic sentence from *each group* and write a brief paragraph based on each topic sentence. Use reasons for paragraph development. When you have completed the paragraphs, check each sentence carefully to make sure that it supports the controlling idea.

Group A

1. American automobiles have many advantages over the foreign imports.

2. Woodworking is a lost craft.

3. This country needs more skilled automotive mechanics.

4. The "do it yourself" craze has practically taken over in every aspect of our daily lives.

5. Flying is an exciting and challenging hobby.

6. Everyone should have a hobby.

7. Land is the best investment for the future.

8. The small, independent farmer is being squeezed out of agriculture.

Group B

1. The current minimum wage is sufficient (insufficient) to maintain an adequate standard of living.

2. If we are to save our natural resources we must act now.

3. We must (must not) support federal aid to education.

4. Personal income taxes must be lowered.

5. We must change (maintain) our current foreign policy in Latin America.

6. We should (should not) legalize gambling in the United States.

7. We should (should not) have a guaranteed annual minimum wage.

8. The government should do something to control the rising cost of living.

Definition

Definition simply answers the question: What is it? In 1782 Crevecoeur concluded that

> The American is a new man, who acts upon new principles;
> he must therefore entertain new ideas, and form new opin-

ions. From voluntary idleness, servile dependence, penury, and useless labor, he has passed to toils of a very different nature.

He has used definition for development.

When we define a word we usually place it in a class to show its general characteristics (in order to make the unfamiliar familiar), and then point out how it specifically differs from other things of the same class.

> The V-8 engine is an internal combustion engine. [We have placed it in its larger order—engines.] It has eight cylinders placed in a V-shaped configuration. [We have differentiated it from other internal combustion engines.]

> The Shakespearean sonnet is a poem composed of fourteen lines of iambic pentameter with a rhyme scheme of *abab cdcd efef gg*. [We have included its relationship to all of poetry and its own distinctive characteristics as well.]

It is quite possible to complete some definitions adequately in a single sentence, but most of the time more space is needed. If you were asked: "What is democracy?" your explanation would most likely be a definition of the word *democracy,* even though the question did not specifically ask you to define the word. The following concepts would all be needed to define the term: It is a form of government in which the power remains with the citizens. This power can be exercised either directly or indirectly by means of elected representaton. A social system based upon equality and mobility usually goes with it. It is, in effect, a government "of the people, for the people, and by the people."

Chronological Order

A clear development of ideas in a paragraph or an essay can often be achieved through the use of chronological order, by listing events in the order in which they occurred.

> The equipment used for air travel has changed dramatically since 1928, when the Ford Tri-Motor carried fourteen passengers at a cruising speed of 120 m.p.h. In 1936 Douglas

developed the DC-3, which could carry 28 passengers at 180 m.p.h. In the 1940's two major planes were developed: the Lockheed Constellation in 1946 (54 passengers, 310 m.p.h.) and the Boeing Stratocruiser two years later (60 passengers, 300 m.p.h.). The next plane introduced was again similar to its immediate predecessors—the DC-7 of 1953 carried 69 passengers and cruised at 330 m.p.h. Since then, the changes have been even more dramatic. The Boeing 707 of 1958 is able to carry 132 passengers at 570 m.p.h., and 1970's 747 will carry 490 passengers at 625 m.p.h.!

Cause and Effect

There is often some confusion between this method of paragraph development and development that relies on chronological order. Remember that just because one event precedes another, it does not necessarily cause the second event. The Boeing 707 did not cause the Boeing 747!

Last year the university dropped its language requirement, and this year the enrollment is up 10 percent. Dropping the language requirement preceded the increased enrollment, but that does not prove that the deleted requirement was the cause for the rise in enrollment. Usually the cause of an event is a complex interaction of conditions, and *each* is necessary for a specific result. It is quite possible that the deletion of the language was one of many conditions. It might be found that the number of job opportunities available to students increased. Perhaps more loans and scholarships were made available. Perhaps the entrance requirements were eased. Resident high schools in the area may have graduated several thousand more students than in the previous year. In order to determine the cause of any single event, all the possible conditions must be examined.

In the use of cause and effect we can begin with the result, as stated in our topic sentence, and list the causes. Or we can list several causes and end up with the result, again stated in the topic sentence. (In this case the topic sentence would be the last sentence in the paragraph, instead of the first.) The important thing is to always guard against the easy way out.

John stopped for pizza after the basketball game. When he finished the pizza, he started to drive home and was involved in an automobile accident. Therefore pizza causes automobile accidents.

Exercises

Select three of the topics listed below. Develop one of the topics in a paragraph using definition. Develop the second topic in a paragraph using chronological order. Develop the third topic in a paragraph using cause and effect. Be sure to select your topics carefully as some of the topics can be developed more easily in one way than in another.

1. Honesty in business

2. Civil disobedience

3. Drug addiction

4. The importance of good communication

5. The most unforgettable character I have ever met

6. The college library

7. Social Security

8. Growth of the nation's railroads

9. The plight of the American Indian

10. Civil rights

11. Making a pizza

12. Gaining journeyman status in a trade or craft

13. Setting up a small business

14. Vocational training

15. Reloading shotgun shells

CHAPTER 3:   OUTLINING PROCEDURES

Several years ago I had a student who had extreme difficulty organizing his written assignments. Try as he would, he could not grasp general outlining procedures. Although he had much to say and would make valuable contributions to class discussions, his paragraphs and essays seemed almost cryptic. He seemed to skip from point to point, never actually finishing, or even supporting, his ideas. Yet when questioned about his ideas in later conferences he would bubble over with enthusiasm and speak confidently about his point of view.

I happened to see this student one afternoon in the student center. He was sitting at a table, working on a model of an old Chevrolet five-window coupé. I noticed he had several small piles of parts: the running gear was in one pile, engine parts in another pile, and so on. He was quite busy taking the flashing off the parts and smoothing the edges—organizing his efforts in preparation for the actual construction of the model.

I sat quietly watching for some time, and then I picked up part of the rumble seat and placed it in the pile containing the running gear. I don't recall the exact conversation that followed, but it went something like this:

"Hold it, Mr. Sheridan, that part goes over here with the interior parts."

"Why?" I asked.

"Because this pile is for the running gear and you just had the rumble seat, that's why."

"Does it make any difference?"

"Yes," he said, somewhat annoyed by now, "I'm trying to keep all the parts organized."

I smiled and said, "I thought you were the guy who couldn't get the hang of organization."

I asked him if we couldn't try one more time, and although he protested at first, he finally consented.

We put all the parts into one pile and began.

Our subject matter was an automobile. Since it was his automobile and his experiment, I tried to remain as uninvolved as I could. It was his logic that the automobile was broken into the following four areas:

I. Complete engine assembly
II. Running gear
III. Chassis
IV. Interior

From this point on, the job was an easy one. He used the drive shaft as a link between the engine and the running gear and made logical relationships between the various parts and the whole. Our little experiment did not solve the problem by itself, but it was a first step; it broke the ice and the rest was easy.

Many students claim that outlining is dry and boring. It seems like "busy work." If the outline seems uninteresting, it may be that the subject matter itself is uninteresting. If the subject is interesting and the student is involved in it, how can the organization and outlining be uninteresting? It's like saying "I love my new suit, but can't stand the pants and jacket."

Outlining aids in the logical development of *your* ideas. It can save you valuable time, because it helps you to see the integral relationships between the various parts and between the parts and the whole. Outlines help pinpoint weaknesses and problems in the assembly of your ideas. They help keep you from writing yourself into a corner. An outline gives you a game plan.

Decide first on a general subject area. Let's say, for example, the general subject area is

Horses

The overall subject area would include race horses, draft horses, and pleasure horses; breeds of horses; and so on. Obviously, the subject area is too broad as it stands. Therefore, the next step would be to select a portion of that total subject area. We might call this step a general narrowing of the subject area. We choose

Pleasure Horses

We are still faced with the problems of various breeds and types: western pleasure, English, jumping, etc. So we further limit our subject area by selecting

Quarter Horses

Various papers could be written about the raising of Quarter Horses—showing them, working them, racing them, breeding them, recording their history as a breed.

It is often said that a person should write about what he knows. Let's assume that you are currently raising a Quarter Horse colt for a 4-H project. Your chief concern at this time happens to be

The Necessary Steps in Breaking and Training a Colt

The general subject area—horses—has been narrowed to a specific topic—the necessary steps in breaking and training a Quarter Horse colt.

Once a subject area has been narrowed sufficiently, you must decide on the best way to present the material. Perhaps the best way is to look for relationships within the specific area. This aids both in your organization of the material and in the reader's understanding and retention. For instance, in the case of the colt mentioned above, his training could best be explained in a time sequence. From the time he begins his training until the rider mounts him for the first time, several things must take place. Chronological development regarding the training steps will bring the total picture more sharply into focus.

Thesis: There are several necessary steps in breaking and training your Quarter Horse colt.

Intro: There are few bonds stronger than the one that exists between a man and his horse.

    I. Gaining the colt's trust
        A. support
        B. support
    II. Breaking to halter
        A. support
        B. support

   III. Breaking to saddle
       A. support
       B. support
          1. support
          2. support
   IV. Reining your horse

Conclusion: The result of all this patience and effort is a
            well-trained, trustworthy, and responsive horse,
            and the thrill a person experiences from the
            working relationship between horse and rider.

In another instance, a person might want to explain just what
goes into a good family garden. In that case, he might want to consider an organization based on "what" relationships. That is, what
is a good diversified garden? What plants are included? What can
one expect from such a garden? What kind of care is needed?

Besides the four basic relationships of what, where, when, and
why, there is that organization which can be a mixture of two or
more relationships. What are the problems plaguing our assembly
operation? Where are the trouble spots in our assembly operation?
At what point in the operation do the problems occur? Why do
problems exist in our assembly operation? These can be combined
effectively in at least two ways. What are the problems in our
assembly operation and when do they occur? What are the problems in our assembly operation and why do they occur?

Topic Outline vs. Sentence Outline

The topic outline is used more often for short talks or brief written
pieces and shows only the arrangement of material. It does not
summarize the thought content.

SAMPLE TOPIC OUTLINE

Thesis: There are both advantages and disadvantages in
        owning a small foreign automobile.

   I. Advantages
      A. Smaller original cost

B. More economical to operate
1. gas milage
2. tires
3. insurance
II. Disadvantages
A. Service facilities
B. Replacement parts
C. Accidents

The sentence outline does everything done by the topic outline, but in addition shows the author's point of view by summarizing in complete sentences the material listed in each heading.

SAMPLE SENTENCE OUTLINE

Thesis: There are both advantages and disadvantages in owning a small foreign automobile.

I. The main advantages to ownership of a foreign compact automobile lie primarily in the area of economics.
A. A small foreign economy car can be purchased for considerably less money than some of their larger American cousins.
B. The foreign compact car is more economical to operate.
1. The foreign imports offer 10 to 25 percent greater gas milage.
2. You can purchase a complete set of tires for the same amount you might spend for two tires for a domestic automobile.
3. Most insurance companies have a discount rate for insuring compact automobiles.
II. In my opinion, however, the disadvantages of foreign compact ownership outweigh the advantages.
A. There are fewer service facilities available, particularly away from large cities and ports of entry.
B. Lack of replacement parts often causes long periods of delay when repairs are necessary.
C. In case of a severe accident, the lighter foreign compact is no match for the larger, heavier domestic automobile.

Conclusion: In the final analysis, I will cast my vote for the
              comfort and safety provided by our domestic
              automobiles.

Therefore, an outline is merely a breakdown of the whole into
its component parts, with attention given to clear subordination
and coordination.

    I.
      A.
      B. (Means that I. can be broken into two integral parts.)

However, if you have something like this:

    I.
      A. (Means that you have broken I. into one part, which is
         impossible. If you doubt this, try to break a pencil into
         one part, or tear a sheet of paper into one piece. It can't
         be done!)

When you have this arrangement, chances are you have merely
restated I.

Review of outlining procedures:

1. Select a general subject area.
2. Narrow the general subject area to a specific topic.
3. Arrange material into logical groups according to their relationships with each other and with the topic itself.
4. Establish a thesis statement.
5. Check material to make sure that you have included only that material which supports your thesis.
6. Arrange material in the order of logical development.
7. Construct your introduction and conclusion.
8. Re-check your outline to eliminate mixed construction. That is, you should have either a topic outline or a sentence outline. Select the one that best fits your needs and stick with it.

Exercises

1. In order to become familiar with the logical relationships within a subject area, select a topic and write four brief outlines for that one topic. Use the four basic relationships for your outlines: What, Where, When, Why.

2. Select a topic for a brief paper and outline your material first in a topic outline and then in a sentence outline.

3. Choose an article from one of your recent trade journals and construct an outline similar to the one the author may have used in preparing the article.

CHAPTER 4: REWRITING AND
PROOFREADING EXERCISES

An important part of good communication is the review and re-evaluation which precedes the final draft of any piece of written material. It is the writer's last chance to check his work for content and coherence. Has he said everything he wants to say? Has he said it in such a way that the reader will understand it and accept it? Has he eliminated all the unnecessary words? Has he spotted faulty reasoning in time to make changes? Has he corrected his faulty punctuation and misspelled words?

The difference between an effective writer and an ineffective writer is very often in the proofreading. If we could list the two most critical periods in the process of writing, that list would have to include the mental preparation and organization of the material and the rewriting and proofreading preceding the final draft.

The following exercises have been designed for two purposes: (1) to give you some practice in repairing faulty construction and (2) to give you the opportunity for self-review in such areas as verb tenses, punctuation, and usage.

Exercises

Coherence. Rewrite the following incoherent sentences so that the confusion is eliminated.

1. We found the car which had been pushed around the corner by a mailbox.

2. Waiting for us in the living room was a distinguished guest that was freshly plastered.

3. He wore black gloves on his hands, which were made of alligator hide.

4. The dog frightened away every salesman with a growl.

5. I sold the car to that young man who recently got married even though he couldn't afford the down payment.

6. We keep pickles in a large jar for guests in our refrigerator.

7. The famous humorist gave a speech to Congress, which was unexpectedly sober.

8. The displays amazed the children with their brightly blinking lights and eerie electronic sounds.

9. I saw the young man who had recently been married on the bridge in a mood of deep despair.

10. I talked to George after he had eaten lunch in the elevator.

11. You will find the coffee I bought in a small can in the cupboard.

12. The snake was long and green with rattles on its tail which bit me.

13. He wore a yellow hat on his head which had large holes in it.

14. She took a picture of every cow with a polaroid camera.

15. I saw Wilbur Spelvin dancing on Thelma's television set last night.

16. Skiing down the mountain side, a large pine suddenly fell across my path.

17. To kiss a girl properly, one's nose should be turned slightly to one side.

18. After swimming in the icy lake, the enormous fire on the shore felt very good.

19. Flying at 40,000 feet, the mountains seemed tiny and far away.

20. To climb a rope, the hands should be perfectly dry.

21. When preparing for a formal date, tie and socks should not clash.

22. Running up the stairs, her necklace broke.

23. When peeling onions, the windows should be open.

24. Playing golf, the trees kept getting in the way.

25. Finding the elephant that had been shot by the waterhole two days before, the stench was unbearable.

Wordiness. Rewrite the following statements, taking care to eliminate the excess words.

1. I think I ought to tell you here and now that everything I'm telling you here is my own thoughts, and I thought I ought to tell you that.

2. Many problems in our community ought to be considered and I intend to bring them up for your consideration.

3. Many phases of this business' operations should be evaluated and you can be sure that these shortcomings will come under the committee's evaluation.

4. My childhood days will never be forgotten which is reflected in the fact that I am constantly reminded of things that happened during my youth.

5. In size, John is several inches taller than his shorter roommate, Bill.

6. The house I live in is an older home.

7. The car I drive is a 1966 model automobile.

8. When a person takes up bowling as a serious hobby, he needs much bowling equipment such as bowling shoes and a bowling ball and a bag.

9. Hiking, as an outdoor recreation, offers a person the opportunity to enjoy the outdoors.

10. There are three parts to the problem; part one, part two, and part three.

Rewrite the following paragraphs by combining some of the materials and eliminating the wordiness.

There were several reasons Jane decided on practical nursing as a career in which she would become involved. Jane wanted to become involved in a career in which she could deal with people and be of some service to people in need. Since her funds were limited and she had little money to spend on education she needed to receive her training at the community college in her community. This would allow her to remain home and save some of the money it would cost her for room and board if she went away to college. Lastly, and finally, Jane wanted a career that would enable her to pick her working hours later in life when she would have a family and responsibilities when she was married.

Jack found law enforcement to be both challenging and rewarding for a profession to be in. He had to keep up with the latest developments in law enforcement and study and work to keep abreast of the changes taking place. He knew he had to set an example in the community by being an outstanding citizen and someone the people in town could look up to and respect. He felt extra special good about doing his share to keep the town a safe and happy community in which to live and grow up in. All in all, these are the main reasons for Jack feeling the way he does about things in general.

Punctuation.   Rewrite the following sentences, taking care to insert the proper punctuation.

1. Historians may disagree with me but my list of outstanding presidents would include Thomas Jefferson Abraham Lincoln Franklin D. Roosevelt and Harry S Truman

2. One of the questions asked at the Chamber of Commerce seminar was what does this community need to attract new industry

3. Al Jim asked Did you finish the lube job on the Ford

4. Mr. Graham the drafting teacher drives a bright red Alpha Romeo

5. After the movie Mike Sally Terry and the rest of the crowd went to Harris Hall where the Sophomore Class was having a sock hop

6. Teaching students to read for greater understanding and to communicate more clearly are the two basic objectives of this course

7. The short story The Sons of Martha appeared in the February 1967 issue of Harper's

8. The problems of farm subsidies price controls Soil Bank and land reclamation are just a few of the problems confronting the Department of Agriculture

9. One of the most often asked questions at the hearing was Do you think the U S Government will provide the same financial support to the airlines that it does to the railroad industry

10. I don't care what anyone says the Yamaha is still the best imported motorcycle.

Rewrite the following paragraph supplying the proper punctuation.

There are somewhere around 200 million people in the world who are considered American citizens There are about 200 million different ways in which they choose their heroes too Any time you are dealing with people there are variables No two people will look at any situation the same way or if they do somebody somewhere has been brainwashed or hypnotized Even when looking at so called national heroes such as George Washington everyone to one degree or another has a different vantage point and thus a different outlook Americans are also a unique people and thus their criteria for choosing their heroes is going to be different from the criteria set down by other national groups Russia has its Peter the Great and England has its Wellington Both these examples of heroes have to do with what these men did for their countries while American national heroes Washington Lincoln etc have to do with ideals that they represented as well as what they did for their country This shows in some respects the character of the American people in their search for identity in ideals as well as the more materialistic aspects of human development such as superiority in science industry space military power and just being plain "American" ie baseball apple pie mom motherhood and the stars and stripes

Verb Form. Rewrite the following sentences using the appropriate forms of the verbs in parentheses.

1. You could have (write) a fine report if you had (take) more time.

2. Hank (lay) his tools on the work bench and went into the kitchen and (sit) down for dinner.

3. My sister has never (fly) in a jet plane.

4. I have never (know) a machinist as clever as George.

5. Our Indian guide (eat) his dinner on the shore.

6. When the truck (break) down, we were forced to walk the rest of the way to town.

7. Mr. Favors has (teach) shop for twenty years.

8. The flag was (raise), the cannon (fire), and the chuckwagon race (start).

9. The young colt (become) frightened and (run) to the old mare's side.

10. The car (speed) around the corner and out of sight.

11. The infielder (miss) the relay from center field and the runner (race) for the plate.

12. He (jump) into the river and (start) (swim) for the opposite shore.

13. Jim (start) the saw and (begin) (rip) the plank.

14. The Board of Directors (choose) the new Chairman.

15. I have not (write) a theme for over a month.

16. I have (check) the tires and (recommend) immediate replacement.

17. He (call) out but it was too late.

18. The workshop was closed by the time he (arrive).

19. The dog (flush) the rabbit from a brush pile near the old barn.

20. Baxter (slip) and (fall) on the slippery walk.

Pronoun Agreement.   Rewrite the sentences supplying the proper form of pronoun to insure agreement.

1. He is the kind of mechanic who takes their work seriously.

2. I know a lot of interesting things, but when I go to write it down, I forget it all.

3. Find out if her or him will be attending.

4. It will be difficult for he to do it without some help from she and the others.

5. The baby was angry because it couldn't find it's bottle.

6. Whomever made this mistake will find out that they can't get away with it.

7. Ask who you want to come to the party, it's okay with I.

8. The Board of Directors are not able to agree on their course of action.

9. No one should allow their emotions to govern their better judgment.

10. The foreman spoke to Flanagan and I about the strike vote.

11. The members of the union had its problems getting the kind of representation it wanted.

12. The spaniel went to its master and wagged his tail.

13. The cows were nervous but the farmer decided to milk it anyway.

14. Everyone who attended the workshop knew they would benefit greatly from the demonstrations.

15. A person who enters the apprenticeship program knows they will have to work hard to succeed.

16. The garage is closed on Mondays so you will have to take their business to someone else.

17. Should we take you're car or him's?

18. The farmer got mad at the rooster and he lost his head.

19. The number of buses needed for our trip will depend on whomsoever will be going.

20. The nurses will be upset to learn that the hospital Administrator turned down the proposal to raise its salaries and fringe benefits.

PART IV

Shaping The Oral Response

SHAPING THE ORAL RESPONSE

Before we get into construction of a speech and its delivery, it would be wise to set the record straight in regard to some popular misconceptions about speakers and speech-making.

"A good speaker is a born speaker." There is a great deal of difference between a person with the gift of gab and an effective speaker. Similarly, there is a great deal of difference between a man who can throw a football fifty yards and a great quarterback. Stories have been circulated that the legendary professional golfer, Bobby Jones, never had a golf lesson and was simply a natural. While all that is well and good, for every natural golfer or speaker, there are thousands who become proficient only after hard work and practice. Most people can speak. Likewise, most people can improve their existing speech skills. YOU can improve your speech skills, or your bowling average, or your handwriting, or anything else, if you will make an honest effort to do so.

Improvement of your speaking ability will not improve your personality, just as a new suit of clothes will not. On the other hand, it can help you achieve greater poise and self-confidence. Self-confidence by itself will rarely get you a job, but it can get you through the front door and past the personnel director's office. And once on the job, it can help you to establish better relationships between you and the customer, you and the boss, you and your fellow employees.

Confidence can be acquired! Many speech problems (such as sweating, loss of voice, and loss of memory) are psychosomatic in origin—outward, physical expressions of fear. You may never overcome that fear, but you can learn to control it and convert that nervous energy into a positive force—enthusiasm. Brief and informal speech exercises can help you build your confidence. As your successful experiences grow in number, your poise and confidence will also increase. Confidence ought to become a habit; it is the one habit you will never have to break. Remember, the fear you may have of appearing before an audience is a social fear, not too much different from the fear you may have felt before your first date or before your first prom. You are afraid you might receive an unfavorable response from the very people you wish to impress. Many public figures, including Red Skelton, Elvis Presley, Ella Fitzgerald, Elizabeth Taylor, Kim Novak, Roger Maris, Billy Graham, President Truman, and President Eisenhower, have felt these same basic fears and have managed to control them.

If you have ever participated in organized sports you will understand that many obstacles can be met and dealt with more successfully if you will get yourself "psyched-up."

Let's pause for a moment and take stock of the situation. You are about to make a speech and just before you go on, you ask yourself, *"What do I have going for me?"*

Audiences usually identify with the speaker. They want you to do well. The better you do, the more comfortable the audience will feel. They will be more interested in how well you bounce back than in any mistake. The fact that you made a mistake only proves to the audience that you are, in fact, human. But when you bounce back, you are re-enforcing that old part of the American Dream: An American is NOT a quitter.

You will always appear more confident than you feel. Since you will not be holding hands with the audience, the fact that your hands may be sweaty should not affect you in the least. The fact that you are the only person standing on your legs should assure you that no one will know your legs feel weak or wobbly.

If you have studied your material and are truly interested you will probably know just as much, or more, about your subject than anyone in the audience. The fact you are an "authority" on your particular topic should add to your confidence.

Each speech is also a learning experience. The more speeches you give, the better they will become.

The Impromptu Speech-or-"C'mon in, the water's fine."

For most people who have little experience in public speaking, the thought of having to deliver a speech without time to prepare

Remember—you are only carrying on an enlarged conversation.

can be terrifying. An *impromptu speech* is a speech delivered without previous notification and without preparation time. Sound frightening? You say you can't do it? Nonsense! If you have ever responded when asked a question in a classroom, if you have ever stood up in a club meeting to make a comment, if you have ever made your feelings known in a church or civic group, you have delivered an impromptu speech. These can all be considered mini-speeches.

Remember there is always time to prepare if you will utilize those few precious moments that elapse between when you are asked to speak and the actual beginning of your reply. Do not waste that energy on a feeling of despair. The initial shock of being asked to make a few remarks should start your adrenalin flowing. Turn that adrenalin flow into a positive force working for you, instead of against you. Learn to harness that energy.

If you are asked to deliver a brief speech, approach the situation with an air of confidence. Rise and walk with assuredness to the speaker's platform, take a comfortable position, establish audience contact, take a deep breath, and begin. At least 30 seconds have elapsed since you were called upon to respond. If you have used your energy and controlled your emotions, you have had time to prepare.

The most important part of this brief preparation is the formation of a thesis statement that contains a controlling idea. (Remember the time you spent grasping the controlling idea concept?) The controlling idea will set the course you will follow in this brief speech. Several statements in support of this thesis will probably be sufficient to fill the few moments of your impromptu speech. Perhaps you can draw upon your past experiences and come up with a brief example or a story to add to your support. All that remains is to restate your point of view in a concluding remark and your impromptu speech is finished.

Introduction: State your thesis and controlling idea in a complete sentence.

Body: State why your point of view is valid. Offer some evidence, examples, reasons, illustrations, to support your thesis.

Conclusion: Summarize your remarks and restate your thesis.

Some Self-Starters for Impromptu Speeches

Fill in the blank and you have the opening for an impromptu speech exercise.

1. How many of you really understand the importance of _____?
2. Are you aware that _____ affects every one of you in your day-to-day living?
3. Every person here could have his health problems solved almost overnight by paying attention to _____.
4. Presidential primaries are _____.
5. The thing that really burns me up is _____.
6. The most swinging city in the world must be _____.
7. My idol is _____.
8. The most shocking event in years was _____.
9. More people are concerned with _____ than with any other topic of the day.
10. Silence is _____.
11. English people are _____.
12. The United Nations ought to _____.
13. The best automobile on the road today is _____.
14. Color is _____.
15. The most inspiring event in years was _____.
16. Let's all work together and make _____ a part of our daily lives.
17. My favorite meal is _____.
18. _____ will never work!
19. The occupational field that provides the most opportunities for a young man is _____.
20. _____ was the most important single event in the first two-thirds of the 20th Century—if you understand the background and causes.

CHAPTER 1:   SOME SPEECH MECHANICS

Notes

Notes are designed to increase your chances of delivering an effective speech, not to decrease your chances. Therefore, notes need not interfere with the speaker/audience relationship.

Both of the sample note cards on p. 120 took the same amount of time to construct.

The first note card would be an asset, the second note card a liability.

Here are a few basic guidelines which may help you in the construction of your note cards.

1. *Use small note cards.* 3″ x 5″ note cards are easy to handle, but there is no magic size. Use the size that makes you feel comfortable. Large sheets of paper have an embarrassing tendency to flutter from the lectern, as well as being noisy.

2. *Number your cards.* As a speaker, you will have enough to think about without having to shuffle through your notes searching for your place.

3. *Write on one side only.* Just another precaution to insure a smooth, trouble-free delivery.

4. *Do not camouflage the use of your notes.* Everyone recognizes that a carpenter uses his saw as a tool, and that a draftsman uses a T-square for the same reason. Notes are part of the speaker's selection of tools. Time and effort spent trying to hide your notes would be better put to use in establishing good contact with the audience.

BETWEEN THE YEARS 1940-1960,
17,400,000 PEOPLE LEFT RURAL AMERICA AND
HEADED FOR THE CITIES.

THIS MOVEMENT CONTINUES AT A RATE OF
500,000 per year.

Many people moving from farms and small towns
to big cities; between 1940-1960 -- 17,400,000
left from the country to the industrial centers
and large cities. This movement is still taking
place at a rate of 500,000 each year. Reason
is that many small farms are going under
because farm help is hard to come by. Fewer
farms on shares; high cost of land; high cost
of machinery; better wages in city.

5. *Limit the material on each note card.* Some speakers will limit
   the material to one key point to each note card. You may not
   want to be this restrictive, but try to keep all the material on a
   card closely related. Typing in capitals and double spacing will
   make the notes easier to read and lessen the possibility of confusion.

These are only suggestions and you may want to make some changes. Remember, whatever *works best* for you *is best* for you. Each speaker must arrive at his own technique through trial and error.

Rehearsals

People who are successful, particularly in a creative activity, are usually those people who spend adequate time in preparation and practice. The question is not really "Should I rehearse?" but "How much time should I spend in rehearsal?"

Anyone who has arrived early at a ball game and watched the players chasing fungos and taking field and batting practice can not dispute the value of practice. The whole point of apprenticeship programs is to allow the apprentice the time to develop the proper techniques of the trade. It also exposes him to some of the problems and situations he will encounter along the way. The speaker uses his rehearsal for much the same reasons.

The location of the rehearsal is really of little importance and should have little effect on the final delivery. It is said that Abraham Lincoln used to practice his speeches before rows of corn in a field. Daniel Webster rehearsed while fishing; John Kennedy, while in an automobile. More than one speaker has confessed that he rehearsed while shaving.

The time of the rehearsal is important and often vital to the success of a speech. Don't attempt to rehearse your speech until the ideas and the basic outline of the speech have become definite. Allow time for these ideas to jell. Once you have the points clearly assembled and recognize the relationships between points in your speech, you are ready to begin. Take time to avoid the pitfalls of last minute preparation. It has been proven time and time again that last minute rehearsal only increases tension and does little to increase the speaker's effectiveness. As a student, you have no doubt had the experience of waiting to study for a test until the last minute. The resulting panic of trying to cram all the material into your head in a couple of hours should go a long way to prove this point.

There are only two basic parts to the actual speech rehearsal: (1) fixing the general speech idea in your mind, and (2) polishing the delivery.

The first phase, fixing the speech in your mind, is really no more than a general familiarization with the particular speech you are about to rehearse. The speaker begins by reading his entire outline several times silently without hesitation. This is followed by several oral readings of the outline. The purpose here is to see the speech from beginning to end in its skeletal form and to recognize the relationships of the key parts of the speech.

At this point you may want to try to deliver the speech without referring to the outline, but by simply trying to remember the key points. If you stumble and miss certain points, make a mental note of the trouble spot but do not stop. You must make every effort to go on. Repeat this process several times.

In order to avoid being discouraged, remember that the aim here is for a firm grasp of the sequence of ideas, not a finished speech. With this in mind, continue until you can recognize a clearly related progression of ideas.

The second phase is to polish the delivery. Some people say that practice makes perfect and still others add that practice makes permanent. Now that you have the sequence firmed up, you may begin to rehearse the speech in its entirety. If you think a mirror or a tape recorder will be of help, use them. However, if these things make you nervous, quit using them.

The number of rehearsals will vary according to the ability of the speaker, but a starting point might be between two and six. A good indication of when to stop rehearsals is when you feel you are losing your spontaneity. When the material begins to sound stale and lifeless, stop. Use the remaining time to make minor changes. You may want to consider adding better illustrations, adding material, or checking your transitions for clarity.

Introductions

There are several techniques used by speakers to introduce their topics. Although there is no formula to point out the best introduction for any given speech, and any speech can begin with almost any of the methods of introduction, it is important to be familiar with the assets and liabilities of each particular method.

One of the most common techniques used in introducing a speech is *humor*. It is a paradox that this most popular method is also the most dangerous to the unskilled speaker. Very often a fledgling speaker will begin with a very funny story that has little relationship to the actual speech. The problem then becomes one of transition. A quick and easy transition such as "seriously, folks" or "all kidding aside" is not enough. A very funny story may put the audience in a mood for more funny stories and not for a serious speech.

If you decide to use humor, you must make absolutely sure that the humorous story has a bearing on the speech topic; it would be wise to point that out in the transition from the story to the speech. If you have established this clear relationship you will avoid embarrassment should the audience fail to see the humor in your introduction. However, all these things must depend on your ability to control the audience, the ability that most often is associated with the experienced and polished speaker.

The *question* introduction, on the other hand, is much easier to control and just as effective. For instance, in a speech delivered before a conservation club, a speaker might word his introduction like this.

> There are an estimated 75,000,000 fishermen in this country. Do you know that by the year 2000, it is estimated that there will be no lakes, no streams in this country capable of supporting marine life? The question is: What can *we* do to prevent this needless destruction of one of our most precious commodities—clean, fresh water?

The obvious value of this kind of introduction is that you start the audience thinking in terms of solutions to a problem. It is like priming a pump, and your question becomes the primer. You have suggested that there is a problem and that there is a solution, *and* that the link between the problem and the solution is the audience. Now it is up to you, in the body of the speech, to bring these relationships into focus.

It is also possible to begin a speech with a story or *narrative* introduction. Many speakers have used the story of George Washington and the cherry tree to introduce a speech about the importance of honesty. This story has been used so often that it now lacks freshness, as does the story of Abraham Lincoln rising from the humble log cabin to the nation's highest office. We can still cherish the stories themselves, but as introductions to speeches, they are better left alone.

The main concern in the use of the narrative introduction must be in relating the piece of narration to the topic of the speech. If it does not bring the topic more sharply into focus, it should not be used. It also should not be so long that the audience will begin to wonder when the story will be over and the speech will get under way.

You may also want to try a *quotation* for the introduction to a speech. Again, the quotation should have a direct bearing on the speech topic and aid the audience in its understanding of the point you wish to make. If you use a quotation, try to select material from a source which could readily seem reliable. For instance, if speaking about the need for more skilled tradesmen, it would be better to quote the Secretary of Labor than a neighbor who had a leaky sink and who had trouble getting a plumber to fix it. Your neighbor's problem might well point up the need expressed by the Secretary, however; and could be used as a supporting illustration. You should also consider the relevancy of the material when selecting a quotation. The Wright brothers no doubt had many ideas about the need to develop air travel, but a quotation from the current head of the Civil Aeronautics Board would most likely be more effective.

The introduction is a tool; and, like any other tool, it has certain functions. The introduction to a speech should capture the audience's attention and set up a favorable relationship between the audience, the speaker, and the topic. It is from this introduction that the audience receives its initial impression. If the speaker can gain the audience's acceptance as an individual, his chances of getting audience acceptance for his material will be greatly increased.

Conclusions

Now that you have decided on exactly what you are going to say and how you are going to get into your material, you must decide on the most effective way to conclude and make your exit. You should leave the audience with the feeling that you fulfilled the promises made by the introduction.

It is possible to conclude with any of the techniques used in introductions: humor, question, narrative, or quotation. It is also possible to use other techniques for the conclusion. In the *formal summary* of a speech, the speaker moves into the conclusion with a transition from the main body of the speech. A transition, or bridge, may go something like this: "From the evidence I have presented, it should be evident that . . ." or "After reviewing the facts, we can hardly deny that . . ." This kind of transition is much more polished than the easy way out: "In conclusion let me say . . ."

If, as in the case of the speech on water pollution, you have indicated there are certain steps an individual can take in order to turn the tide of pollution, you would recount these steps in the formal conclusion. If your speech was about the pre-flight ground check in flying, your conclusion would restate these checks. If you used a story to open, refer to that story in the closing. In referring to the introduction you will give the audience the feeling that the speech has come around full-circle. It is like tying together all the loose ends at the close of a mystery story. All questions should be answered; all doubts erased.

There are a few obvious mistakes often made during the conclusion of a speech. One of the most common errors is introducing new material that has little to do with the particular speech in progress. It would be absolutely ridiculous in the speech about pre-flight ground checks to conclude with remarks that would introduce problems facing the pilot once he became airborne. If you are delivering a speech about the savings afforded a hunter by reloading his own shotgun shells, what would be the value in mentioning the use of decoys in the conclusion?

The anticlimax is another example of poor planning in the conclusion.

> And so, my friends, it is true. Only you can prevent forest fires. . . . And if I didn't believe in the concern of the individual, in his desire to preserve our forests, in his willingness to cooperate, I wouldn't be here speaking to you right now. Why, perhaps the greatest resource we have in this nation is people. . . .

People may represent a great resource, but that information should be put before the climax. The speaker has led the audience to believe that the speech has come to an end and then has continued for several more minutes.

An audience that has been attentive and cooperative can quickly change its attitudes toward you and your material if you lead them to expect a conclusion and then cross them by going on and on. When you are finished, stop!

The Importance of Bodily Action

It is difficult to fully explain the use and importance of gestures as they relate to a good speech. However, this is a certainty: everyone uses a certain amount of bodily action whenever they communicate orally, whether with one other person or a large audience. This action no doubt varies from individual to individual, but it is always present, from a simple nod of the head or shrug of the shoulders, to complete animation including arm waving, foot stomping and nervous pacing. We must now relate all of this to the speech situation and assign it some value.

The value of bodily action should never be underestimated. Total inactivity for any extended period of time increases muscle tension, particularly when you are under an emotional strain. Trying to ignore this tension will not make it go away. If your knees begin to shake, locking them more tightly into position will only increase their tendency to shake. Therefore, we might conclude that one principal reason for bodily action is to lessen muscle tension. This in turn allows you to concentrate more on the speech itself and less on emotional difficulties.

Another value of movement is the variety added to a speech and the increased audience attention. A voice that lacks variety— a monotone—tends to put the people in the audience in a trance or, in extreme cases, puts them to sleep. Unchanging posture does the same thing. The audience must never get the impression that they are being addressed by a robot or a statue, or, even worse, that the speaker is merely getting it over with. If you think back to some of the speeches you have seen and heard, you will surely be able to picture some of the activity and inactivity we are about to discuss.

Good bodily actions are valuable in helping to achieve emphasis and clarify meaning. Instead of involving the audience through their use of a single sense—sound—you bring into play the use of another sense—sight. The more senses you can involve, the better your chances of helping the audience to visualize concepts of size, shape, and speed. Action can also indicate your emotions.

You should not use bodily action for its own sake. That kind of exhibitionist activity merely draws attention to itself at the expense of your ideas. The visible action does not replace the speech; it supplements it. If you continually substitute gestures and facial expressions for words, you run the risk of turning the speech into a display of sign language, a pantomime.

Bodily action itself can fall into four distinct areas: eye contact, facial expressions, posture, and movement.

Eye contact is extremely important in a well executed speech and must not be overlooked. It is not always true that if a speaker is nervous he should avoid the audience by fixing his gaze at something else in the room, like a clock on the back wall. Speech is a human activity and must be directed at human beings, not clocks. The term *communication* indicates that there will be a response of some kind, that response comes from other people, not clocks or chairs. An audience knows when a speaker is avoiding them and does not appreciate it. If a speaker avoids making visual contact with his audience, he runs the risk of not recognizing when he has lost the group, or when he has touched upon a point of vital concern. Although an audience will not normally be responding aloud, they do respond through facial expressions, movements in their seats, sighs, and any number of other ways. If the speaker has been avoiding the audience, he will miss these signs; and his speech will lose some of its vitality.

It is equally dangerous to flit around quickly from one person to another without ever establishing contact with anyone. If you take the time to establish meaningful and lasting eye contact with the members of your audience, they will probably reward you with added attention. It is worth the effort.

Facial expressions will come naturally if you will let them. Do not plan or rehearse them; they must be natural, spontaneous reflections of your own attitudes.

There are no set rules concerning posture, but you can ask yourself this one question concerning your own posture: "Does it help or hinder me in achieving my purpose?" Posture may run from the human telephone pole to the speaker who seems to be making love to the lectern—with hundreds of variations between the two extremes. The suitability of your own posture depends on the total speaking situation: speaker, speech, audience, and situation. Movement refers to movements of the entire body. Again, the total situation must be considered. If you are speaking at a dinner, chances are you will simply speak in place. It would be humorous indeed to stroll among the tables like a gypsy violinist. However, it is possible and desirable to lean forward for emphasis or to draw the audience into the situation. It is perfectly natural to shift your weight from one foot to the other. These are natural body movements and are expected. The danger lies in the extremes: the speaker who sways lazily back and forth like a field of wheat in a summer breeze, or the speaker who paces nervously back and forth like a caged animal.

Everything you say and do in front of an audience will contribute to a total mood. When you are uncomfortable, the audience will be uncomfortable. If you are a caged animal, the audience will become trapped also. Therefore, everything you say and do must convey to the audience the impression that they are being addressed by a confident and mature individual who has something important to say and the ability to say it effectively.

Exercises

Select two speech topics: one to be delivered to a special audience made up of people in your particular vocational area, and another topic for a general audience. Now construct several introductions and conclusions for these topics using a variety of the methods discussed in this chapter. Remember to gear the material for the particular audience. (You may wish to take advantage of role-playing here. That is, you might want to briefly describe your particular audience and the situation in which you will be delivering this speech.)

Example: I have just opened a small service station and garage, and the Junior Chamber of Commerce has asked me to address their group at the monthly dinner meeting. They have a campaign under way to attract new businesses to their community and have asked me to discuss some of the problems (such as financing, availability of choice locations, and comparative property taxes in the area) confronting a new business. I now ask you (the class) to assume the role of that Junior Chamber group.

The speech itself is not required—just the situation, topic, opening, and closing.

CHAPTER 2:   THE SPEECH TO INFORM

The informative speech is perhaps the most basic speech and it, along with the persuasive speech, is the one with which you will most often be involved. The term *informative speech* is almost self-explanatory. Taking a look at the various parts of this particular speech will have greater merit than a wordy definition. The basic parts of the informative speech—introduction, body, closing —are actually the basic parts of any speech. Therefore, it must be the content and presentation of these basic parts that will make this speech different from another type of speech.

Introduction to the Informative Speech

First impressions are usually lasting impressions. As was stated earlier, your opening remarks will set the stage for the remainder of your presentation. It is most important that you get off to a good start. A poor introduction places you in the position of having to catch up for the rest of the speech. If you lose your audience at the start, you will be forced to expend your efforts on recapturing their attention, instead of informing them, which was, after all, your main objective.

Getting and maintaining an audience's attention can be learned if you will simply put yourself into their shoes. This part of the introduction is often labeled the *Favorable Attention Step*. You can never assume that the audience will be interested in what you have to say because they ought to be interested. The fact that we all ought to be interested in the stability of the British Pound or the European Common Market does not mean that we *will* be interested. It is also a common mistake for a speaker to identify himself with the subject of his speech, rather than identifying his audience with the subject. Remember the old "you" approach to selling? How might your material affect the audience? Involve them! "You will be interested to know . . ." "You will be amazed to find . . ." "You have probably wondered from time to time . . ."

If any of your material needs clarification, or if the understanding of your presentation rests on a common understanding of certain terms, this ought to be included in the overall introduction to the speech. The important thing is that you are providing worthwhile information in a clear and interesting manner in order to bring the unknown and misunderstood into the proper perspective.

Body of the Informative Speech

A good speaker knows that his materials should be audience-centered, and in constructing his speech he often asks himself: "What is my listener's ability to understand and follow my material? What is his experience and knowledge in this area? How quickly can he absorb material, particularly new material? What is his ability to comprehend new terminology?"

If you will ask yourself similar questions about your particular audience, you will then develop your material in such a way that the listeners will want to follow and understand. They will be reacting to you *and* the material. Their response is what speech is all about. Communication is based on this two-directional idea. Without feedback (or response, as we have termed it), there is no communication.

When we say we have informed someone, we make the assumption that they have carried some knowledge away with them. If they take something with them they have retained some of the information we presented. If this is the process, then we must do everything in our power to make retention possible.

Two different people can tell the same story with amazingly different results. The reason one man succeeds where the other man fails is often quite simple. The successful story teller is the individual who is careful to construct vivid and concrete examples in such a way as to create clear mental pictures of what he is saying. You can insure greater audience retention if you will avoid the pitfalls of vague and generalized phrasing.

> Brand X gasoline will provide improved mileage over Brand
> Z gasoline.

This doesn't tell the motorist anything. Improved mileage to one customer might mean he will double his mileage, while to another motorist it might mean two more miles per gallon. If the Brand X gasoline will improve mileage 2 to 4 miles per gallon used, say so.

If you want to inform the audience of the great value of our natural resources and you were using a sequoia tree as an example, could you expect a great deal of response from a statement like this:

> A giant sequoia tree contains as much as 240,000 square feet
> of lumber

Unless you had an audience of contractors and lumbermen, I think not. Most people don't even know how to figure board feet, let alone imagine 240,000 of these feet. It sounds like a lot of lumber, but how much? A stack? A boxcar full? Your audience is more likely to remember if you were to give them a good mental image.

> There is enough lumber in one giant sequoia tree to construct
> six six-room houses. This includes all the lumber needed for
> flooring, walls, roof, siding—the works!

Helping the audience to see and follow relationships also helps to insure their retention. If you draw relationships in a speech, make sure you point out how the ideas are logically related. It is easier to recall something if it has been presented in a step by step fashion. It would be logical, if talking about the proper way to paint the exterior of a home, to begin by pointing out the ways to prepare the surface.

> You scrape off cracked and peeling paint and remove all dust
> and dirt before you begin the job of repainting. New paint
> will adhere to a clean, dry surface.

The use of props and visual aids can also aid in increasing audience interest, understanding, and retention. Using an actual watch as a prop for a speech about watch repairing may be a good idea from your point of view, because you can examine it up close. But what about the audience? What about the person clear in the back row? We agreed earlier that a good speech was always audience-centered. If you use props, make sure that everyone can see them. Keep all drawings and charts basic and uncluttered. It is better to have several simple drawings than one complicated one.

Your function as a speaker is more than just filling time. To be effective you must take pride in what you are doing. You must be dynamically enthusiastic about your subject and about communicating your material to the audience. Your attitudes will always be reflected in the material you select.

The Conclusion of the Informative Speech

The conclusion of the informative speech must bring all the elements of the speech into a panoramic view and reemphasize the critical points in order to fix them enduringly in the minds of the listeners. We could talk all day about the component parts of a new sports car. But in the final analysis, it would be the completed model on the street that would be the focal point of our interest. We always gain the most when we can view something in its proper perspective.

You made a promise at the start of your speech. You promised to inform the audience, to instruct them. The worst mistake you could make would be to ignore that promise. Take time in the conclusion of your speech to reassure the audience that you kept your word. Stress the importance or immediacy of your material. You might also feel that certain kinds of material ought to be included in the closing in order that the audience might have the opportunity to gain further information regarding the substance of your talk. This additional step is referred to as the *continuing action step.* Where might the audience get additional information? What publications can they use? Perhaps you have seen the public service commercials sponsored by the United States Government regarding water pollution. "If you want to know what you can do to help, write the President's Council on Clean Water, Washington, D.C." The close in this commercial is an example of the continuing action step. If your speech was about model railroading, and you were informing the audience of the popularity of the hobby, perhaps you would provide them with the address of a model railroading club so they might go and see a model railroad in action. The names and addresses of hobby shops that specialize in model trains would also be helpful. There are also some magazines published for the model railroad buff. The audience can now follow up on the material you presented.

One final note: It is quite obvious that we all possess a certain amount of personal bias, but in an informative speech we must try to be objective. Avoid indoctrinating your listeners while posing as an informative speaker. This approach is more suited to the persuasive speech.

Sample Evaluation Sheet for the Informative Speech

Speaker _____

Subject _____

Evaluator _____

Did the opening remarks of the speech arouse your interest?

Did the speaker's material seem to be:
1. _____Readily understood by the audience
2. _____Too complicated for this audience
3. _____Too elementary for this audience

Explain what you liked most about this speech:

Explain what you liked least about this speech:

Do you feel the time spent listening to this speech could have been put to better use?

Suggestions for improving this speech:

Adequate pauses?

Adequate volume?

Adequate eye contact?

Overall evaluation:

CHAPTER 3:   THE SPEECH TO PERSUADE

I drive a Ford; and if you had any sense, you'd drive one too.
I don't care what anyone says, I know the Mets have the best
team in professional baseball.
Why don't you vote for Senator Smudge? He seems to be the
only politician who makes any sense.
If you're so set against smoking, you ought to do something
to help people quit.
That system will never work here at Amalgamated Steel and
Wire.
Blotto is the best beer on the market.
Unless you want your taxes to skyrocket, you better vote
against increase in millage.

Points of view, opinions, positions—whatever we choose to
label them, it all boils down to this: someone is always trying to
convince someone else that he has the right answers. It only seems
natural for one person to approach another for the purpose of getting that second person to change his mind. Perhaps part of this is
caused by our competitive nature.

Advertising agencies are always trying to convince the public
that they ought to be buying this cheese instead of that cheese,
driving this car instead of that car, using the inexpensive spread
instead of the high-priced spread. The same principles are even
being used to build images for political candidates.

The fact is that we all are entitled to our own opinions. Patterns of thinking, like biting fingernails, can become habit and as
habit, become difficult to break. Like any habit, opinions are reinforced with time and become harder to break.

Whether you are trying to persuade someone to use a particular brand of deodorant or to persuade him to join a particular
political party, the process of persuasion is basically the same.
Most people want to be accepted, to belong to a group, to be suc-

cessful, to be happy, and to be secure. Everyone has aspirations, hopes, and fears. In order to persuade an audience, a speaker must be aware of and appeal to these aspects of human nature. He can do so in three distinct ways, through logic, psychology, or personality. It is also possible to have a combination of the three. The other basic speech principles should be applied as well.

Some Elements of Persuasion

While a persuasive speech must have a *logical appeal* to an audience, the logic need not be flawless as long as it simply makes sense. Most audiences will be looking for those facts and statements which are acceptable. Therefore, in using logic, a speaker must reason with an audience.

One way of reasoning with the audience is the presentation of a conclusion arrived at through induction.

President Franklin D. Roosevelt's speech to the Congress of the United States on December 8, 1941, will provide an example of the inductive method.

To the Congress of the United States:

Yesterday, December 7, 1941—a date that will live in infamy—the United States of America was suddenly and deliberately attacked by naval and air forces of the Empire of Japan.

The United States was at peace with that nation and, at the solicitation of Japan, was still in conversation with its government and its Emperor looking toward maintenance of peace in the Pacific. Indeed, one hour after the Japanese Ambassador to the United States and his colleague delivered to the Secretary of State a formal reply to a recent American message. While this reply stated that it seemed useless to continue existing diplomatic negotiations, it contained no threat or hint of war or armed attack.

It will be recorded that the distance of Hawaii from Japan makes it obvious that the attack was deliberately planned many days or even weeks ago. During the intervening time the Japanese government had deliberately sought to deceive the United States by false statements and expressions of hope for continued peace.

The attack yesterday on the Hawaiian Islands has caused severe damage to American naval and military forces. Very many American lives have been lost. In addition American ships have been reported torpedoed on the high seas between San Francisco and Honolulu.

Yesterday the Japanese government also launched an attack against Malaya.

Last night Japanese forces attacked Hong Kong.

Last night Japanese forces attacked Guam.

Last night Japanese forces attacked the Philippine Islands.

Last night the Japanese attacked Wake Island.

This morning the Japanese attacked Midway Island.

Japan has, therefore, undertaken a surprise offensive extending throughout the Pacific area. The facts of yesterday speak for themselves. The people of the United States have already formed their opinions and well understand the implications to the very life and safety of our nation.

As Commander in Chief of the Army and Navy I have directed that all measures be taken for our defense.

Always will we remember the character of the onslaught against us. No matter how long it may take us to overcome this premeditated invasion, the American people in their righteous might will win through to absolute victory. I believe I interpret the will of the Congress and of the people when I assert that we will not only defend ourselves to the uttermost but will make very certain that this form of treachery shall never endanger us again.

Hostilities exist. There is no blinking at the fact that our people, our territory, and our interests are in grave danger.

With confidence in our armed forces, with the unbounded determination of our people, we will gain the inevitable triumph, so help us God.

I ask that the Congress declare that since the unprovoked and dastardly attack by Japan on Sunday, December 7, a state of war has existed between the United States and the Japanese Empire.

Remember then, in inductive reasoning you move from specific instances to a conclusion.

The most common form of deductive reasoning used in persuasive speaking, on the other hand, relies on probabilities. Briefly, deduction involves the process of moving from general examples to specific conclusions. "All professional athletes are good sports. Jack is a professional athlete. Therefore, Jack is a good sport."

These three statements, labeled *major premise, minor premise,* and *conclusion,* are the parts of the most common kind of deductive reasoning, the *syllogism.* The major premise (general example), "All professional athletes are good sports," is applied to a minor premise (specific case), "Jack is a professional athlete," in order to reach a specific conclusion, "Therefore, Jack is a good sport."

However, persuasive speakers (or people in general, for that matter) rarely use this pure form of deductive reasoning. Instead, they rely on what is called the *enthymeme.* Earlier I mentioned that the persuasive speaker would most likely be dealing in probabilities (this is one characteristic of the enthymeme) and using something less than the three parts found in the syllogism. The usual process is one which moves from some general evidence through a connective to a conclusion, and the conclusion is based on probabilities.

If you will take time to look into the behavior of human beings in their deliberations, you will note that this is a very common form of arriving at conclusions. *"In all probability* this man will win the election over that man." *"Most likely,* the union will call for a strike vote." *"It now seems almost certain* that the cost of living will level off." These are all the result of using specific examples to arrive at some form of probability.

Your main concern regarding this form of reasoning should be: Can I reasonably move from the examples to the specific conclusion? Is my evidence reasonably sufficient to convince the audience? An obvious mistake would be like this one:

> The toaster I recently purchased at the department store has a short in the wiring, and I can't seem to get the store to send out a repairman. The engine in my new car is not functioning properly and there is a four-day wait at the garage. It is impossible to get repair service on merchandise purchased in this community.

It would be almost impossible to convince an audience on sketchy and questionable evidence like that. The argument is not reasonable, and the conclusion is not in keeping with the evidence. There is little to connect these examples to the specific conclusion. (See how many examples of faulty reasoning you can locate in that last example.)

Now compare it with this more reasonable piece of deduction.

> This unpopular bond issue will be financed entirely through increased real estate taxes, and since a majority of voters in

this district are real estate owners and feel they are already over-taxed, it can be safely assumed that the bond issue will be defeated.

A second appeal used in persuasion is the *psychological appeal* and is designed to reach the audience by appealing to their basic emotions. While it is true that some speakers have mastered audience control almost exclusively through psychological appeals, a wise speaker will take care to mix his appeals. A good logical appeal may gain strength when seasoned with a generous amount of psychological and personal appeal. The example used above concerning the unpopular bond issue may appeal logically to the audience, but may gain increased audience acceptance if some psychological appeals are added.

> The increased taxes will mean less money in the family budget. Perhaps it will mean that the long-planned family vacation will have to be postponed for another year. Just when can the 'little guy' expect a break?

Appeals to family, God, home, country, security and creature comforts all fall into the area of psychological appeals.

The *personal appeal* of the speaker to his audience is perhaps the strongest; because in the final analysis, speaking is a human activity, and people are most affected by other people around them. As a speaker, you may present a logical case to your audience, but if they don't like you and respect you, if they don't trust you, all the evidence in the world would have but little influence with their decision to accept or reject your arguments.

Positive thinking and determination, along with a good appearance, go far in establishing a good strong personal appeal between you and your audience.

Another important step in establishing personal appeals with the audience is to build some kind of identification with the audience into the early part of your speech. It is important to do this as soon as possible because it can affect the audience's acceptance of what follows. Once this identification is established you can refer to it from time to time in order that it might be reinforced.

Remember those basic aspects of human behavior, particularly those involving group membership and the need to belong. Members of groups often feel they have a great deal in common; they may share the same hopes and fears; they often feel strongly about their community of interests.

Make an effort in your introduction to establish that community of interest between you and the audience. For example, if you
were speaking with a group composed of scout leaders, parents of
scouts, and youth leaders, you might say:

As a former scout myself, I am delighted to have this opportunity to appear here this evening. Some of my most cher-
ished memories are those of squatting around the warmth of
a camp fire after a hike in the woods. I can remember listening to the endless stories of hunting, fishing and the wonderful life in the outdoors. . . .

In a speech to persuade the Professional Men's Club to support a
citizens' drive to provide better education and recreation facilities
in the community, you could begin:

I am here today as a parent and as a concerned member of
the community. Although your shirts are white and mine are
blue, and though you wear a suit to work and I arrive at work
in coveralls, we share a bond that goes much deeper than the
clothes we wear. The bond we share, the one between a man
and his family, is perhaps the oldest and strongest bond in
mankind.

In 1959, the then Vice-President, Richard M. Nixon, made a
speech while on a tour through Russia. Following is the basic
introduction to his Russian speech. Notice how he established an
identification with his Russian audience.

These are some of the characteristics of the Soviet people which I particularly noted on this trip.

First, their capacity for hard work, their vitality, their
intense desire to improve their lot, to get ahead, is evident
everywhere.

There was another feature about the Soviet people
which I noted which may surprise you, and that is in how
many respects you are like us Americans. We are similar in
our love of humor—we laugh at the same jokes. The people
of your frontier East have much the same spirit of what was
our frontier West. We have a common love of sports; the
name of Vasily Kuznetsov, your great decathlon champion,
is known in the United States as well as the Soviet Union.
We are both a hospitable, friendly people. When we meet
each other we tend to like each other personally, as so many
of our soldiers who met during the last great war can attest.

Above all the American people and the Soviet people are
as one in their desire for peace. And our desire for peace is

not because either of us is weak. On the contrary, each of us is strong and respects the strength the other possesses.

You can see that in all the examples of establishing identification, there is a feeling of mutual respect. If a speaker freely expresses respect for his audience, if he is sincere in his attempt to communicate, and if he believes in what he is saying, the audience will be aware of these things and respond accordingly.

Three Forms of Persuasive Speaking

The emphasis of the persuasive speech can be directed to convince an audience to accept a particular point of view; to reinforce those views currently held by the audience; or to activate an audience in a specific behavior pattern.

In an effort to point out the application of the three forms of persuasive speaking, let's assume for a moment that you are serving on the campaign committee of Barlow Blabb, who is currently running for reelection as the mayor of your city. You are scheduled to make three speeches during the coming week; and to further complicate your situation, the speeches are scheduled before three entirely different types of audiences. On Wednesday you will be speaking to the Association of Women Voters, known to be directly opposed to the Mayor's reelection. In this instance your chief concern will be an attempt to convince the women that Mayor Blabb has done a good job. This will require a defense of his record and a summary of his accomplishments. You will also have to point out his strengths and the weaknesses of his opponent. Perhaps the women favor Blabb's opposition because he has been advocating more law and order. You know that Blabb's strong suit is his wizardry with getting the most benefit for the taxpayer out of each tax dollar, but in this instance it would not be advantageous to stress that point. If law and order is what the audience wants, you will have to convince them that Mayor Blabb is the one candidate who can best provide it.

On Thursday night you are scheduled to appear before a public rally sponsored by the Blabb for Mayor Committee. The Committee has invited all interested voters to attend, although it is expected that most of those in attendance will have leanings toward Blabb or will be moderately in favor of his reelection. Your goal on Thursday night will be to reinforce the audience's belief that perhaps Mayor Blabb deserves their votes. Blabb's opposition has been hurling charges at the Mayor for some time and this would be a good opportunity for you to answer the charges, yell foul play, and reassure the voters that they made the right choice in electing Blabb the last time and with their continued support, Mayor Blabb could continue his drive to make the community a place the citizens could be proud of.

On Friday night you are slated to address a fund-raising dinner which will be attended exclusively by Blabb supporters and campaign workers. A friend of yours has commented that the speaking assignment will be a snap for you. "After all," he continued, "they are already committed, so what is there to convince?" However, you know that there are different degrees of agreement. Although this audience will support Blabb, your concern will be the extent of their involvement. Is a vote enough to expect from a strong supporter? Actually, this may be your toughest test as a persuasive speaker, because it is a speech to activate. Your job will be to get the audience to do more. If they have made campaign contributions, you must persuade them to contribute more toward a winning cause. If they have been ringing doorbells in an effort to reach the voters on a personal basis, they must now ring more doorbells. The next vote they get may decide the election. If they have been passing out literature, they must now pass out bumper stickers and buttons in an effort to garner every possible vote. They have all made commitments to the Mayor; they are all involved in his campaign. Now they must increase that involvement. They are expected to eat, sleep, and breathe Blabb—all, of course, in a winning cause—until all the votes are in, and the victory is won.

All three engagements call for persuasive speeches, but the three differ in type. Some persuasive speeches call for a combination of the three types. The President's inaugural address could be considered an example of a combination of the three. His speech reinforces the actions of those who voted for him, while at the same time he hopes to convince the losers that he will represent all the citizens equally, and that he is, after all, the best man for the job. Finally, his speech is one to activate. He hopes to persuade all of the people to get behind him and actively support his programs.

A hybrid of the persuasive speech is a speech which contains none of the forms discussed above, yet is persuasive in nature. It is the speech to neutralize. Let's assume that on Saturday night you had the opportunity to speak before a group known to actively support Blabb's opponent. You have been warned that the audience will be hostile, and your chances of rounding up a single vote are considerably less than slight. You immediately recognize this as an opportunity, not to convince the audience to vote for Blabb because that is out of the question, but to neutralize some of their hostility toward your candidate.

In any attempt to neutralize an audience's hostility, the speaker must rely heavily on audience/speaker identification. A good rapport with the audience is essential. If the members of the audience like the speaker as an individual, if they feel he is one of them, maybe, just maybe, they will say to themselves: "He seems like a good fella. He's got a lot on the ball and he says he's voting for Blabb. I wonder . . . ?" Mission accomplished!

Exercises

---

1. Select a topic for a persuasive speech. Prepare three outlines for your topic:

   A. Speech to convince
   B. Speech to reinforce
   C. Speech to activate

   Present a finished persuasive speech using what you consider to be the best of the three outlines.

2. Select another topic for a persuasive speech and prepare three introductions to establish identification with three different audiences.

3. Listen to a televised persuasive speech and try to determine the appeals used by the speaker. List his key ideas and the support he used for these ideas. Did you notice any faulty reasoning? Did you detect the psychological remarks used in place of evidence? What were the speaker's strong points? Were there any noticeable weaknesses?

4. List ten controversial topics which you feel would present a challenge to the novice persuasive speaker. Indicate why you feel these topics would be more difficult to present than some others.

Sample Evaluation Sheet for the Persuasive Speech

Speaker ⎯⎯⎯⎯⎯⎯⎯⎯⎯⎯⎯⎯⎯⎯⎯⎯

Subject ⎯⎯⎯⎯⎯⎯⎯⎯⎯⎯⎯⎯⎯⎯⎯⎯

Evaluator ⎯⎯⎯⎯⎯⎯⎯⎯⎯⎯⎯⎯⎯⎯⎯

Was the opening designed to capture audience interest?

Was the speaker creative in his choice of examples and illustrations? How would you grade his originality?

Did the speaker's enthusiasm spread to the audience?

Was the speaker poised and relaxed?

Did the speaker put the audience at ease?

Was the development of the speech a logical one?

How would you rate the speaker's knowledge of the subject?

Would you say the speaker was

⎯⎯⎯very well prepared
⎯⎯⎯adequately prepared
⎯⎯⎯poorly prepared

Was the speaker loud enough?

Was the speaker too fast?

Do you feel that the speaker had an honest desire to communicate with you?

List the things you would have done differently.

Additional comments and overall evaluation:

CHAPTER 4: GROUP DISCUSSIONS

A shortcoming in our society today is very often the inability of people to work together toward a common goal. The more experience we can get in interacting with groups of people, the better prepared we will be to face the problems ahead. This is where group discussion fits into the picture. Simply stated, discussion takes place when a group of people cooperatively exchange information and ideas in an effort to solve a problem or to learn about a topic of mutual interest.

In almost every phase of life—business, civic, social and religious—more and more decisions and policies are being made by groups of concerned individuals working to make the human environment a better one. However, a group of people getting together merely to pass the time in conversation does not constitute a group discussion.

An intelligent individual, armed with sufficient facts and know-how, is often in a better position to solve a problem. Group discussions take on greater significance when we consider them in light of our democratic process. A group of people is less apt to be trapped by a single point of view. That is, each member of the group is likely to bring his own point of view into play. Thus several aspects of a single problem will be considered. Most people enjoy the opportunity to assist in decision-making and are more likely to support policies and decisions they helped to frame.

Familiarity with the process of group discussion and the problems of leadership will usually increase the effectiveness of a group. This chapter is designed to introduce you to the group discussion and the mechanics involved with successful discussion.

Learning discussions, problem-solving discussions, and panel discussions are the three types of discussions in which you are most likely to become involved. In a learning discussion, the members of the group present information in an attempt to broaden their knowledge and understanding of a subject. In a problem-solving discussion, the aim is to analyze a specific problem regarding its importance and history, and to arrive at a solution or future course of action. The panel discussion is designed to be held before an audience and is therefore a public discussion.

Learning discussions most often involve individuals with similar interests who have gathered to exchange information related to those common interests: mechanics may gather to discuss the new anti-pollution devices on the new automobiles and how to service and repair these devices; printers may gather at a convention and exchange information on new printing techniques; contractors may sit down to discuss the use of new synthetic building materials. The purpose is to discuss materials of mutual interest. The atmosphere is most often one of informality.

Problem-solving discussions can take on many forms: members of the union's executive committee meet to resolve labor/management problems within the plant; selected members of the college's Agricultural Club get together to plan a way to raise funds for some new soil testing equipment; the Community Betterment Committee plans a series of group problem-solving discussions in order to resolve racial conflicts within the community. These serious deliberations call for more than the ordinary pattern of thinking; they call for critical or reflective thinking. The decisions and policies resulting from these discussions may have some serious, long range effects.

Panel discussions are presented before audiences for the expressed purpose of exposing that audience to a complex and meaningful discussion of a clearly defined topic. The members of the panel are selected because they represent different views and can supply the necessary facts to insure thorough coverage of the topic. Since the various viewpoints usually represent those held by members of sub groups in the audience, the panel members are actually representing other individuals and can be considered as spokesmen for members of the audience.

Example: Your community is considering various ways of raising money to provide additional funds for your city's hospital. The funds will be used to provide extensive care facilities, raise the salaries of nurses and hospital aides, improve the facilities in the maternity ward, expand and improve the hospital's laboratory, and add a twenty-bed wing to the existing hospital building. The City Council has voted to sponsor a municipal bond issue to raise the needed funds.

A panel is scheduled to be held on three successive evenings in the high school auditorium. There is a great deal of interest in the community over this bond issue and many citizens have chosen sides and taken public stands. There have also been many misconceptions about the cost of the bond issue and the need for the additional facilities.

The Junior Chamber of Commerce has invited several members of the community to participate in the panel discussion. The cross section of the panel is designed to allow all sides to express their views. The members of the panel include Mr. Harvey Planner, the Hospital Administrator, representing the Board of Trustees' position; Dr. Mortimer Getwell, representing the general practitioners; Dr. H. Globin, a heart specialist; Sally Sheets, who will speak for the nurses and nurses' aides; Bob Gladhand from the Chamber of Commerce; Dave Yardly and Mary Cook join the panel as concerned citizens and taxpayers; and Mr. Charley Gogetter, President of the JC's, who will serve as the leader of the panel discussion.

The panel has been constructed so as to provide ample expression of all views in an attempt to expose the community to the facts it needs to make an intelligent and educated voting decision.

Elements of Effective Discussions

The individual participants in the group discussion should take their responsibilities seriously. They have no doubt been asked to participate because of their knowledge of the subject under discussion and should therefore make adequate preparation prior to the actual discussion. At the same time, they should recognize that other members will also want to express their own views, so it would be both unfair and impolite for a member of a discussion to try to monopolize the discussion. The reverse of this problem is the participant who sits smugly by, relatively sure that his position is the best position, thus killing the need to discuss. If you are asked to participate, it is because someone feels that you have something to contribute. Your failure to do so would constitute a betrayal of this confidence shown you.

The group itself should reflect a cooperative spirit. Members must be willing to share the time and treat each other with respect.

This does not imply that the discussion must be formal and highly structured. On the contrary, an informal atmosphere is much more desirable. However, the informality must not cause the discussion to slip into a bull session. If a conflict exists within the group, the members must try to resolve it so the group can continue in an orderly fashion. The group must remember they are involved in a discussion, not a debate.

The key to a successful discussion might well be the leader, and great care should be taken to insure that the selection of the leader is a great deal more than a popularity contest. The leader must be able to control the discussion and see that the participants confine their discussion to the defined topic. This will require the ability to see through ambiguous statements and put them in their proper perspective.

Should conflict arise, the leader must take an active part in resolving that conflict. Therefore, impartiality is vital. His questions should be phrased objectively and designed to draw all sides into the discussion. The leader must attempt to sum up the facts presented. To do this he must be able to think clearly in order to separate the facts from the opinions. A good leader is a fair leader; and as a fair leader, he is in a good position to gain the respect and cooperation of the individual participants.

Finally, many leaders will present the group members with an outline based on the kinds of questions they will ask. This in no way should be interpreted as prompting, but rather an attempt to achieve the best possible participation from the group. To guarantee spontaneous participation, this outline would include only a representative number of questions. It should seem obvious by this time that a good leader is one who is basically familiar with all aspects of the topic and has done a fair amount of research on his own.

Group Problem-Solving Discussion: A Case Study

SELECTION OF THE PROBLEM

The Ajax Metal Stamping Company is concerned over the poor safety record in their Madison Plant. Top management people claim that the accidents are the result of carelessness on the part of the factory workers. Factory Workers Local No. 33 blames the accidents on the failure of the company to install needed safety equipment. Middle management personnel counter by stating that the "equipment is adequate, but the workers do not take advantage of the equipment provided." Tensions begin to mount at the factory, and there is talk of a work stoppage.

There is no doubt that a problem exists. If the problem is not resolved, the losses to both sides, in terms of lost salaries and lost revenues, will be great. The Vice-President in charge of Industrial Relations for the Ajax Company decides to attempt a resolution to the problem through a series of group problem-solving discussions.

SELECTION OF THE PARTICIPANTS

Mr. Holloway, Vice-President for Industrial Relations, calls a preliminary meeting between labor and management to ask for their cooperation and to select the participants for the discussions. Top level management takes the offensive by requesting that the plant manager serve as the leader of the discussion. The labor representatives find this totally unacceptable. They have no desire to see the plant manager in the role of discussion leader. They claim he is entirely "management." After an hour of deliberation, the two sides compromise, and the manager is selected to serve as a member, not leader, of the discussion group.

The selection of the shop steward is met with approval from both sides. However, management balks at the suggestion of a union official being placed in the group, claiming that the problem is an internal one and that the union official will only bring outside agitation into the picture. At this point, the factory workers are prepared to walk out of the preliminary talks. They feel that management is trying to stack the group against labor. They further feel that the union has prior experience in dealing with these problems, referring to the problems at the Wilmont Trucking Company earlier in the year when the union was successful in bringing unfair labor practice charges against the Wilmont firm. They further contend that receiving union counsel is one of the reasons they have a union.

Mr. Holloway agrees in principle with labor on this issue and urges the management representatives to accept a union official into the group. Management continues to have second thoughts, and again there is a threat to the preliminary talks. At this point, Mr. Holloway proves his worth as a good industrial relations man, as well as a man with keen sensitivity. He suggests that what management really fears is the chance that the union official selected may be an excessively hostile individual, a trouble-maker. He poses the following question to the management representatives: "Will you drop your objections if *you* can select the union official who is to serve as a member of the group?" Management agrees; and, after discussion among themselves, the labor representatives also agree.

Both sides then agree that one man be selected by the factory workers from within their own ranks. It is also agreed that the plant's Safety Engineer should participate. After some additional politicking, the Production Manager is added to the group.

The time has come to select a group leader, and both sides automatically shift into defensive gear. Some nervous sparring takes place, and a management man jokingly suggests, "Holloway would make a good leader." Labor takes the suggestion seriously and accepts the proposal. The decision is unanimous and Holloway consents.

Labor's acceptance of Holloway as the leader of the problem-solving group is not a very surprising one when we consider the facts. Even though he is a member of top-level management, his unique position places him somewhere between the two sides. His skill as an arbitrator became apparent to both sides as they watched him handle the preliminary meeting. And, perhaps most important, he proved his impartiality by stepping in on several occasions and making suggestions acceptable to both sides. Both sides evaluate him to be a strong personality, a man who will keep the group heading toward a solution.

DETERMINING THE ISSUES

At their first meeting, the group sets up some guidelines which they will follow in their subsequent meetings. These guidelines will serve as the playing field and rules for the problem-solving discussion.

1. It is agreed that all the issues will be posed as questions to further stimulate response. Example: Instead of an issue being

listed as "Safety equipment provided by the company," it would be restructured as a question: "To what extent is the company obligated to provide safety equipment to its employees?"

2. Only those facts and statistics which can be supported by proof will be used in the final analysis of the problem and the proposed solution. In other words, emotional appeals are irrational only when they replace rational supports. Example: "Are we going to continue to risk the lives of the factory workers?" This question, by itself, represents nothing more than an emotional appeal and as such, is irrational. However, if there is proof that lives have been lost through carelessness and because of the absence of safety equipment, the appeal can be considered rational, even though it has emotional overtones.

3. Each participant will become familiar with *all* the issues. It is hoped that the group can increase its objectivity if they have to see the problem from each other's point of view. Example: The employees are asked to consider the pressure on management to keep production up and costs down. The fact that the stockholders are far removed from the problem of safety and the costs of restructuring a safety program should also help labor to recognize management's dilemma. Management is asked to put themselves in the shoes of the worker on the assembly line. If the worker loses his hands or the use of his eyes, he loses his skill—his bread and butter. The employee's concern is with his welfare, not the cost of that welfare.

4. One of the group's final steps in preparation for the problem-solving discussion is to decide on the nature of the problem. It is determined that the nature of their particular problem is both one of fact—an investigation of actual conditions—and one of value—if these conditions are found to be undesirable, what conditions would be desirable?

5. What are the basic assumptions? (An assumption, you'll remember, is a belief that can be accepted as true without proof.) Example: In this case, the group accepted the following as assumptions. The employees suspected the company of cutting corners when it came to employee safety. The accident rate was up, and prospects were that it would continue to rise unless something were done to stem the tide. There were many other assumptions, far too numerous to list here.

It is important to note that these same assumptions may have been challenged by a different group. Each group must decide on their own assumptions.

6. Listing the actual issues was the final step in this initial meeting. (An issue is a point of controversy that must be settled in order to resolve the main problem.) Here is a representative list of the issues decided upon by this particular group:

A. What are the characteristics of a good safety program?

B. Does our plant measure up to adequate safety standards?

C. Is employee carelessness at fault? If so, should some additional incentives be provided to combat this carelessness?

D. Have the employees hired at this plant been carefully screened in regards to their past performances and safety records in similar jobs? Can the problem be solved by raising the hiring standards?

E. Does worker fatigue increase the accident rate? Are these workers fatigued? If so, should production standards be decreased? Should more rest periods be provided? Should overtime limits be decreased?

F. Would an increase in safety equipment automatically lower the accident rate?

G. What positive actions can be taken to raise the morale of the factory employees and enhance the working relationship between labor and management?

PREPARATION FOR THE DISCUSSION

Since objectivity has been mentioned as an element necessary to the success of a problem-solving discussion, the participants must investigate the problem thoroughly. This means that all issues must be viewed from as many angles as possible. Each member of the group must be in a position to approach all the issues pro and con. Simply showing up for the talks is not enough. As a matter of fact, more preparation is probably required for the problem-solving discussion than for any other speech situation.

Many people agree that a good approach is to review the information on hand and organize this material into an outline.

Wherever possible, participants supplement these points with statistics, quotations, and whatever else they can accumulate as support. On the basis of this material, a tentative opinion can be formulated, and the foundation can be laid for a solution.

A brief analysis of the group is also desirable. What effect will these findings have on the rest of the group? How will they respond? What objections might they raise? What counter-proposals might they make? What approaches are they apt to take? What attitudes will they have towards the proposed solution? These questions are a must, because the group and its members represent a variety of viewpoints. If a group member can accurately evaluate these views he can almost predict certain responses and be in a position to handle rebuttal.

The Safety Engineer may be concerned with fatigue as a major cause of accidents and may want to reduce overtime limits, while the Shop Steward might be expected to fight vigorously to uphold these overtime limits as an integral part of the labor contract. The Plant Manager, who is known to have a forceful personality, may try to monopolize the discussion. On the other hand, the Secretary of the Union is a quiet, reflective individual.

A complete analysis of the problem, the issues, and the members of the group goes a long way in insuring meaningful and productive participation.

THE ACTUAL PROBLEM-SOLVING DISCUSSION

At this point we can only assume what might have taken place in the Ajax discussions. An actual transcript of the discussion would no doubt fill many volumes. There are certain assumptions that can be made about what went on in the mind of each group member. As a statement was being made by one participant, the others were asking themselves: Is this statement being made as the result of personal prejudice? Does the speaker have facts to back his statements? Is he speaking as an authority? If he is quoting an authority, is the authority an acceptable one? Are these findings consistent with the findings of others? Do I have a comment, or a fact in support of this statement? If I disagree, do I have information with which to refute his findings? Is my agreement or disagreement based on emotion or rational thought?

At one point in the discussion, Mr. Holloway had to interrupt a heated debate between the Shop Steward and the Production Manager about the influence of the unions in regard to production quotas. He did this by pointing out that the subject was undoubtedly a problem unto itself and could very well be discussed under different circumstances, but reminded them of the fact that the stated problem under discussion concerned safety records and not production standards or union shop.

Another time, the Secretary of the Union stated that a large number of workers were upset over the working conditions at the plant. In order to evaluate that comment, Mr. Holloway asked if the Shop Steward had records of grievances having been filed by the workers regarding safety standards. Holloway said, "These records would go a long way in separating fact from hearsay."

Several times Holloway had to interrupt emotional discussions and suggest that they be tabled until the members involved could provide some substantial facts to back up their statements.

The individual members increased their own awareness as the discussion progressed. They actually began to police themselves and each other in the attempt to limit inference and supposition, to differentiate between fact and fiction, and to separate rational from irrational thinking. When a group reaches this point, they have stopped playing cat and mouse and are in a position to get down to the serious business at hand. (Almost every problem-solving discussion goes through an initial period of sparring. It is the group's way of establishing a climate for discussion. This initial period may take on many different forms, from small talk to joking, but eventually the group gets down to business.)

THE SOLUTION

There are certain considerations closely related to the solution of a problem. Two of these considerations are common to almost every problem: immediate solution versus long range solution, and whether eliminating the cause will eliminate the problem. There can be other considerations depending on the nature of the problem. These considerations will always be determined by the group itself. In the case of the Ajax discussions, these two considerations were applied. They also used certain criteria for judging their solution:

1. Is this the best solution for our problem?
2. Will the solution satisfy all sides?
3. Will the cost of the solution be prohibitive?
4. Is the solution consistent with the evidence presented in the discussion?
5. Is the solution a workable one?

Findings of the Ajax Group

1. The accident rate at the Ajax plant was approximately three times that of factories with similar operations.
2. Safety equipment was, in fact, sufficient and, in some areas of the plant, more than the minimum required to provide for the welfare of the employee.
3. What had been previously considered carelessness was in actuality a lack of familiarity on the part of the employees regarding the use of the safety equipment provided by the company.
4. There was a definite morale problem resulting from the rift between labor and management.
5. Communications between labor and management were practically non-existent.

Solution Suggested by the Ajax Group

Based on their findings, the group arrived at a solution based on three principal areas which they felt were at the root of the problems in the Ajax plant. The three areas were accident rate, morale, and communications. They also felt that the three areas were so closely related that the solution would necessarily overlap the three areas.

In an attempt to lower the accident rate, they proposed a cycled retraining program to familiarize all employees with the available safety equipment. The slight reduction in production during the initial safety training would surely be offset by long range increases in production due to the decreased down time resulting from accidents. They further proposed semi-annual seminars in Plant Safety Procedures. The twice-yearly half-day programs would be held on company time, and the employees would receive full pay for the sessions.

The group felt that morale would be lifted as a result of the interest taken in employee welfare. In a further attempt to decrease accidents and raise morale, the group suggested a bonus system based on safety record. Funds for the bonus program would be accumulated in a dollar reserve fund based on increased production and lower insurance premiums stemming from an improved safety record and safety program.

The group also submitted the basic outline for a revitalized communications program which would include a plant newspaper, an improved grievance procedure, and a factory-wide contest to stimulate interest in plant safety. The contest included competition in safety posters and safety slogans.

One final, long range suggestion urged that management look into the possibility of an employee stock-purchase plan.

SUMMARY

A close look at the Ajax case study and a review of the problem-solving procedures should make quite evident the need for objective, cooperative interaction among men in a variety of situations. The problem-solving techniques can be applied in almost every situation involving groups of individuals sharing different and conflicting points of view.

Exercises

1. List several occasions in which the group problem-solving discussion might be helpful.

2. Outline a general plan for a panel discussion. Confine this plan to a need within your own proposed occupation.

3. Select small groups within the class. Each group should plan and execute a panel discussion.

   Several small groups may also be formed to present problem-solving discussions. Imaginary problems could be agreed upon and the members of the groups could proceed with the discussions, using the role-playing technique. The views you present need not be your own personal views, but merely in keeping with those that would be consistent with the character you represent. The Ajax case could be used for a model.

Sample Evaluation Form for the Group Discussion

Subject ―――――――――――――――――――

Listener ―――――――――――――――――――

Problem ―――――――――――――――――――

(rate from 0% to 100%)

Problem adequately defined   ――――――

Clarification of terminology   ――――――

Group rapport   ――――――

Quality of leadership   ――――――

Willingness to participate   ――――――

Quality of argument   ――――――

Preparation of members   ――――――

Resolving group conflict   ――――――

Suitability of solution   ――――――

Check the items below that apply to this discussion.
――――――Some members monopolized the discussion.
――――――Members did not think objectively.
――――――Discussion became a debate or bull session.
――――――Arguments were inconsistent.
――――――Leader was unable to control the discussion.
――――――Solution was not consistent with evidence.
――――――Poor reasoning.

Other comments:

PART V

Selected Readings

Auto Biography

Richard Armour

Automobiles played a large part in our family life. In San Pedro, where I was born and where my father had a drugstore from 1904 to 1912, he took on the Hupmobile agency on the side, expecting to make some easy money. To get the agency, he had to buy two cars, a blue roadster and a somewhat sportier red one. Having no showroom, he parked both vehicles in front of the drugstore, where he could keep an eye on them and on anyone who seemed interested.

My father demonstrated Hupmobiles to countless "hot prospects," driving them up and down the hills of San Pedro and along the waterfront until they cooled off. There was no lack of interest. Any time he could get away from the store for a few minutes, there was someone willing to be shown how the Hupmobiles would "take" the hill past our house. It would chug a third of the way to the top before my father had to shift to intermediate and another third before he had to shift into low. At the top the radiator would be spouting a geyser of steam and rusty water, but my father said this only proved how well the circulation system worked.

Demonstrating cars was good for my father. It got him out into the open and convinced him that he was the best driver in San Pedro, if not in all of southern California. As he drove past our house in his cap, duster, and goggles, with a prospect in the seat alongside, he squeezed the bulb of his horn and waved a gauntleted hand in a gesture of confidence. This time, he wanted us to know, a sale was as good as made.

My mother, who had no enthusiasm to start with, lost all hope very early, and it got so that I was the only one who waved when my father drove by. It seems that many who were curious about the horseless carriage were not quite ready to own one. My father tried hard, but finally gave up the agency. In all, he had sold just two cars, both of them to himself.

When we moved to Pomona, in 1912, we took with us the two Hupmobiles, and we also had the use of my grandmother's Overland, which she could not drive. Since the Hupmobiles were small roadsters, the Overland, a touring car, was the one we used when the whole family had to go anywhere.

The Overland was open at the sides, as all touring cars were, but could be closed up quite cosily with side curtains. These, with their isinglass windows, could be installed in half an hour, if everyone lent a hand. It was necessary only to get the curtains out from under the back seat and fasten the sections together with metal fasteners that were poked through slits, like buttons in buttonholes, and then turned half way. Of course there was always the question of which was the outside and which the inside, which was the top and which the bottom, and which curtain fitted into which space. Meanwhile, the yellowed isinglass cracked and splintered with each manipulation and, once installed, let in more wind and water than light.

The upholstery was leather, filled with horsehair that kept working out through the holes and was stiff as wire. Horses might be gradually disappearing from the scene, but, thanks to horsehair in automobile seats, they continued to make themselves felt.

Unlike the modern car, with its four headlights and six taillights, our Overland had a single small taillight and two feeble headlights, each of which cast a faint yellow spot on the road about ten feet in front of the car. The faster the motor went, the brighter the lights, and when we wanted to see how deep a rut was or whether there was a turn in the road up ahead, we raced the motor. There was never any need to dim our lights for oncoming cars. Instead, we revved up the motor so that they would be sure to see us.

On the running board we kept a rack of cans containing gasoline, oil and water. The water could be used for drinking, but it was mostly for the radiator, which was thirstier than any of us passengers and much more important. Also on the running board was a metal box full of patches, rubber cement, and other materials for coping with punctures. We carried an ax and a shovel for other kinds of emergencies. The shovel was frequently employed when we got off the edge of the road into sand, but I do not recall that we ever had occasion to wield the ax. What sort of situation would have required this awesome tool, I do not know. But, as my grandmother said, "You can never be sure." She had something in mind, and I am glad it never happened.

All of us—my father, mother, grandmother, Uncle Lester, and I—wore goggles and dusters when we ventured outside the city limits. In addition, the women wore veils that held on their hats and protected their faces from the sun and wind and insects. The dusters, made of linen or pongee, were not merely to shield our clothing from dust but to impress fellow travelers (a term then without political significance) with our seriousness of purpose. We were as determined to reach our destination as were our pioneering forefathers in their covered wagons, no matter how often we might have to "get out and get under." I don't know what my father thought about as he gripped the steering wheel and, on a good stretch of road, shot up to forty miles an hour. As for me, I turned my cap around and imagined myself Barney Oldfield.

Every other Sunday, when my father did not have to go to the drugstore, we had a day for rest and recreation. Often we planned a drive into the country, or even to the beach, fifty miles away, but by the time my mother had prepared a picnic lunch that was elaborate enough to satisfy my grandmother, who was still sure to find fault with it, and by the time my father, who had gone back to bed after breakfast, had got up for good, it was usually too late to go anywhere. Another deterrent to travel was my father's pessimism. Having systematically kicked each of the tires, he would look worried and say he doubted they would get us there and back.

My father was as unmechanical a man as ever lived, and the gasoline engine was a complete mystery to him. Sometimes he would go so far as to lift the hood and stare at the engine, or maybe reach in and wiggle a wire to see whether it would wiggle. But mostly he confined himself to kicking the tires. It was never clear to me, and I doubt that it was clear to him, what he expected to learn from this, but he was very serious and professional about it. His attitude was that of a doctor thumping a patient's chest. I wonder that he never placed a stethoscope to the casing or stuck a fever thermometer down the valve stem.

Another reason we rarely drove out of town on Sundays was that my grandmother would expect to go along. Granny, my great-grandmother, preferred to stay home with her rocking chair and spittoon, but my grandmother loved to ride and, after all, it was her car. If we took her, she was sure to throw a tantrum, and we would come home Sunday night in high gear and low spirits. My mother and grandmother would not be speaking to each other and my father would be disinherited.

Disinheritance by my grandmother, which was something like excommunication by the Pope, was always her ace in the hole. She kept her last will and testament in the kitchen cupboard, within easy reach, rather than in the safe deposit box at the bank, since she wished to be ready to strike out a name at a moment's notice.

I myself, being a cowed youth and her only grandchild, was disinherited only once. This was when we were on a trip and I got out of the car and slammed the door behind me, not noticing that my grandmother was gripping the doorpost.

"Oh-h-h! You have cut off my finger," she screamed without looking to be absolutely certain.

"I'm awfully sorry," I said, realizing at once that this was inadequate.

"You did it on purpose, you ungrateful boy," my grandmother cried, forgetfully pointing the supposedly amputated finger at me. I looked with fascination, expecting to see it fall to the ground. "Just wait till I get home," she continued menacingly, "and see how fast I take your name out of my will. You'll never get a cent of my money."

As it turned out, my grandmother's finger was only mashed a little and she ultimately lost a blackened fingernail. But I assumed I had been disinherited and so did my father, who had had hopes for me if not for himself.

But if we made a trip on Sunday and left my grandmother behind there was hell to pay. Against my mother's advice, my father would always feel that he should call her up and say good-bye, this being the least a son could do. Whatever my grandmother said to my father in the course of their conversation, she invariably hung up on him, and he turned away from the phone wild-eyed and shaken. Thus, instead of coming home annoyed and depressed and possibly disinherited, as we did when we took my grandmother along, we started out that way.

"It's six of one and half a dozen of the other," was the way my father analyzed it, relying on one of his favorite observations. Or sometimes he used another, "You're damned if you do and damned if you don't." As I learned later, when we studied mythology at school, it was like being between Scylla and Charybdis, except that my grandmother was both of them.

Actually we did not have two Hupmobiles, the two my father sold himself, but only one, because Uncle Lester had been either lent or given the red one, the racier model. The ownership of the red Hupmobile was a matter of considerable uncertainty and difference of opinion. Shortly after we moved to Pomona, according to my father, my grandmother had suggested that he let Uncle Lester drive the red Hupmobile around town to impress potential clients for his architectural services. After fourteen months, during which he apparently had not been any too impressive, Uncle Lester was still driving the car as if it were his own.

"Isn't it about time you gave me back the red Hupmobile?" my father asked Uncle Lester one day in the drugstore, when he had dropped in to watch my father work. Unlike my grandmother, Uncle Lester never criticized whatever my father was doing. He just watched.

"But you gave it to me," my uncle said, reaching into the large glass jar next to the cash register and helping himself to a hoarhound drop. "Don't you remember?"

"Frankly, no," my father said, resting his hand on the top of the hoarhound jar as if needing support. He only wished he had been a little quicker. "Can you tell me when I gave it to you?"

"Two or three years ago," my uncle said. "I don't know the exact date. If you can't remember, how do you expect me to?"

"I tell you I never did give it to you, and I want it back."

"You gave it to me."

"I didn't."

"You did."

"I didn't."

Despite his 240 pounds, there was always something of the small boy about my uncle, and at times like this he made a small boy out of my father, too. They were just at the point of sticking their tongues out at each other and snarling, "Oh yeah?" "Yeah!"

Uncle Lester ended matters by walking out and driving off. This was disconcerting to my father, not so much because of the car as because he was always the one who walked out on an argument. But he could hardly have left Uncle Lester alone in the drugstore with a full jar of hoarhound drops.

My uncle finally settled things by selling the car and using the money for a trip East. What caused him to sell was not his fear that my father was closing in on him but a harrowing experience he had at the wheel. He tried to get across the railroad tracks near the center of town while the black-and-white striped wooden gates were descending. He almost made it, but not quite. The gate came down just as he started under it, and the iron supporting stake pierced the canvas top of the car and came to rest on the seat alongside him. There, until the gates were raised, he was pinned like a butterfly in a display case. Had the car had a left-hand drive, Uncle Lester would have been spitted for fair, making an interesting specimen for the Southern Pacific.

I doubt that any other incident ever gave my father so much satisfaction. Years later he would remember it and his usually sad face would brighten and break into a half smile. Even if it was only a near miss, it almost made up for the loss of the red Hupmobile.

A Boyhood in Ras Tanura

William Tracy

It always amused me to see people's reactions in the States when I told them where I lived. "Saudi Arabia?" they would say. "You mean in the desert?" And I would say, yes, in the desert, and they would say, "Well, gee, that must have been interesting!" Then they would hurry away to tell their friends about this oddball who grew up in an oil camp on the Arabian Gulf.

At the time I thought they really did consider it interesting. I didn't realize that to many people in the United States growing up anywhere but in America seemed more peculiar than interesting. "How," they sometimes asked, "can a boy grow up without, oh, football games on Saturday, snowstorms, ice skating, cutting the lawn in summer or burning leaves in the fall or going walking in the spring, or, well you know . . ."

As it happened, I did not know, not really. I went to Saudi Arabia when I was only 11 years old. Oh, I do have vague memories of a few things in Illinois—frost on the windows, maybe, the smell of fresh cut grass, the Memorial Day parades, or the sight of tall trees against the sky. But for the vivid memories, the bright warm memories of boyhood, I have to go back to Saudi Arabia, to the night the plane from Cairo dropped out of the darkness onto the Dhahran airstrip, the night our new life in an old land began . . .

It was 1946. The war was over—World War II, that is—and my mother, determined to join my father after a year's separation, had packed us off to New York and onto a freighter bound for Alexandria (it was called *"The Black Warrior,"* I remember). Then we took a train for Cairo and, after a week of false starts, a plane for Dhahran. When we landed we straggled across the airfield like a small untidy parade. My mother was first with my baby sister Sally cradled in one arm on a bulky WAC's purse. I was second, clutching her hand, and my brother Jimmy was last, trotting along at the end of a sort of leash with which, I felt, I had dragged him half way around the world.

It was terribly hot and very dark, I recall, and the loud speaker from the Dhahran Airfield was just broadcasting the beginning of

From *Aramco World Magazine*, 19:4 (July-August 1968). Reprinted by permission.

"Inner Sanctum," one of my favorite programs at home. I remember the sound of the creaking door. And then I saw my father. He was standing on the apron waiting for us, a tall thin man, almost a stranger after our year's separation. He was dressed in white, I remember, and he had sunglasses strapped to his belt. We ran to meet him . . .

Later, my father introduced us to the Snyders with whom we were to spend the night before going on to Ras Tanura, a new community where Aramco had built a refinery. One of the Snyders was a boy named Myles who was two years my senior and who, in the 15 minutes it took to drive to the Snyder house, became my closest friend.

"See those flames?" he asked in a low voice. I looked out through the darkness and saw the dancing lights of the gas flares from a gas-oil separator plant. "They're volcanoes," he said. "Live volcanoes, really!"

A few minutes later he pointed to the silhouette of twin minarets on a mosque near the road. "Cactus!" he hissed. "Saguaro cactus!"

And both times I believed him.

In the months to come, Myles was to teach me all sorts of new things: how to find green scorpions under driftwood on the beach, how to catch lizards behind the neck so that you weren't stuck with a writhing lizardless tail between your fingers. He was to introduce me to spiny-tailed "dabbs," meat eating "warals" and suction-toed geckoes; to desert hedgehogs and foxes, and even once—on a wilderness trip with a geologist—to a hunchbacked striped hyena. It would be Myles too who would, one year in Dhahran, lead me under the camp fence on daring hikes to distant flat-topped hills, and to the charred crater blasted by a misplaced Italian bomb. But that would come later. The first night he contented himself with making the new kid think that the flares were volcanoes. As I dozed off in the Snyders' living room, I heard his voice echoing in my head, "Live volcanoes, really!"

The next morning we headed for Ras Tanura in a four by four army surplus truck. We drove past Aramco's Dammam Seven, the company's first producing oil well, past pyramid-shaped Jabal Shamal on the left, and past the fishing villages of al-Khobar and Dammam. Later, we saw crystal white salt flats and scattered palm groves over which loomed towering dunes. As the truck drove along, occasionally shifting into four-wheel drive to push through patches of drifted sand, we saw flocks of long-haired black goats,

clusters of low Bedouin tents, and the huge stiff-legged white don-
keys of the Eastern Province, with spots of orange dye on their
backs. We saw our first camel standing against the horizon and
noted a sign by the road cautioning us that "camels have the
right-of-way."

All this, which would become so familiar to us, was new that
morning. Some of it, unstirred by centuries, had begun to disappear
even then; all of it would change a little in the next few years. All
except the searing heat and the scorching beige glare of the desert
which reached halfway into the sky. Beside the road were the
catalysts of the change; the high-tension power line, the flares of
the gas-oil separator plants ("Live volcanoes," huh?) and the rows
of pipelines with mounds of clay for the camel caravans to cross.
Then the towers of the new refinery appeared beyond the long
finger of Tarut Bay and we drove onto the narrow Ras Tanura
headland to the house where we were to live.

We had one of the first group of 30 stucco family houses built
in "American City," now Nejma. The houses, painted in brilliant
colors as if to challenge the monotony of sand and sky, were ar-
ranged four deep along the shore. They had spacious yards of
white beach sand, and patios of flat "faroush" stone taken from
the bottom of the bay. From our dining room we could watch the
changing moods and colors of the Gulf: misty silver and mirror-
still at dawn, clear aquamarine and violet at mid-day, chalky green
during a storm and washed lime-blue when the storm was over. It
was unforgettably beautiful.

In Ras Tanura, in those days, most of the early facilities were
located in temporary wooden barracks. There were a clinic, a
laundry, a barbershop, a mail center, and a recreation hall in which
were located a library, a snack bar, a billiard room and a bowling
alley.

For the hard-hatted sheet metal construction workers, the
recreation hall was the center of their off-duty life. Here they balanced the day's sweat with a night of pre-prohibition beer drinking
and high-stakes poker. Across the street was the Mess Hall which
served all the bachelors, including married men whose families
had not yet arrived, and "bachelorettes," the first few nurses and
secretaries who had been persuaded to come out to Saudi Arabia.
Nearby were flood-lit tennis courts (used by us kids surreptitiously
for roller skating). There was also an outdoor theater, with straw
mat sides to keep out the strong north wind. We went to the
movies winter and summer, although in winter it meant wrapping

up in blankets. But often on mild nights in the spring and fall the sky and its stars offered a better show than the one on the screen.

The refinery, I remember, had just gone "on stream," as everyone soon learned to say, and little Ras Tanura began to celebrate its ever-increasing post-war production with splendid holidays on the beach every time we racked up a 100,000- or a 150,000-barrel day. These were most often Employee Association picnics with donkey races (the big white ones were safe bets), buried coin hunts for silver riyals and Indian rupees, and, on very special occasions such as the 4th of July, feasts of watermelon from al-Kharj, southeast of Riyadh.

Other big occasions in those days were the monthly (or sometimes semi-monthly) arrivals of the refrigerator ships, for the ships brought fresh vegetables. I remember the sight of the women hurrying to the commissary carrying heavy canvas bags of clinking silver coins since paper money had not yet been introduced.

There was always construction underway and that meant lots of bricks and planks that enterprising boys could manage to "borrow" despite the efforts of the Safety Department to keep us at bay. Rightly or wrongly we considered Safety Department personnel and "Security" our mortal enemies. They discovered our board-covered tunnels beneath the sagebrush hillocks at the edge of town and bulldozed them under. They discouraged our long bicycle rides on the hard-packed beach at low tide by building a fence. They cut us off from the deserted coast where huge shells dried in the sun, where oar-tailed sea snakes warmed themselves on the sand and sand crabs tunneled below, leaving little castles by their front doors. We were never completely foiled, however, and swam outside the fence to walk as far as the magnificent sand dunes where we could somersault down to the bottom without harm, or play "king of the mountain."

Meanwhile, as we explored Ras Tanura and its environs, my mother was making a determined bid to tame the desert. In our first house the only garden we had was an accidental growth of tiny palm shoots that sprang up when dew dripped from the sloping roofs onto date pits left by construction workers who had made a habit of eating lunch in the shade of the house. But when we moved to a new house and when soil had been trucked in, Mother planted the beginnings of a garden and between the sandstorms which periodically swept across the beach wall, nursed it to life. First she planted a crop of alfalfa. Then she put in creepers of Bermuda grass which had to be poked into the earth one by one and painstakingly sprinkled with the hose each evening. Then she put in oleander bushes and tamarisk and acacia trees, buried dried seaweed and fish near the roots to fertilize them and, because of the wind and the shallow soil, tied them upright to sturdy poles. Some flowering plants could be obtained from the company's nursery: frangipani, climbing red, orange, and purple bougainvillea, hardy periwinkle, dwarf poinsettia, but there were also four o'clocks grown from seeds sent out from my grandpa's farm in Ohio. I remember how strange Ras Tanura looked the first year green trees began to poke above the roofs all over town, throwing circles of shade onto the ground and softening the skyline.

Before then we had spent a year in Dhahran. It was the year my sister Sue was born. We lived in a house on a hill from which you could see the smoke from the flares on the island of Bahrain. On the other side of the house in Dhahran, I recall, lived a boy named Jim McCarthy who introduced me to an intriguing little book about the facts of life. Another neighbor, Louella Beckly, lent me scores of Carolyn Keene's Nancy Drew mystery stories. They were both "big kids" like Phil Braun, who could swim faster on his back than most of us could crawl. But big or little, there were plenty of them since the families in Saudi Arabia were young and large. There was always a new wing under construction at the school and new faces on the bus or at the mail center. Since someone was always leaving for long vacation or going "outside" to school, there were also familiar faces disappearing too. Myles Snyder, for one.

After the year in Dhahran we moved back to Ras Tanura and I made new friends. One was Joe Studholm and the other a boy named Jim Mandaville. Jim was a genius of many talents, we all knew, because he threw shoes at his brother Jack (who could pinch you with his toes when wrestling), identified desert plants and fragments of pottery, rode horses, and built radios and model airplanes. He was a "girl hater" at the time and a party hater. To his chagrin, his mother helped organize the Teen Club.

Since we lived on the shore, I guess it was inevitable that we would come to know the sea and its inhabitants. Some of us, at least, like D. T. Gray, my cousin, and Miles Jones, with whom I ranged up and down the coast in quest of all that it had to teach us.

Miles lived in a house in the Marine Terminal area on the tip of the Ras Tanura peninsula. Because the house was the oldest in town it was infested with earwigs and centipedes and for some reason that I can't remember we were convinced that there was a mongoose in the attic which had escaped from one of the tankers from India.

When D.T. and I spent the weekend with Miles we would hike across the narrow sand spit to the abandoned arrow-shaped palm frond fish traps there, and wade cautiously in the slimy sand, watching for sand dollars and sea urchins and feeling mud sharks and skates slither across our nervous toes. We caught baskets of fish for fertilizer and great blue crabs, and quantities of huge pink shrimp which we cleaned and ate doused in tomato catsup. We also decimated the population of a certain snail which had the bad luck of shutting itself in with a dime-sized trapdoor of some beauty which we called cat's-eye. We held our noses as we boiled kettles of them, pried their protective seal from the sticky body, dried them in the sun, and bathed them in glistening olive oil. We ran our fingers through piles of them like misers. They were too chalky to be valuable, of course, but to us they were priceless.

But great as it was, there was more to life than just leisure and mischief. There was also school. School then was held in a portable building on a steel frame that was hauled in on a truck and perched on four large concrete blocks. Sam Whipple was the principle but he was also our teacher, and our friend. He was short and balding and could run faster than any of the boys in junior high.

One day, when the seasonal wind had whipped around and under the school for several weeks, we felt a sudden window-rattling jolt and the building lurched. The sand had blown away from the base of one of the concrete supports. The Safety Department moved in at once and took precautions and put out bulletins, but we thought it had been great fun when all the volleyballs and baseball bats behind Mr. Whipple's desk began to roll lazily down to the far corner of the room.

In cool weather in our school we frequently went out on excursions, sometimes driving all day on sand tracks to the Hofuf oasis with its maze of caves and eroded sandstone pillars, its hot springs, donkey drawn wells, covered *suqs*, and old walls. We took the three step journey by dhow, rowboat, and donkey cart to Tarut Island where thousands of tiny turtles lived in the irrigation ditches beneath jungles of palms. We climbed like lizards over the crumbling Portuguese forts in Dammam and Qatif, and visited the last of the great winter encampments of the Bedouins.

Like all American boys, of course, we had a Boy Scout troop, but although we learned our first aid and Morse and semaphore in the prescribed fashion, our company trips were quite different. We always had an extra truck loaded with firewood and water. No amount of woodsman's lore would have provided either in that territory. In Tarut Bay we camped on uninhabited Za'al Island which was separated from the peninsula only by a broad mud flat and narrow reef channel, but gave us a splendid feeling of freedom and remoteness when the water rose and the tidal current was running. There we skinny-dipped and hunted tern's eggs, and at night herded schools of needlefish onto the beach by sweeping a powerful three-battery flashlight beam along the dark surface of the bay.

Ras Tanura was so small that having a party meant inviting every kid in camp. The girl hater clique was not big on "scissors," "walking the plank," "sardines," "inchy pinchy," or "country club." They once fled from a party with Nancy Bradfield's birthday cake in tow. But I think even the girl haters were secretly impressed by Mary Beth Harrity when she floated on her back in the Gulf. Of course she was a "big kid" and only came to Ras Tanura during vacations from the American Community School in Beirut, Lebanon. She brought back stories about boarding school which we all believed and could hardly wait to experience for ourselves. In the meantime, enjoying our last year at home, we made dribble castles on the beach, threw sun-dried stinging jellyfish at each other, ran barefooted across melting asphalt roads, and chased locust swarms from the gardens, knocking them down with tennis rackets.

We thought ourselves to be special breed of kids in those days. And maybe in some ways we were. We spoke Arabic, we had met the famous King Ibn Sa'ud. We knew real Bedouins and all of us had been around the world at least once. Our thick green passports were gay accumulations of visas and permits from as many nations as there were pages, and our arms and inoculation certificates were both full of shots. We had, furthermore, lived through the incomparable excitement of watching a town come to life in what, to us at least, was a new and exciting land.

But now, suddenly it was time to leave again—off to high school in Beirut. It wasn't really very far and we were coming back every holiday, but still, when the special red and silver Kenworth bus headed out to the airport that day, there was more than one red-eyed mother and silent father aboard.

We drove past the same dunes, and the same palm groves, and even, I thought, the same herds of goats that I had seen that first day when we left the Snyders' house. My father had become noticeably quiet as we passed the halfway coast guard house and as Jabal Shamal appeared on the horizon, he began to fidget uneasily.

"Er, ah, Billy, . . ." We bounced past the gas flares ("Live volcanoes, really!"). "Well, Bill . . ." We jolted past the main gate of Dhahran and down past the twin minarets ("saguaro cactus") towards the airfield. It was 1950. Had it only been four years? "Son," my father gulped and looked around and leaned towards my ear. A gargled whisper: "Is there, er, anything you'd like to know about, er . . . girls?"

Which is as good a place as any to end my memories of those, yes, innocent years growing up in Saudi Arabia.

The Hawks

Alan Devoe

On days like this the hawks cry down the wind, and I hear them as long as I can—trying to take no notice—and then I put on my wool-lined coat and my heavy boots and climb up the mountain that rises behind my farmhouse and is called Phudd Hill. It is easy to take life very casually, almost not to notice it, but the presence near you of death is not easy to ignore; and what the hawks cry down the wind is death. We are so accustomed here to hearing the thin voices of nuthatches and woodpeckers, and the lusty quarreling voices of starlings, that we pay them no heed; or if momentarily we do, it is to listen as people have ever listened to the customary thing, with half an ear. But the voice of the hawks is not like these. It cuts the bitter winter air with a sharp stridence, and we always feel somehow—hearing it—as though it were the sharpening of a knife.

And so, as I say, today I stayed as long as I could at my writing beside the stove, pretending that that edged cry was not in my ears, and then I threw down my pad and went and got my coat and my boots and went out. A north gale was blowing down the valley, so hard that the chimney smoke streamed parallel to our farmhouse roof, and the ground under my feet was as hard and granular as pebbles. It has always been on days like this that we have heard the hawks, making the cold air clamorous with their hunger for hot blood. I knew, from other times, which way to walk, and set out up the southeast face of the hill. There is a kind of cleft there, called Miller's Gully from the name of a long gone farmer whose land it once was, and at the head of it the hill grows sharply steep. Here there is a great growth of pine and hemlock, and high in these is the roosting place of the hawks. The pine trunks are smeared white with their dung.

I climbed up the Gully slowly, for the icy air hurt in my lungs, and all the while over my head a hawk made his sound. I stopped presently, to rest from pushing my way through the frozen tangle of last season's wild blackberries, and looked up and watched. The

From *Down to Earth* (Coward-McCann, Inc., 1940). Reprinted by permission.

hawk was not very high. Here on Phudd Hill they have grown bold, and are not afraid. Almost I could make out the notching of his outer primaries as he wheeled in slow spread-winged arcs above me, peering and crying. The red-tails are always leisurely, even at their killing. Sometimes—once or twice in a season—we surprise one of those slaty hawks called Cooper's in the thick pine woods on the mountain, and always they flash from sight almost before we know what they are, and there is only the harsh staccato of their cac-cac-cac! receding in the far distance. But the red-tails, seeking their meat from God, move with so slow and indolent a grace that it would not be hard to imagine it were a studied thing. With unbeating wings they sidle down the wind, and the scream wells slowly from their throats.

This one today, as I watched him, seemed to lie as effortlessly on the swirling wind as a gull on calm water. The tilt of a wing, the flex of a muscle in the root of that fulvous tail—it was thus suavely done.

When you live in a country place you learn to endure the constant company of deaths around you—the rip and twist of the knife in hogs' throats in December, the snap of the chipmunk's spine between the weasel's teeth—but I have not learned to look without a flinch when the red-tails are at their work. And this although I know that death in woods and meadows is mostly not so horrible a thing as the poets like to recite it. It has no foreshadowing, and it is a quick clean thing, stripped of artifice and ritual. When it comes, it comes in haste, and honestly. Animals do not often die long deaths, of broken hearts and inner sickness and slow despair, but mostly fast and uncomprehendingly, with torn jugulars or cracked spines or the breath crushed out of their lungs. Their terror is only for a little while.

As I stood chilled on Phudd Hill this afternoon, watching the lazy dip and tilt of those tawny wings, I felt a conviction I have often felt before, and this was that the hawk had long since sighted his prey, and, having marked well the spot of fancied shelter to which his first scream had sent it scuttling, was idling unhurried now, savoring in gourmand-like anticipation that mite of quivering flesh far below him. Slow and rhythmic as a pendulum the hawk glided in his effortless arcs, crying his shrill screams down the wind. Unmistakably this was not the chase itself, but the time of exultation. The chase was long over and ended. Somewhere now in Miller's Gully, flattened against the frozen rubble or cowering at the base of one of these wind-whipped pines, some small thing was run to earth. It was there now, its ribs swelling with the pounding of its tiny heart, in its small furry ears the shrilling of an edged cry, full of exultation. I stood very still, bitterly cold for all my great coat, and stared up at the hawk and hoped he might be done quickly with his playing.

Slowly, almost imperceptibly, the arcs of his gliding flight grew smaller, and each leisured spiral brought him closer to the earth, as though he were following in his slow descent the outline of an invisible funnel in the air. He had stopped crying now, and eddied earthward as silently as a leaf. Soundless, too, and incredibly quick, was the final sudden veer and swoop. He seemed no more than to brush with his wing-tips a little clump of frozen bittersweet, but as he rose again he struggled laboredly against the gale, for he was carrying a weight.

I could not see what it was, but among the dead creepers of the tangled bittersweet I found a little place where the frost had been thawed by the warmth of a small body, and one tiny jet of bright red blood lay smeared across the brittle leaves.

Ready or Not, Here Comes Jumbo

Time Magazine

The high white contrails of cruising jets are bright symbols of the promise and pleasures of air travel. When the big ships descend into sight and sound, their aspect alters. Their great engines foul the air with noise and noxious fumes; their proliferating numbers crowd the airways with dangerous traffic jams. Each new plane seems to bring more problems than the last. But the newest and largest product of this technological age is built to a different pattern. The Boeing 747, first of the generation of superjets that will dominate the skies in the 1970's, is quieter and cleaner than its predecessors. Its huge capacity will help airlines keep ahead of their expanding roster of passengers. The new planes should alleviate rather than increase the clutter aloft. In the process they will bring new comfort, convenience and economies to ever greater numbers of travelers.

Boeing's 355-ton superjet is 231 ft 4 in. long—three-quarters the length of a football field, longer than the Wright brothers' first flight. Its 20 ft-wide cabin is almost twice as broad as the largest passenger plane now in service; it can be fitted with up to 490 seats. More like a small cruise ship than any familiar aircraft, the big plane brings to mind comedienne Bea Lillie's comment on the *Queen Elizabeth*: "When does this place get to England?"

If all goes well, the 747 will get to England next week, when Pan American World Airways has scheduled the initial flight of paying passengers from New York to London. By the end of June, at least 30 superjets should be regularly crossing the Atlantic, the Pacific and the continental U.S. With their remarkable efficiency, they will help hold fares down at a time when everything else is going up.

Risking the Future

For all such benefits, the superjets will create some giant problems all their own. Airport managers nervously await the great clots of passengers that will be disgorged from a single flight. Practically no terminal is prepared. In the first months of 747 service, baggage handling and ground transportation—already overstrained—may be utterly swamped.

Airline managers are equally concerned. The 747 is so costly that its advent has plunged the industry deeply into debt. When one line buys a new generation of aircraft, all feel the urge to follow. At a time when profits are down, credit is expensive and other costs are climbing, the airlines feel that they have no choice but to order the 747's. So far, 28 of them in the U.S. and abroad have ordered 186 of the superjets at around $23 million each. That amounts to a capital outlay of $4.3 billion.

The initial cost is only the beginning of a new round of expensive investments that the superjets make necessary. Airlines must spend another $2 billion for new facilities and equipment in the next four years, including 54-ton tractors to tow the big planes and new boarding ramps to lift passengers to doors that are 17 ft off the ground.

The airline that will be first with the most 747's, and thus must cope with every one of the bumps in what airmen call a new plane's "learning curve," is Pan American. As if that were not enough, the company is already experiencing more than its share of turbulence. Last year it lost an estimated $23 million, $7 million in the month of November alone. It is getting much tougher competition from archrival Trans World Airlines on the North Atlantic route, and it faces a flock of new competitors on transpacific routes that it once all but monopolized. Now, with the 747, Pan Am is taking one of the larger risks in business history. It has committed $1 billion to buy 33 of the jumbo jets and create the facilities to handle them. The company is staking its corporate future on the big ship.

Expert's Assessment

The man who must make the wager pay off is Najeeb Elias Halaby, 54, Pan Am's new president and chief executive. Halaby has not yet had time to demonstrate that he can lead a losing airline back to solid profits, but he has sound credentials for that difficult job. Before he landed at Pan Am, he was in turn an outstanding pilot, a practicing lawyer, a corporate executive, and an imaginative, activist chief of the Federal Aviation Administration. He also showed himself to be accomplished in personal public relations, seldom failing to remind audiences that he was President Kennedy's principal advisor in all aviation matters. Pilots who met him at the gossip sessions known as "hangar fly-ins" took to greeting him with the line: "Halaby thy name. Thy will be done, on earth and in the heavens."

One of Halaby's major assets is the fact that he probably knows more about the 747 than anyone outside of Boeing. As FFA administrator, he framed many of the Government rules that will regulate the plane's flights. Last year, when reports filtered through the industry that the big ship was in trouble, Halaby went to Seattle to take the 747 on a test flight. Settling into the left-hand command seat, he piloted the plane through its paces for two hours, then gave a singularly satisfied description of its virtues.

Confidence Building

"You keep thinking that you have 170,000 lbs of thrust in four little levers," he said. "You've got your hands on a hurricane on the ground. You have to be careful, because the blast could blow in a hangar door. Another thing: you've got 355 tons of momentum when you're taxiing that machine, and you don't go charging around. So you have got to plan ahead while taxiing. But once it's airborne, it's absolutely superb." Halaby took the 747 through high-altitude stalls and a series of landings and takeoffs. "You become integrated with the ship. That big fin and so much rudder contribute to stability and control." The plane was so bulky that he found that it seemed to dwarf the runway. Landing, he reported, was "like training for carrier landings." When he taxied back to the hangar, the feeling was "like docking a patrol boat—you've got to sail it in, and very carefully."

"It's a confidence-building machine, straight-forward and honest," adds Halaby with unbridled enthusiasm. "Once passengers get aboard, they will have such a feeling of space, of strength, yes, even security, that any early anxiety will disappear. It is going to be, for older people, like going back into an ocean liner. For the youngster, it is going to be a different kind of life in the sky, where he can move around, go up and down the deck, feel less inhibited and constrained than he was in previous airplanes."

Stepping into the 747's passenger cabin is indeed like walking onto the passenger deck of a luxury cruise ship. The aisles are wide, the walls nearly straight, and the ceiling an unconfining 8 ft high. Economy-class seats are 10% wider than on an ordinary jet. Coats and carry-on baggage are stowed in large overhead storage compartments. The cockpit is in the prominent bulge atop the plane's front end, along with a surprisingly spacious bar and lounge for first-class passengers, reached by a winding staircase. On the main deck below, the cabin extends out into the nose of the aircraft. In the economy section—which is separated by galleys into cabins so large that TWA recently held a board meeting aloft —passengers sit nine abreast in rows of two, three and four, divided by two wide aisles. The total effect is of roomy comfort. In flight, the 747's heft helps to smooth out some of the turbulence but, as in every other airplane, passengers in the rear are subject to the most movement in bumpy air.

To many people, the sheer size of a superjet raises the horrifying image of a supercrash. The thought of as many as 500 passengers and crew members going down at once seems too appalling to contemplate. Even so, actuaries in London, where most airline insurance is written, forecast three 747 crashes in the first 18 months of service. Each accident would cost the insurers up to $65 million. Balanced against their projection is an actuarial fact: though 98 of the 3,012 jets that have gone into service in the past dozen years have been lost in accidents, air travel—measured on an aircraft-mile basis—is five times safer than it was a decade ago.

Moreover, judged by its extensive new equipment, the 747 ought to be the safest aircraft ever built. The superjet has three inertial-navigation systems—the same sort that has guided Apollo flights—lest one, or even two, should fail. There are two auto pilots instead of one, a redundant supply of communications gear and an advanced radar with a 300-mile range. The 747 even has an automatic landing system designed to bring it safely to a runway in any weather without the touch of a pilot's hand.

Gaps on the Ground

As its biggest boosters are all too well aware, it is on the ground that 747 passengers will find what Halaby calls "a surface-transport gap, a hotel gap, and a parking-lot gap." There is also that conspicuous airport gap. The 747 can land in the same length of runway as a 707, but its sheer size makes many other changes necessary. The only airport in the world that claims to be fully prepared for the 747 is Paris' Orly, which has already built one separate terminal and has another under way. By June, London's Heathrow will be the second adequately equipped airport, with an expanded terminal and twice as many customs officials. Tokyo's Haneda airport, probably the world's most crowded terminal, has made preparations only on paper, and no one knows how its thoroughgoing customs officers are going to handle the crush. J.F.K. airport in New York will not be fully prepared until 1973.

Ground transportation of every variety is already overloaded. Authorities at Kennedy and other airports may eventually have to ban private cars altogether, allowing only buses and taxis to drive up to the terminals. New York's Metropolitan Transportation Authority plans a rail line on an unused right of way of the Long Island Rail Road between J.F.K. and Penn Station to whisk passengers to midtown Manhattan in 20 minutes. But the first trains probably will not be ready until 1974.

Winning by Losing

Congress is moving belatedly to supply funds to equip the nation's airways and airports for the superjet age, and most of the load will fall squarely on the air traveler. By spring Congress is likely to pass legislation to raise nearly $1.8 billion a year in new revenues. The ticket tax on domestic flights will rise from 5% to 8%, and there will be a new "head tax" of $3 on passengers flying overseas and a 2% tax on air freight. The money will be used to improve airways by adding new navigation and communications aids; airports will also be improved.

Perhaps the most surprising fact about the 747 is that the plane that promises to accomplish so much actually began its existence as a loser. In 1964, Defense Secretary Robert McNamara ordered a competition for a giant military transport and an advanced jet engine to power it. Lockheed and General Electric won the plane-and-engine competition, and their entry became the C-5A. The two losers, Boeing and Pratt & Whitney, were eager to find a market for their rejected designs. Boeing's chief, William Allen, decided to risk what turned out to be $1 billion in turning the military reject into a commercial success. Pan American's founder, Juan Trippe, who had ordered the first 707's a decade before, was still in command. He backed Allen by placing the first order for 25 of the 747's and taking an option for more.

To get production under way, Boeing had to construct one of the world's largest buildings—a plant covering 42.8 acres at Everett, Washington. Inside that vast space, the engineers encountered vast problems. The aircraft's weight grew by 15 tons from its projected 340 tons, and Pratt & Whitney had to rush development of a still more powerful engine. Because it burns its fuel more efficiently than other engines, the 747 is virtually free of the greasy smoke that trails ordinary jets on takeoff like ink from a frightened squid. Its engine is only half as loud as a 707's, though the difference will be less noticeable during takeoffs than landings. The new engine was not put into production as fast as the plane. Boeing last week had 15 expensive airframes sitting powerless outside its plant.

Once attached, the new engines brought another serious difficulty. As the turbines thrust forward in flight, the rear casing was bent one-twentieth of an inch out of shape, letting jet gases leak around the turbine. Result: the engines lost some of their power and fuel consumption rose a costly 5%. Pratt & Whitney finally found a solution by modifying the mounting, in effect adding an extra strut to carry the thrust. The new part will not be ready until the first 30 aircraft have been built.

Middle-Age Spread

Early design difficulties are inherent in building any plane, and the 747's major troubles now seem to be overcome. Two weeks ago, the FFA gave the plane an airworthiness certificate, the final approval needed to fly passengers. Recalling a recent conversation with Pan Am's best-known director, Charles Lindbergh, Halaby says: "Slim Lindbergh and I were sitting in the 747, and we decided to list the greatest civil air transports of all time. We picked the German JU-52, the DC-3, the DC-6, the 707 family of jets, the DC-8s—and this airplane, the 747."

That assessment had better be right, because Pan Am needs a major new success. Almost as soon as it started flying from Key West to Havana in 1927, Pan Am became the high and mighty among U.S. air carriers. Patrician Boss Juan Trippe maintained what was virtually his own state department to negotiate landing rights with foreign governments; at home, he had the political clout of a board of directors that has always included more former high Government and military officers than that of probably any other U.S. company. Among the current crew: Cyrus Vance, Alfred Gruenther, William Scranton, Robert B. Anderson, and Lindbergh.

In recent years, though, Pan Am has been overtaken by symptoms of middle-age spread. It faces a fleet of increasingly nimble U.S. and foreign competitors, and has suffered a series of reverses in Washington. Last summer Pan Am lost out to National Airlines on the award of a Miami-London route that it coveted, and President Nixon's award of Pacific routes allowed a host of competitors onto Pan Am's most profitable runs, Unlike TWA, Pan Am has no domestic routes to feed passengers onto its overseas flights. But that does not explain why its regular passengers last year deserted to TWA by the planeload and TWA for the first time carried more passengers across the Atlantic than Pan Am. Strike threats and a brief labor walkout last summer badly hurt Pan Am. As its popularity dwindled, TWA stewardesses somehow earned a reputation for giving more considerate service. TWA, in fact, manages to maintain such service while spending less per passenger mile than Pan Am.

While Halaby is very much the boss, he delegates authority among several close associates and has brought in a cost-conscious new vice president to operate the airline and make day-to-day decisions. He is Richard Mitchell, former head of Pan Am's aerospace division at Cape Kennedy, where Pan Am fills a housekeeping and maintenance role. Together, Halaby and his top managers are trimming the line's payroll, laying off 1,730 of 45,500 employees, including 450 of its 3,590 pilots.

Halaby expects that Pan Am's lead with the 747 will help the line to turn a quick if temporary profit this year; 1971 will be a tough year because by then so many competitors will have their own fleets of superjets. To make more money, Halaby plans a wide-ranging diversification, particularly by expanding a subsidiary, Intercontinental Hotels. Pan Am already owns 45 hotels around the world, mostly in the luxury class, and is building 60 more, largely for the middle-income group that it hopes to attract with the 747. "We'll let our beds match our seats," says Halaby, who also plans to open low-price hostels. Says he: "We will provide a clean, wholesome austerity."

Squalls of Competition

Pan Am is not alone in feeling the profit crunch that, in the year ending last Sept. 30, held U.S. airlines' investment return to 3.7%, down from 9.5% in 1967. "Nobody can make money in the goddam airline business these days," says C. R. Smith, chairman of American Airlines until 1968. "The economics represents sheer hell. Practically everybody is in trouble."

The economics of aviation was little better eleven years ago, when the 707's first flew into service. Then, airline executives wondered how they could possibly fill the expensive new jets or pay for them in a time of economic slowdown, slackening passenger growth, and steeply diving profits. For several years, the planes flew with too many empty seats. Not until 1963–64 did they achieve their full potential. Then the jets became the airlines' biggest moneymakers ever; airmen called them the "flying cash registers." Now Halaby and other industry chiefs hope that history will repeat itself, and the chances are that it will. The CAB predicts that passenger travel on U.S. lines will more than double by 1980. The notable economies of the 747 should enable airlines to wring more profit out of that increase. The jumbo jet can be particularly productive as an all-cargo carrier, and could cut the cost of sending a ton of air freight from Dallas to Tokyo, for example, from $340 at present to $135.

The immediate outlook, however, is for a few years of costly overcapacity. Pan Am will have 362 seats to fill per 747 flight, and TWA has ordered 15 superjets with 342 seats each. Even Ireland's little Aer Lingus has asked for two 400-seat versions for jam-packed all-economy flights between Dublin and New York, presumably relying on Irish loyalty and cut-price deals to fill them. Besides overcapacity, the 747 will bring higher operating costs. Pan Am's senior pilots will get paid $58,000 a year to fly it; airport authorities are asking for triple the landing fees that airlines pay for a 707.

Meanwhile, the industry continues to be troubled by fare-cutting competition from unscheduled airlines. So-called "supplemental" lines carry passengers at fares far below airline rates, passing on to their customers the economies that result from having every flight a 100%-full charter. During Halaby's term as FFA administrator, Washington set rigid new rules for the proliferating —and sometimes unreliable—supplementals. The Government weeded out the weaker ones, reducing their number to about a dozen. In the years since, they have burgeoned again, cutting deeply into the scheduled-airline business.

The scheduled lines' answer has been to offer "bulk" fares. The lines sell wholesale blocks of tickets to travel agents, who retail the seats for as little as $175 for a New York-London round trip (provided that the passenger also pays $100 in advance for meals and services at his destination). Another bargain is the new "group inclusive tour," which reflects the power of foreign government-owned airlines in the International Air Transport Association. International fares are now designed to encourage tourists to make fairly long visits to individual foreign countries in which they will presumably spend more money. As a result, tour fares, which include round-trip ticket, hotel room, some meals and theater tickets, can supply a remarkably inexpensive two-week stay in many a European city.

The 747 may allow even more attractive package deals. Regular fares, however, are unlikely to be cut; businessmen and others who stay abroad for fewer than 14 days will continue to pay relatively high prices for airline tickets. On domestic runs, U.S. airlines were granted two increases totaling more than 10% last year, and some lines are now rallying lobbyists to press for another boost, on the order of 3%.

Talking Merger

Executives of the supplemental lines argue that they serve the public interest by helping to reduce fares. They are calling for looser regulation, and are asking the State Department assistance in negotiating new landing rights abroad. In rebuttal, Halaby makes the point that scheduled airlines are already tightly regulated and overwhelmed by a surfeit of competition. As he puts it: "We should abandon the recent trend toward multiplication of carriers and the inevitable addition of deficits."

In an effort to reduce extreme competition and improve profits, many airlines are talking merger. The U.S. hardly seems in need of a score of trunk and regional lines. American Airlines has discussed merger with Western; ailing Eastern, admits President Floyd Hall, is "studying every other U.S. carrier" as a possible merger partner. TWA has considered both National and Northeast. Pan Am executives have held informal talks with American, Eastern, Delta, and Continental.

Pan Am could compete on better terms if it were allowed to feed into its overseas routes from inland gateways like St. Louis and Dallas, or permitted to acquire a medium-sized domestic line to give it a home base matching TWA's. The Justice Department may well fight tie-ups between any two of the very biggest lines, but there is little doubt that the Administration will permit some mergers. Most airline executives agree that there will be fewer carriers surviving by the end of the 1970's.

Debate on the SST

The financial benefits of togetherness will be all the more important because the lines will have to raise so many billions to pay for the 747 and other superjets in the future. Next summer, test pilots are scheduled to take up the first of the huge, three-engine "air buses"—McDonnell Douglas' DC-10 and Lockheed's 1011. Both are expected to enter service by 1972 and carry 250 to 350 passengers in comfort comparable to that of a 747. So far, 382 of the air buses have been ordered. Originally designed for shorter-range routes than the 747, the trijets are now being offered in stretched intercontinental versions as the two manufacturers compete for orders. In the continuing competition of bigness, Boeing has designed a 747 that can carry up to 750 passengers. Eventually, the jumbo jets are likely to reach capacities of 1,000 and 2,000.

Last month Congress voted $86 million—of an eventual $1 billion or more—to underwrite development of an aircraft of less obvious benefit: Boeing's supersonic transport, or SST. It is the U.S. answer to the British-French Concorde and Russia's TU-144. The SST will, as Halaby says, "turn the Atlantic into a river and the Pacific into a lake." But it will be much less economic than the 747, and passengers will have to pay premium fares.

The SST has divided the industry. Halaby, who as FAA administrator supervised the original competition for an SST design, says that he is an unabashed "supersonophile." He seems confident that the plane's problems can be solved. Pan Am Director Lindbergh has questioned the SST as a potential despoiler of the environment. Unless there is a breakthrough in design, the SST will spread a sonic boom beneath its path up to 50 miles wide. "Slim and I are in constructive debate on the SST," says Halaby. "I'm for it and he's not."

So far, the supersonophiles are winning, and the U.S. SST is likely to be in service by the late 1970's or early 1980's. The lines are expected to have a broad mix of planes and fares: premium prices on the SST, regular tariffs on jumbo jets, somewhat lower fares on older jets. By then, the problems of air travel will have multiplied, creating an even greater need for improved control of airspace, more airports, better ground transportation and bigger, more efficient terminals. Halaby worries because public investment in such facilities has always lagged five to ten years behind technological innovation. As the 747 takes to the air, its first and most important lesson is that the disparity must be corrected.

The Problem Passenger

Chaytor D. Mason

I believe it was a railroad man who once said, "The most difficult package of any to transport is that package called 'the human
being'." As we all know, the railroads have found that package
exceedingly hard to transport and to understand and so have given
over their burden wherever possible to the air lines and to the bus
companies. They have happily withdrawn to the business of handling freight in as automated a fashion as possible. Freight after
all is much easier to deal with. It doesn't complain about a little
rough treatment. It doesn't get drunk in transit. It doesn't get upset
about a little deviation of schedule—it's the people who do! The
only problem the railroad has to worry about is the breakage. How
easy it is for the railroads these days!

Well, we inherited the railroad passengers, and we are getting
more and more of them each year. Even the runs where rail transportation is faster than air line are losing their passengers to the
air lines. But along with our inheritance of the passenger, we have
also inherited all of his problematic behavior as well as a special
bonus.

Our problematic passenger checks in late, wants to arrive
early so that he can make his too-close connection. He wants to
travel only during rush hours, yet he complains if he can't have the
seat he desires. He flies economy but expects first class treatment,
and if he flies first class he wants to be treated like a king. He
wants very much to have a safe flight but all this stuff about oxygen masks and life jackets irritates him. He looks grown up but in
many ways acts as irrational as a child.

Not only did we inherit all of the usual problems in dealing
with the passengers that the railroads so happily gave up, but we
also got a little bonus along with the deal. Our passenger has a
new attitude which adds greatly to the difficulty in dealing with
him—stark, gripping, unreasonable *fear!*

When our passenger rode the cushions of the parlor car of the
Congressional Limited on the Pennsy, or when he rode the coach
seats of the Challenger, he rode in security. The railroads were

From *Air Line Pilot,* 38:11 (November 1969). Reprinted by permission.

safe! The railroads were as safe as the ground on which he walked, and they weren't very far from it either. The passenger whom we inherited felt very secure on the old railroad train. But it wasn't always thus on the train. Back in the older days of the railroad he had his fears too. There were boiler explosions when the Hogger tried to belt a few extra miles per hour out of Old Betsy by tying down the safety valve. There were head-on collisions when Casey ran the red board. And out on the U.P. there was always the danger of attacks by Indians. But even at worst, he wasn't too far from his old familiar Mother Earth. Besides, if necessary, he could always hit the cinders. Many passengers did.

Although the passengers at first had many fears, and many of them were pretty reasonable, through one hundred years of improvement the fears lessened as did the reasons for them. In recent years the railroad passenger could approach the parlor car as calmly as he could sit by his Atwater-Kent listening to the baseball game. Trains had become pretty unthreatening. The violent period of the railroads was a part of the dimly remembered past.

But we haven't had one hundred years of aviation. Although it is true that we have advanced in design, operations and control further in the past twenty years than the railroads did in one hundred, the wild period of aviation is not so long ago! It wasn't so long ago that DC-6's were exploding mysteriously. It was only about twenty years ago that two airliners showing their passengers the Grand Canyon collided. Well, we never did have the Apaches as the U.P. did. But then today we have Cubans. Happily the Cubans don't take scalps. Even they are not as great a threat.

True the wild period of aviation is over. No longer do we expect to see a friendly P-38 pilot put his wing tip under the tip of our DC-3 and flip it up gently. We have grown much more civilized. But the memory lingers on. Many passengers aren't even sure it has passed. Many passengers don't know the cold emotionless preciseness of today's air line pilot. Many passengers don't know how exhaustingly trained is the team that flies him from Kokomo to Keokuk. Many passengers don't realize that twenty years in aviation is a lot longer than one hundred years on the railroad. Many passengers don't know that aviation is as safe as it is.

One of the reasons that people don't know how safe aviation is, is the fact that there are not really very many accidents. We have so few accidents that when one occurs it gets full treatment by the news media. It is unique. It is unique enough to attract attention and comment. For several days after an accident there are stories, comments, and cries to Congress to "stop this carnage in the air." These the air line passenger remembers. Even six months later he remembers as if it were yesterday. If air line accidents were as frequent as car and bus accidents, they would probably attract as little attention. If they were investigated as poorly as car and bus accidents, they would get less attention. But all of the publicity keeps our passenger from realizing how safe this form of transport is today.

But there are other features of aviation also adding to his insecurity. The railroad passenger could always get off and walk. He was close to his old familiar habitat, the ground. Our air line passenger is not sure what supports him up there. He's heard some vague stories about some mysterious forced called "lift" but he's really not sure what the devil that is. In the railroad days if he got really tensed up about things, he could get up and walk off his tensions as he made his way forward to the bar-car. There he could finish off his tensions with six or seven belts of Rye and sink into a semi-conscious reverie. Unfortunately in aviation he must remain in this aluminum tube which is only about as long as one railroad car and he can't even pace up and down the aisles. Whereas most trains, even the first class ones, are far more rough-riding than an airliner in fairly turbulent weather, the roughness was in only two dimensions, not three. He could be thrown forward or to the side but not upwards!

Then there is another thing—closeness. If he was in the Parlor Car, he had a seat all to himself. If he was in the coach, he might have to sit next to another person—but not quite so close. And if he couldn't stand the prattle of the old lady next to him, or her devilish grandchild, he could always change seats. There were usually empty seats. Or he could retreat to the Bar Car. He could move. He could get away. How about our air line passenger in that middle seat? Does he ever get that close to another person in his normal everyday living? Only in certain romantic interludes! And then it is in most cases not a stranger! In any case the partner is one of his choice. Here he is in the middle seat, between two strangers and he can't get away. Even if he could, there is no place to go.

All of these situations set the passenger on edge. All of these situations and memories threaten him. All of these memories, restrictions and unique environments stimulate the machinery of the body to produce that unpleasant physical and psychological state known as *fear*. Fear of heights. Fear of death. Fear of restriction of movement. Fear of novelty. Fear of unexplained activities of the crew. Fear of closeness. Fear of strangers. Fear he may smell bad to his neighbor.

Fear does many things to the body and the psyche. It makes many changes. One general change that it makes in all of us is that it makes us more extreme. It makes us stronger. It makes us quicker. It makes us louder. It makes us think faster (it may even make us wittier). It makes us more single-minded. It makes us more self-centered. It makes us take the gloves off and be ourselves. It makes us use defenses that we might normally cover up under layers of more sociable behavior.

One of the primary reasons why the business man was such a tyrant on the flight was that he was afraid. One of the reasons he apologized so sheepishly on the ramp was that he was now more secure. He was back on Mother Earth again—he was out of the big aluminum tube. As a matter of fact, we can look at any problem behavior on the part of any airborne passenger and learn something about him if we use fear as a bench-mark. It all starts with fear. Fear of something or of some situation. If we recognize that fear generates problem behavior, then we can formulate ways of dealing with that problem behavior.

In the course of writing a text for air line cabin personnel—*Aviation Psychology for Cabin Attendants,* I decided that a very necessary chapter would be one on how to deal with the problem passenger. How to deal with the various problem passengers and personalities with whom we fly. Sort of a short course on human misbehavior and behavior. I felt that as a psychologist, I should come up with some answers for the problems that have perplexed the railroads these many long years and which eventually caused them to withdraw from the problem.

As I began to list the various types of problem personalities (and ways of dealing with them), I noticed that a pattern was beginning to form. I had a primer to the human personality. A veritable A B C of human behavior. In fact, the finished product is just that: A B C to Z. Admittedly some of the categories are a bit tongue in cheek but anyway, let's have a short course in the A B C's of passenger psychology.

A is for Angry passenger. He is angry because something now or recently has threatened his security. He is scared about something. It may be his last appointment. It may be bad words with his wife. Something has made him feel weak and ineffectual and he is normally a person who feels secure when he feels powerful and only then. So by his angry expressions and angry demands, he is trying to establish his potency. Naturally anger on our part will threaten this image further and catapult into further excesses. Frankly although he's not very lovable, this is a time where he needs it. If we remain quiet and friendly in spite of his ire, we are most likely to reduce his feeling of impotence and increase his security.

B is for Bantering passenger. He "kiddingly" tries to top us and engages in endless verbal competition to prove that he is not really afraid. But he is afraid—of something. If we ignore him, he has nothing to think of except his lonely isolating fear and so for a while he'll try harder. But if even then he does not get communication, he'll sink into a blue funk. The best method of handling him is to let him win a round or pass him off to his seat-mate.

C is for the Critical one. This person has always built his image and his security by being on top of things through finding fault. It seems to me that even some women might fall into this category. When this person is in a state of threat or fear he tries to get on top in the old familiar way. He may criticize the pilot's technique, the company's equipment, or your service. Anyway, doing so reduces his fears and gives him a direction, and because he is able to look down on someone it makes him feel a bit Godlike and thus invulnerable. If you yourself are pretty secure, you can let him have this round and recognize that this hopped-up fear has made him hyper-critical.

D is for Dependent. This person has handled fear ever since babyhood by running to Mommy and here he is running to you. You can't cradle him in your arms and so he'll keep running back for more love in the form of attentions. The more frightened and impotent he feels the more he'll be calling for "Mommy!" Although his Mom probably fostered his dependency because it made her feel important, he can be encouraged to do things for himself, that it is really all right for him to help himself. If you put it on that basis rather than an outright refusal, you will keep from further threatening his already weak ego.

F is for Familiar. This person has always, especially in times of isolation and threat, tried to get close to people to increase his security. As scalps used to prove the potency of the Indian warrior, so too first names and familiarity increases his security. It makes him feel less alone and unloved in his time of need, and he can say, "See folks, someone does love me." Help him get familiar with his seat-mate. He may have been afraid of rejection by her and so that's why he tried you. He'll be forever grateful if this is the case. If not, it still gives him another scalp.

H is for Hostile. Unlike the Angry one he is cold, distant, and unapproachable. He is unresponsive because he is afraid. Some people spend their entire lives in this condition. Any added threat will increase his isolation—and here he is in an *Aeroplane!* Don't let his rejection fool you. A little extra pat or attention may warm up his cold, bleak world and make him a devotee.

P is for the Paranoid. Books by the score have been written about this man. And it is most often a man, too. He often looks like the Hostile one, because he is Hostile. But he has another thing going for him. He lives in a world in which power is the only answer and frankly he doesn't feel that he has the necessary power to cope with it. As a result, he is always in there trying to think out the problems and people that he must cope with. As a result, he is continually suspicious and suspicious of motives. To him there is no altruism, only power. Any threat to his security will cause him to respond with a power play in the form of a letter to the company (but he doesn't really expect them to read it). A little TLC will probably be wasted on him but it's worth trying because he might be a Hostile. But if there is an emergency *this* is the man to look out for. He often becomes the leader of a panic-flight and at times of this sort must be put down with any force necessary.

X is for that guy with the X-Ray eyes. He, like the V for Voyeur, handles threats by trying to know more about the world. Notice how extra romantic men get in the hospital and on airliners. It keeps them from thinking about the real threats to their existence. Our man with the X-Ray eyes is doing that too, but the reason he visually undresses women and lets them know he's doing it is that one of his main threats in life has been women. He has always felt lesser than they and his way of neutralizing the threat was to undress them. He may have learned this from his college speech professor who told him that if an audience threatened him, then he should mentally undress them. Anyway it is a way of reducing a threat, and if he pays attention to you, he doesn't have to look out the window. Some of the air lines, as you may have noticed, have capitalized on this technique and given him something to occupy his attention. (On WPA air lines *everyone* wants an aisle seat), but don't let him bug you; all he sees about you is his own fantasy and because he builds women up so much anyway his fantasy is probably more flattering than your own tape measure.

Well, we could go on through the whole alphabet, but if we did, then I wouldn't have any customers for the book, so let's leave the alphabet and sum up some of the major features of the problem air line passenger.

In a study by Bryan and Rigney (also from the University of Southern California) who surveyed 156 stewardesses, it was found that the average air line passenger is generally well-behaved, as an individual (although group behavior and charters can be something else) and as an individual tends to act in the air pretty much the same as he would on the ground in his own realm. Because of the confinement in a strange environment and flying in what he considers to be a void, in close proximity to many strangers, he tends to express more of the dependent side of his nature. He asks permission to do things which are obviously permissible. He asks questions which he could answer himself. He asks for services that he could himself perform. His behavior is in general more childlike.

The average air line passenger continues to fly scared, and this is not necessarily reduced by experience. His fears wax and wane during the flight as he passes the various mileposts which he feels are the areas of danger. His behavior increases or decreases along with them.

These fears vary with the passenger, whether he fears the rush of the takeoff roll with its noise and surge of unleashed power, whether he fears the sharply tilted attitude of the climbout, the possible collisions of the high-density area, the vague invisible world of the clouds or the IFR letdown and landing. Although he most often conceals these fears they are often evident in his behavior and the many little things he does. These evidences become more remarkable the more his threat is increased.

The air line passenger depends for his security on various signs and signals which he has learned on previous flights; the normal activities of the stewardesses, the lack of sound from the PA system (his greatest threat may be when the PA system comes on and the captain says "Uh . . ." and then waits 10 seconds before he continues) and finally the service of drinks and meals on schedule. These things, little as they may seem, serve as the mileposts which reduce the threat and reduce the fear that makes every air line passenger a potential "Problem Passenger." If we knew the proper mileposts for each passenger, we would produce them as we saw the symptoms of fear and thus reduce his threat. If we keep trying, we may be able to continue to run with the ball that the railroads dropped years ago.

The Civilized Engineer

Samuel C. Florman

Those of us who are engineers in the last third of the twentieth century are among the most fortunate.

In a time of widespread despair our constructive work gives us reason to be sanguine. In an age when most men are confused by the complexity of the scientific revolution, we are uniquely equipped to understand and enjoy the marvelous technological happenings all about us. It is said that the condition of man in our era is one of increasing alienation. But we engineers are needed by our fellow men; our place in society is secure; we feel at home in the world. Our work brings us comfortably in touch with the real world of "things"; our days are spiced with the tang of novelty and inventiveness. Financially, although we might not always consider ourselves adequately compensated for our efforts, we need never know want.

Nevertheless, we are not content. We can see that the world is teeming with treasures of the arts about which we know little. We find ourselves somehow excluded from the intellectual and philosophical discourse in which the values and goals of our society are shaped. Not only are we not participating in the artistic and intellectual life of our time, but we find that our professional product, the technology of which we are so proud, is being misused and misdirected, dominated by forces beyond our control. We are unhappy about our "image" and about the fact that we are not receiving our proper share of respect.

In sum, we may be busy and secure, but we are far from satisfied. Anyone familiar with the literature of our professional journals knows this to be the case.

Our dissatisfaction seems related to a certain flaw in our professional personality, a flaw that limits both our capacity to experience life to the full and our ability to play an important role in the political, cultural, and social developments of our time. The source of both our inadequacy and our discontent is rooted in our lack of a civilizing education in the liberal arts.

According to Webster's dictionary, civilization consists of

From *Engineer* (March-April 1968). Reprinted by permission.

"progress in education, refinement of taste and feeling, and the arts that constitute culture." If we take this definition literally, the average engineer today is simply not civilized.

I am not talking about superficial refinement but about something more fundamental. It is not an exaggeration to say that liberal education for engineers could improve the quality of their lives, contribute to the sound development of the engineering profession, and help to preserve and enrich society. As a noted educator has said, liberal education helps "to cultivate those skills and habits of reasoning which constitute intellectual competence, the capacity to think logically and clearly, the ability to organize one's thoughts on any subject on which essential facts are possessed or obtainable."

If we need the liberal arts to maintain and improve our intellectual competence, we need them even more to develop imagination, for without imagination reason is not equal to even the minimum demands of our exploding technology. Lewis Mumford has warned us that a concentration on pure technical training "might defeat even its immediate purposes by depriving original minds of the stimulus and enrichment of wider interests and activities."

As liberal education improves our intellectual competence and expands our imagination, it also develops those qualities of intellectual curiosity and general understanding, those traits of grace and wit and poise that characterize the leaders among men. Too often engineers are found lacking in these attributes. Scientifically-made personality studies have revealed engineers to be "socially conforming, impersonal, introverted individuals." In industry the effectiveness of engineers has been found to be limited by their lack of "people-wisdom," their reliance on "coldly rational judgment," and the recurrent appearance of a "noncommunicative syndrome."

The president of a large corporation has said succinctly what many leaders of American industry have come to recognize as fact: "The specialist cannot function effectively at the top level of management if all he brings to it is his specialty. . . . The qualifications needed for leadership in industry are developed largely through a liberal arts education."

In addition to helping each one of us to do his job more effectively, liberal learning yields great riches to the individual. Knowledge and understanding provide pleasure that needs no practical justification. Beauty evokes joyousness that is its own reward.

We engineers pride ourselves on being members of a profession that engages our energies and challenges our capacities. We are usually too much absorbed in our interesting work to be overly bothered by the doubts and anxieties that plague many of our less fortunate brethren. This concentration on work is a blessing, but it contains a hidden flaw. Our questioning and doubting are liable to be postponed, only to emerge in later years, sometimes with disturbing effect. It is better surely to expose oneself early and often to the eternal problems of philosophy and art than to be awakened with a start in one's waning years by the sudden asking of the questions: "What is life about? What have I been living for?" Socrates' admonition still rings true. "The unconsidered life is not worth living."

As the individual engineer profits from acquaintance with the liberal arts, so will the entire profession. Our lack of "status," our unsatisfactory "image"—these are concerns which gnaw away at our collective professional contentment. Only a vastly increased number of liberally-educated engineers can remedy this situation. Self-praising pronouncements emanating from our professional organizations surely will not suffice.

The public relations problems of the engineering profession already existed in the days of ancient Greece. Xenophon spoke for most of his fellow citizens when he said that "the mechanical arts carry a social stigma and are rightly dishonored in our cities." A hundred years ago Ralph Waldo Emerson looked at the technologists of his day and spoke sadly of "great arts and little men." Even Thomas Henry Huxley, nineteenth-century advocate of science and technology, expressed concern about technologists becoming "lopsided men." "The value of a cargo," he pointed out, "does not compensate for a ship's being out of trim."

In the early twentieth century, engineering achieved a certain level of prestige, although the profession was still regarded warily even by its greatest admirers.

Today, in spite of the most spectacular engineering achievements, this galling tradition persists. An American science editor informs us that "the image that has been projected of the engineering profession—and images are very hard to change—is of a prejudiced, conservative, non-involved group."

Engineers are certainly not insensitive to public opinion, nor do they engage in self-deception. A study has shown that "engineers themselves are convinced that the general public does not hold them in as great esteem as other professions."

Only liberally-educated engineers can bring the profession the esteem it craves and, in so many ways, deserves. For one thing, only liberally-educated engineers will possess the eloquence with which to impress upon their fellow citizens the inherent worth of engineering and its importance to society. It has been charged, and rightly so, that the engineering profession "has not been in touch with the people and by default has permitted a working partner (science) to capture the imagination of the nation."

But there is a more important goal than telling the story of engineering to the public. If engineers themselves, as individuals, become truly cultured—that is, become educated in the liberal arts —then the word will spread without a good press. If engineers become increasingly wise, sensitive, humane, and responsible, we will not need public-relations techniques to sell us to the public.

And as the engineering profession gains prestige and authority, society as a whole will benefit. For the world is desperately in need of the leadership that only engineers can give. "The politicians, and even the statesmen," as James Reston of *The New York Times* has put it, "are merely scrambling to deal with the revolutions in weapons, agriculture and industry created by the scientists and the engineers."

The world must listen to the engineer or it is doomed. Buckminster Fuller has stated the facts in the simplest terms:

"If humanity understood that the real world problem is that of upping the performances per pound of the world's metals and other resources, we might attempt to solve that problem deliberately, directly and efficiently. . . . But I find that approximately no one realizes what is going on. That is why we have been leaving it to the politician to make the world work. There is nothing political that the politician can do to make fewer resources do sixty percent more."

We engineers already possess most of the technical knowledge required to provide food and shelter in abundance, restore purity to our air and water, heal the blight of our cities, untangle the snarl of traffic, harness our rivers, reap harvests from the oceans, husband our resources, and develop power from the sun and atom. We can—if called upon—contribute to the preservation of peace by assisting the undeveloped nations and by devising improved means of arms control.

But unless we achieve a position of leadership, our talents will continue to be largely wasted and misdirected. The world will persist in demanding our blast furnaces but not our smoke-control devices, our highways but not our parks, our bombers but not our hospital ships.

Admittedly, there is a school of thought which holds that the world's ills are not attributable to lack of leadership by the technologists, but rather to leadership heading in the wrong direction. Nor is this sentiment restricted to apprehensive artists and intellectuals. In his farewell address President Eisenhower warned the nation that its public policy might "become the captive of a scientific-technological elite." Senator Bartlett of Alaska has complained that "faceless technocrats in long, white coats are making decisions today which rightfully and by law should be made by the Congress."

Someone must step forward to say, "We can afford to make that automobile a little safer." "Let us consider the possible harmful effects of that insecticide before we market it." "Let us make that machine a little quieter." "Let us not demolish that historically precious old building." "Let us build a rapid transit system for this city rather than a freeway that will bring more cars into an area already choked with traffic."

This "someone" cannot be an ordinary citizen of good will. He must be able to bolster his arguments with facts—technical, scientific, and economic. His recommendations, in order to be persuasive, must be founded in a knowledge of resources, materials, and energy conversion; statistics, probabilities, and decision theory; computers, controls, and systems engineering. Moreover, this "someone" must be concerned, articulate, esteemed, and possessed of a highly developed moral and esthetic sense. In short, he must be a liberally-educated engineer.

A generation of such men would inevitably play an important role in the debates that are instrumental in shaping the public philosophy. Engineers are already developing techniques of decision making that will enable the leaders of society to choose rationally between alternates. When we are as wise as we are smart, we will be qualified to talk about new goals as well as methods.

With the coming of a civilized technology, the world will discover that engineering is not merely a means to an end, but rather an inherently worthy way of life.

In what has been said so far it has been assumed that we are all familiar with what is meant by a liberal education. And indeed we are, in a broad sense. Liberal learning, we know, concerns itself with the eternal quest for truth, goodness and beauty. It grapples with such ultimate concerns as the meaning of justice, liberty, virtue, honor, love, and happiness. Its method is to study the works of scholars and artists, both past and present.

There are some who consider the ultimate purpose of liberal education to be the transmission of our cultural heritage and the creation of good citizens loyal to the ideals of our society. There are others who stress the development of the independent, sensitive, questioning mind, who see the liberal arts as having a critical, almost revolutionary, function. However, all agree that the ultimate goal of liberal learning is wisdom and a reverence for beauty.

Literally, arts that are "liberal" are those studies deemed fit for liberated, or free, men. In past ages only a few men were truly free; the vast majority lived as serfs, chained to soil they did not own. So liberal education has an aristocratic tradition. Because it was restricted to the upper classes, it came to serve the purpose of artificially defining the upper classes. This "snobbish" side of liberal learning becomes an anachronism in a democratic society.

A truly liberal education includes the study of pure science and mathematics. In these fields the average engineer has received a considerable amount of instruction. Liberal learning also embraces the social sciences: sociology, anthropology, psychology, political science, economics, and the like. No man can consider himself educated without some knowledge of these subjects.

But when we say that engineers lack an adequate liberal arts education, we do not really mean that they need more training in the social sciences. For one thing, to the extent that engineers take liberal arts courses in college, they often select the social sciences, which appear to be more useful than such studies as, for example, literature. Also the social sciences, whatever their merits, have a certain illiberal quality about them. They are, after all, sciences, and their approach is essentially clinical. The social scientist is more a statistician than a philosopher. He is liable to make the engineer more lopsided rather than less.

We are left then with those subjects that constitute the true core of liberal learning: history, literature, philosophy, the fine arts, and music. These are the so-called humanities about which the average engineer has always known little and cared less. These are the subjects with which we must now try to gain some familiarity.

Our problem is not unlike that of the world traveler who is constantly torn between the impulse to see as much as he can and the desire to linger in one spot in order to know it well. How much shall we survey in breadth and how much can we plumb in depth?

Certainly we want the overall view, superficial as it may be. But the overall view becomes meaningless unless we stop here and there to investigate in detail, unless we find something to linger over and make our own.

The problem of selecting particular works of literature and art from the myriads which surround us in this age of mass production is extremely vexing, almost paralyzing.

We must learn discrimination and self-restraint. A single work of art, studied with love and understood well, may contain in microcosm and by implication as much as a thousand other works together. At least this must be our hope and our expectation, since we are busy professional men, and cannot delude ourselves into thinking that our experience in the arts can ever be comprehensive.

A further dilemma involves the question of whether we should be guided by what is said to be worthwhile or follow our own inclinations. We must do both, of course. Acknowledged masterpieces should not be foolishly ignored; we cannot rely exclusively on our taste, which is, after all, also our ignorance and prejudice. But neither must we follow the herd. Our taste should be challenged, refined, and stretched, but never overwhelmed. Ultimately it must prevail.

And this brings us to the question of how we, as engineers, should best approach the liberal arts. Eric Ashby, author of "Technology and the Academics," leaves no doubt about the course to be taken: "The path to culture should be through a man's specialism, not by by-passing it."

Unless the liberal arts can be approached through engineering they will seem lifeless and frivolous to those of us who are professional engineers. Engineering educators are grappling with this problem now. They are agreed that liberal education for engineers is essential, but they are fearful of having it degenerate into mere appreciation or ornamentation.

We need to seek a bridge between engineering and the arts. From such a bridge we can look back over our own profession and ahead to the new world to be explored, observing the similarities of terrain, and discerning the common ground on which all worthy human endeavor rests. There is much talk these days about building bridges between the two cultures. These bridges do not so much require building as discovering; they already exist.

One such bridge has been discovered only recently and is being enthusiastically reconstructed at this time. It is at the frontier where engineering and history meet, and it is called the "history of technology."

A bridge between engineering and literature has been long sought, and I think rather fruitlessly, in such desert areas as "engineers as writers" and "report writing for engineers." A better link might be "the engineer as a protagonist in fiction."

Across the gulf between engineering and philosophy is suspended "the truth of science," a fragile structure, scarcely known to most engineers, although it is well traveled by many scientists and philosophers.

Engineering and the fine arts are joined by the age-old link of utility and beauty, often crossed by architects and designers but all too seldom by engineers.

Between engineering and music we find "sound as environment," a span which lately is attracting attention from people in many disciplines.

Let us together venture upon these bridges, and then let us cross them into the alluring lands that lie beyond. We may enter these new lands as relative strangers, but we will know who we are, why we have come, and the route we have traveled. With this sense of confidence and purpose we may soon find ourselves very much at ease in our new surroundings. The liberal arts, after all, have nourished and delighted men since the beginning of civilization.

The City

Genevieve Ray

"Ladies and gentlemen, you are now in East Harlem. One of the nation's worst slums, East Harlem is home for 120,000 people, mostly Puerto Rican." The bus tour passengers peered through tinted glass, air conditioning—125th Street, 124th, 123rd—"Look at them," the lady from Iowa whispered to her seat mate.

Swarms of people, random movement, broken glass, faces all shades, white to brown to black, plump brown arms rest on second story window sills, the faces look down. On side streets, gray rows of sooty tenements. 117th, 116th—past outdoor markets, racks of cheap bright cloths, bins with costume jewelry, kitchen utensils, plastic crucifixes, stalls of fresh vegetables, corn on the cob, beer, cruchifritos, pasteles. 113th, 111th, 110th—high-rise housing projects, barefoot kids direct the full force of fire hydrants on the bus windows. "Destructive, all of them. Look at the men, standing in lines by the liquor stores. You don't see them standing in lines at the employment agencies. And they've got cars!" 96th Street, and the beginning of a change—more white faces, cleaner streets.

"Ladies and gentlemen, we are entering Yorkville, New York's old German section. In the next block you will see the site of the old Jacob Ruppert Brewery. . . ." Faces peered through tinted glass.

We all have tinted glass of one kind or another. The outsider's view of poor communities is limited to flashing impressions—from a bus window, a newspaper, a TV screen, or a book—impressions of physical difficulties. He learn little about the thinking patterns of the poor. The young man on the corner says, "Everybody in East Harlem has the same problems. We all live with rats in crummy buildings, where they turn the heat on in the summer and turn it off the first day it gets cold. We all know somebody in trouble; ask anybody who grew up here what happened to the guys they used to hang out with. They'll say, 'Well, these three guys are in jail, and this other guy got shot, and so-and-so is on dope.' Nobody has enough money. We lose jobs even before we get them because the Man sees the name Diaz or Perez, and he says, 'No, we can't hire him. We can't trust him.' All of us have been called 'spic'—the old

From Vista *Volunteer* (September 1969). Reprinted by permission.

ones, the young ones, the little kids. None of us are different on these things. The real community is in people's heads, and if you really want to understand us, you'd better find out how we think about our problems, and what we do about them."

There are probably as many solutions to problems as there are people in East Harlem. The people seem to approach these solutions in three basic ways.

The first group drops out: Some exchange tedium for euphoria, through drugs. Some become the drunks known simply as Victor or Alfredo—no last names—who sprawl on the sidewalks muttering to themselves. Some convince themselves that they are just temporarily dwellers here. "Someday I will go home to Puerto Rico."

Most East Harlem residents would like to believe that their lives could be better, but have no idea of how to effect change. Mrs. Ana Figueroa came when she was eighteen and has lived in the same block for 46 years. She raised nine children and lost four. She has never voted. She has learned almost no English. She goes to church and confession every week and played Bingo every Wednesday night until she got sick. Now TV is her entertainment. "When I have an extra dollar, I bet it on a number. Someday I will have *buena suerte* and can go back to the island to see my sister." She complains about rising drug use in her neighborhood. She is convinced that nothing will solve the neighborhood's problems. "The rich people—the landlords, the men in city hall—they can do what they want. But there is no respect for me. I am old and sick. If I can make it through today, I've made it through today, that's all. I don't have the energy to think about tomorrow."

The dropouts are constantly assaulted by messages from a second group—the organization people. There is an agency on every corner. New York City Department of Social Services, East Harlem Recreation Center, Casita Maria, East Harlem Community Corporation, Aguilar Sub-Community of M.E.N.D. (Massive Economic Neighborhood Development), Youth Employment Service, LaGuardia House, East Harlem Tenants' Council, Barrio Nuevo, Inc., Mayor's Task Force, New York City Health Department, Bureau of Pest Control, Summer in the City. There is not a block in the area which does not have at least one storefront window plastered with leaflets advertising welfare rights groups, summer programs, job training opportunities, meetings around some issue.

The "corporation" spirit has carried over to other areas of life, often in rather startling ways. One can see storefront churches marked "Iglesia de Dios, Inc." A restaurant on 119th Street has apparently taken heed of the many acronyms on neighborhood storefronts. The homemade sign reads, "L.R." for Lopez Restaurant.

Some of the agencies and settlement houses were formed as long ago as the 1930's by outsiders. Possibly because East Harlem is a mixed area (predominantly Puerto Rican, but with many blacks and Italians), its mood is not as hostile to whites as the mood of some all-black areas. There are still many white social workers in the community.

But now a healthy-sized group of Puerto Ricans is involved. They are generally between 30 and 50 years old, women who speak English well and might talk more comfortably with a suburban housewife than with a militant youth.

They are active and concerned. They have telephones with blinking extension lights, desks with stacks of reports and forms, meetings to attend several nights a week, and a thousand details to remember. They have managed the task of thinking about seven different projects at once.

But ironically this penchant for forming organizations is one of East Harlem's problems. Willie Vasquez explains: "The workers are genuinely dedicated at the beginning. They are good, creative, active organizers. But their creativity is stifled by formal organization, and they become 'sophisticates.' They become organizers who want to define the problem instead of letting the people define their own problem and helping them find solutions. It all has to do with the paycheck. Most of the agencies are either government-sponsored or run by outsiders, and they control their employees by controlling the money. You can understand it—it's only an extension of the fight for survival. For a cat who's been eating peanut butter all his life, he's going to hold on to what he's got. But he has lost what he was hired for in the beginning—contact with the community. So people go to the agency and spill out their problems, but leave knowing that it will all be filed under G—for Garbage."

Angel, a community worker who talked about setting up a new multi-service agency in East Harlem, spoke sincerely about not wanting to gain recognition for himself. He wanted to pull together the efforts of all the programs in the community. But the next minute he said, "We can be bigger than M.E.N.D. We'll get the anti-poverty money, and they'll be coming to us, begging for our help!"

The final result is a flurry of independent activity which leaves not only the community but often the workers confused.

There is yet another group in East Harlem which presents a way of thinking which is different from that of the dropouts or that of the organization people. These are the new breed—the young men and women, roughly 17 to 30, who see other ways of making changes.

Many went to college, often with the aim of making it out of the ghetto into suburban, middle-class society. For the first time they were able to see the world of the "haves" with all its falterings and hang-ups.

They, along with many of their middle class contemporaries, feel a commitment to a larger group. So the former street kids return to the streets, but with a different perspective. Some become the furious militants, angry young men. Some find jobs in existing agencies and work to reactivate and re-direct their focus. Some form new groups.

One of the most exciting new groups calls itself The Real Great Society. RGS was founded in the spring of 1964 by a few young men on Manhattan's Lower East Side. The idea was to form an organization for—and run by—Puerto Ricans. By January of 1967 it was felt that RGS could expand to open a headquarters in East Harlem. This was necessary, since omitting East Harlem would have meant ignoring a large portion of New York's Puerto Rican population.

The members of RGS insist that they are not just "another storefront agency" and that they are not trying just to make peoples' lives a little more bearable. They emphasize skills, ingenuity, creativity, vision, and the pride of a people. Angelo Giordani, Executive Director of East Harlem RGS, says that theirs is the first organization which is interested in building East Harlem as a total community. "We place the emphasis on three aspects—social, economic, and political. We are the first organization in East Harlem which stresses and makes it blatantly clear that we are interested in Puerto Ricans and Puerto Ricanness. We are the vanguard of the Puerto Rican militant movement. We are taking the initiative, carrying the ball."

At the Real Great Society, speech carries to action: buying and renovating two tenements which house a community center, apartments, and the RGS East Harlem Prep School, starting an art workshop, beginning an Economic Development Planning Studio, and running an Urban Planning Studio.

Luis Apote, a 23-year-old VISTA Volunteer from Humacao, Puerto Rico, is an architect in the Urban Planning Studio. Luis considers the educational task of RGS to be most important:

"Education is THE thing. We are working today on plans for five years from now—development for the area. And five years from now, the ones who will be using that development will be the young people of today. Now they are uneducated or mis-educated and have negative attitudes about everything. What we stress is starting from the basic elementary education for these young people so they will have some definite wants and goals which are positive. We want them to improve their area and keep it up because it means something to them."

Luis works in a team with a community organizer and an urban planner. He stresses that this approach is essential. "None of us could work on our own. Every problem is interrelated—the social, the economic, the educational, and the cultural—they're all one package."

The team approach is nothing revolutionary, but it is relatively new in ghetto planning. It is certainly new to restrict the group to specialists who are indigenous to the community. Traditionally, city urban renewal offices have hired outside planners and architects whose finished work has only served one purpose—to illustrate their utter lack of knowledge about the needs of poor communities. The people who would live in those buildings and walk those streets had no voice in the planning and no access to the expertise which would allow their submitting alternate plans. Their environment was necessarily controlled by people whose interests lay in other areas. RGS believes that by utilizing the various skills of their own members, they can provide not only a sensitivity to the needs of their community which was missing before, but the skills to answer some of those needs.

RGS thinks big, while other groups tend to be shackled by more limited scope and less effective planning. There are two groups in East Harlem, for instance, which are both interested in buying apartment buildings.

One, an incorporated tenants' organization, wanted a particular tenement on their block. They found a lawyer who would explain to them the procedures, bicker with the landlord, and help them get through the rigmarole of government funding. But after working up the interest and enthusiasm of people in the neighborhood, they ran into a hang-up: the building will not be available for sale until the old woman who owns it dies. After months of planning, the group had to abandon their hopes and release the lawyer. Maybe after the owner dies they can start again.

The other group, a conglomerate of agencies in the 14-block Barrio Nuevo area, asked RGS to help them work out a system for owning their own buildings. RGS could have helped them select one building and told them how to concentrate all efforts on their securing that one. But they didn't. Luis and his team have set up a step-by-step plan for not only owning many buildings, but for establishing an economic base in Barrio Nuevo—complete with skills training for community men. The first step is to develop a management-maintenance corporation which will bid competitively on maintenance, then management, contracts with city and privately-owned apartment houses. Along with this is a training program in carpentry, plumbing, general repair and upkeep, and building management. As this progresses, the group will gain an economic cushion which will allow them to begin buying buildings with their own money, independent of private funding or government aid.

Luis is excited about it, and hopeful. "This is the first major economic program that the Barrio Nuevo community will have. It is the first stage in finding a source of income for the community. The basic idea is theirs; we go in as technicians and try to figure out the best way of letting their idea survive—independently."

Power is what it is all about—power and pride. Willie Vasquez, who will take over as Executive Director when Angelo leaves for Harvard Business School, stresses the need for continually developing new leadership. He has seen what happens when power is concentrated in too small a group. "I came to RGS two years ago and learned what I needed to know. In the fall I will take over. In another year or so, I will move on to something else, and will have someone to take my place. We aren't going to make the same mistake that a lot of the older agencies make—keeping the same people in the same jobs forever. What happens is that a community guy will develop a loyalty to his agency which is stronger than his loyalties to his own community. The important thing is always, always to keep new people, new ideas developing, and then spread out to other things. The people of this community must run this community, and that isn't done by just a few guys."

When you look at East Harlem as a whole, the many people who are involved in RGS, or in their kind of thinking, seems small. They may have overwhelming success, or they may fail. They will undoubtedly make mistakes. But East Harlem—the drop-outs, the organization people, and the new breed—these three East Harlems will never be the same.

The Billion-Dollar Disease

Charles Straub

At height of the foot-and-mouth epidemic in England last fall, a pair of manure-caked boots was found by government inspectors in the international lobby of Chicago's O'Hare Airport. Investigation revealed the owner of the boots was a young lady who had been riding in England and was returning to a ranch in the United States.

Such an incident, by bringing the dreaded foot-and-mouth virus to this country, easily could have triggered a billion-dollar tragedy in the United States livestock industry. Top officials of the Agricultural Research Service, USDA, are convinced that despite all efforts to keep the virus from our shores it could gain admittance at any time—if it has not done so already—and, ironically enough, through the activities of those most intimately connected with the livestock business, those who have visited farms and stock shows abroad and return with no thought of the contamination they could be carrying on shoes, clothes, and other belongings.

Should an outbreak of foot-and-mouth disease (FMD) ever occur in this country the all-important question arises: how will American livestock producers and their governmental agencies fight such an epidemic? The official answer is brief: by stamping out, meaning the slaughter of all infected and exposed animals. Drastic, yes. But the reason for such action can easily be understood when the nature of the disease is understood.

Known also as aphthous fever, epizootic aphtha, and at times referred to incorrectly as hoof-and-mouth disease, it is, according to the *Merck Veterinary Manual,* "an acute, highly communicable virus disease chiefly confined to cloven-footed animals. Cattle and swine seem to be most susceptible, with sheep and goats only slightly less so. Next in order of susceptibility are the buffalo, American bison, camel, deer, llama, giraffe and antelope. The dog, cat, rabbit, mouse, rat, chicken and other fowl can be infected artificially, but probably do not contact the disease, nor play an important role in its spread, under natural conditions. Man, despite his

From *The Farm Quarterly* (Spring 1968). Reprinted by permission.

frequent and sometimes intensive exposure in some countries, rarely becomes infected. Horses are resistant to infection."

Clinically, that is, from general observation, the disease is indistinguishable from two other vesicular diseases, vesicular exanthema of swine (the last known case of which anywhere in the world was reported in 1956) and vesicular stomatitis. The infected animal slobbers sticky, stringy saliva, goes off feed, becomes lame and refuses to walk, and in the early stages of the disease experiences a marked rise in temperature.

The slobbering and the lameness are caused by painful vesicles or blisters which form on the tongue and the membranes of the gums and lips; and the lameness is caused by similar vesicles on the coronary band and between the claws of the foot. Vesicles also form in some cases on the teats and udders and on the snouts of swine. These vesicles are filled with a clear or cloudy fluid quite distinct from the pustule matter that characterizes pox diseases. After the vesicles have erupted they leave raw, eroded areas surrounded by fragments of loose tissue. While these areas heal rapidly they are often subject to serious secondary infections.

Mortality is low in attacks of FMD, usually not more than 5 percent, though in an outbreak in Tierra del Fuego, Argentina, early in 1967 the mortality was more than 35 percent. Animals affected by the disease lose a considerable amount of flesh, there is a severe reduction in milk production in dairy herds, abortions are common, and mortality is sometimes high among young stock. It is estimated livestock production is reduced by at least 25 percent in those countries in which the disease is endemic. And, unfortunately, those countries represent most of the world. The only major land areas which USDA recognizes as free from the disease are North America, Central America, Australia, New Zealand, Japan, Iceland, Greenland, Norway, the Republic of Ireland, North Ireland and the Channel Islands.

There are seven types of the virus that causes foot-and-mouth disease—type A; O; C; S.A.T.1 (South African Territory); S.A.T.2; S.A.T.3; and Asia type 1—and some 40 subtypes. There are at least 22 subtypes of type A alone. Each of these is immunologically distinct from every other subtype, making it possible for an animal which has recovered from an attack caused by one subtype to have a recurrence of the disease when exposed to another subtype of even the same type of virus. This is also one of the factors which makes it extremely difficult to fight the disease with vaccination. Vaccination against A22, for example, is completely ineffective against O1. Type O1, incidentally, is the one involved in the current epidemic in England and Wales. It is also one of the prevailing types in Latin America, and in swine and cattle in the Netherlands and other European countries. The virus is present in the fluid of the vesicles and in their coverings and during the early stages of the disease it is found in the blood. It is also found in the saliva, milk, urine, and other secretions and is present in the carcasses and meat of slaughtered animals. It is even able to survive curing processes. Animals which have recovered from the disease are known to carry the virus for long periods afterwards. The Probang test (in which a special cuplike device is used to scrape the membranes of the throat) has revealed the presence of the virus in cattle as long as 14 months after recovery.

The disease is spread most readily, of course, by the infected animal itself. The virus is also carried on bedding, litter, feed, straw, tires, wagon wheels, boots, shoes, clothing, utensils, and so on. But man himself is one of the most serious offenders in mechanically carrying the disease from farm to farm and from country to country, particularly in this day of ultrarapid travel.

Dr. Frank Mulhern, now deputy administrator for regulatory programs, Agricultural Research Service, and one of a team of cooperating veterinarians sent by USDA to help fight both the Mexican and Canadian FMD epidemics in the 1940's and 1950's, still recalls the feeling of horror that struck those directing the Canadian fight when they learned, at the height of the epidemic, that a hired man working on a dairy farm hit by FMD had quit and was headed for the United States border. "We put out an immediate alert," Mulbern says, "and the Mounted Police launched one of their characteristically comprehensive manhunts. The disappearing milking hand was finally found on a farm just 18 miles from the border. There he was questioned in detail about his wanderings, and his clothes and all his belongings were disinfected before he was released." Fortunately he had not been in contact with the livestock on the second farm and another outbreak was possibly averted.

Of the many ways the disease can be spread, that which caused the 1902 and 1908 epidemics in the United States was most unusual: contaminated smallpox vaccine from Japan. The 1902 and 1908 outbreaks were two of the six which have struck this country since 1900; the others were in 1914, the most serious, and two in 1924 and 1929.

Fighting an Epidemic

Definite diagnosis of the disease demands prompt and coordinated action on the part of farmer or rancher, veterinarian, and state and federal livestock officials. Say, for example, symptoms similar to FMD were to appear among cattle on a farm in Iowa. In such a situation the farmer would call his local veterinarian who would immediately summon a state or federal veterinarian.

Should the diagnosis be foot-and-mouth disease, the farm where the outbreak had occurred, together with all farms in that vicinity, would be quarantined immediately, meaning that not only would movement of livestock be prohibited, but the movement of humans as well, would be restricted in the area. Even the groceries of the families on those farms would be delivered by sheriff's deputies or others authorized to travel through the quarantine lines. To stop the spread of the disease the movements of all animals, including man, must be halted.

The diseased livestock and all other cloven-footed stock exposed to them would be humanely slaughtered, and buried on the premises. State and federal indemnities would be paid for the slaughtered stock; not enough, however, to compensate for the loss of valuable, purebred animals.

The premises would be thoroughly cleaned and disinfected and while the quarantine was in effect all vehicles permitted to pass through the area would be sprayed with disinfectant and all persons leaving the area would be required to walk through disinfectants.

Thirty days after the premises were cleaned and disinfected, assuming that no subsequent outbreaks took place on adjacent premises, test animals, particularly hogs, whose rooting proclivities make them especially good disease detectives, and young calves, which are most susceptible, would be put on the farms. If, after a sufficient time, probably some 30 days, they showed no symptoms of the disease the farms would be declared fit for gradual restocking. If no evidence of the disease appeared after 60 more days, the farm would be declared clean and eligible for complete restocking.

It is easy to imagine the damage that would be caused by such a localized break; the direct loss of the slaughtered stock; the loss in milk, meat, wool and byproducts; the loss of income to the producers involved during the outbreak itself as well as during the long post-outbreak quarantine; the salaries and wages of veterinarians, health officials and others involved in fighting the epidemic and maintaining the quarantine. Projected on a national scale the damage would be almost inconceivable. The latest figures on the recent English epidemic show that some 369,000 head of livestock have been slaughtered and the total indemnity paid to owners has been estimated at more than $50 million.

The Mexican Experience

During the last FMD epidemic in Mexico from December 1946, to April 1954, the United States spent about $136 million as its share of the cost. The Mexican Government bore a similar burden. Over 900,000 head of livestock were slaughtered, export markets were lost, cattle prices dropped to drastic levels, and the cattle population in areas in northern Mexico outside the quarantine area built up to an unwieldy density. At the height of the campaign some 8,000 men, Mexicans and United States citizens, were employed in fighting the disease.

The Mexican epidemic had started in late 1946 in the State of Veracruz, apparently brought in with some Brahman bulls imported from Brazil. While the outbreaks quickly spread from the Gulf of Mexico to the Pacific, the infection area was confined to central Mexico. Strict quarantines kept the disease from spreading to the United States border which was closed, of course, to all cloven-footed animals.

By November 1947, more than 880,000 head of livestock had been slaughtered and while it had been hoped to whip the epidemic by the stamping-out process, it had become apparent by this time that the pressure of continued slaughter would be too much for the Mexican economy. Thus it was decided to implement the campaign with an auxiliary program of vaccination. More than a million doses of type-A vaccine were purchased from Europe and South America and by July 1948 a new plant for producing the vaccine was put in operation in Mexico itself.

Quoting from a government publication detailing the fight: "Vaccination teams worked in successive waves inward (from the north and from the south) from the periphery of the quarantine zone. This line of attack was designed to limit and reduce the infected area by building up an immune population. To maintain resistance against the infection, the plan called for revaccination of susceptible animals every four months. When infection was found within the quarantine zone, the program of regularly scheduled vaccination was supplemented by slaughter of animals known to be infected and exposed. In addition, 'ring' vaccination—that is revaccination of animals in all herds around a seat of infection—was followed. The plan also called for disinfecting premises that were possibly exposed, then testing with healthy animals to see if any infection remained."

This was a much tougher job than the bare outline of the report even suggests. It meant that 17 million cattle, sheep, and swine had to be vaccinated every four months. To do this the 17 states in the quarantine area were divided into sectors which a team of inspectors, a Mexican and an American, could personally cover every 30 days. This team lived in the sector, became well acquainted with its people and accepted by them, and had a thorough knowledge of the whereabouts and makeup of the livestock population. During the monthly patrols of these teams all stock that could be rounded up were run through chutes for inspection and the range was checked for cases that might have escaped the chutes.

"By August 1950," the government report continues, "60 million doses of vaccine had been administered and the vaccination program was terminated. In nine of the ten districts in the quarantine area, all susceptible animals had been vaccinated at least four times and the fifth round initiated in at least one of the nine. In one district, vaccination was discontinued after three series had been completed. During the vaccination program more than 10,000 infected and exposed animals were destroyed."

"After termination of vaccination, the program went into a phase of inspection and vigilance which was to continue for a year." Two outbreaks were detected during that time and more stock were slaughtered. Finally, in September 1952, after 12 months without any known infection, Mexico was declared free of FMD and the United States border was opened.

But this was not the end. In May 1953, another outbreak was discovered, the border was re-closed, and final eradication of the disease was not achieved until April 1954, after the slaughter of an additional 23,000 head of infected and exposed stock.

An interesting note in connection with the Mexican experience is that while the epidemic was entirely of the type A variety, an outbreak of type O suddenly occurred in an isolated herd within the quarantine zone during the vaccination phase of the fight. The cause of the outbreak has never been determined. Fortunately it was discovered and put down immediately. The incident, though, highlights the possible complications that can arise during a campaign and the hazards of fighting a multitype virus with vaccine.

International Status

At the present time the Western Hemisphere is free of FMD all the way from the Panama-Columbia border to the polar region. The disease is endemic through South America where it is estimated that it exacts a toll of $400 million a year, not including the loss of markets in countries free of the disease. To insure effective control of FMD, at least 80 percent of the cattle population must be vaccinated three times a year. According to a recent report of the Pan American Foot and Mouth Disease Center of the Pan American Health Organization, only Venezuela and Argentina have managed to reach this level. Uruguay and the states of Rio Grande do Sul, Santa Catarina and Sao Paulo, in Brazil, also have achieved a high level of vaccination but it is estimated that the other nations of the continent vaccinate no more than 40 percent of their cattle and those only once or twice a year. According to Dr. Pedro Acha, chief, Veterinary Medical Service Branch of the Pan American Health Organization, efforts are being made to increase the budget of the Pan American Foot and Mouth Disease Center in Brazil, the principal supporting institution of the FMD control and prevention programs being carried on in Latin America.

International credit institutions such as the InterAmerican Development Bank, the World Bank, and the Agency for International Development (AID) are linking their livestock development loans and programs to campaigns to combat the disease.

One discouraging note is the currently uncertain condition of an agreement between Colombia and the Republics of Central America, Panama, Mexico and the United States under the auspices of the International Regional Animal Health Agency (OIRSA), and the Pan American Health Organization. This agreement calls for Colombia to keep its Chocó area, to the west of the River Atrato and along the Panama border, closed to cattle from other areas of the country or from other South American countries. Unable to purchase cattle from disease-free areas, Colombia has been wavering in its resolve to comply with the agreement. The President of Colombia, however, Dr. Carlos Lleras Restrepo, recently promised that his country would do everything it could to protect its neighbors.

Early in September last year representatives of these countries met at Bogota, Colombia, to discuss a possible agreement, and a specific document is now under study by each government. From April 8 to 11 this year an InterAmerican Conference of Ministries of Agriculture and Directors of Animal Health will be held in Washington, D.C., under the auspices of the Pan American Health Organization. The principal objective of this conference will be the FMD situation in this hemisphere and the measures to be taken for its control and eradication.

Europe is in hardly any better condition in relation to the disease than South America. Through August 1967, for example, West Germany had experienced 3,264 outbreaks (types A, C, and O), the Netherlands 196 (types C and O), Spain 12,400 (types C and O), and the Soviet Union 2,123 (types A and O). Even greater outbreaks hit Russia and the eastern European countries late in the year while the epidemic was raging in England and Wales. All these countries, except the British Isles, pursue a policy of vaccination. But vaccination alone has never eradicated the disease.

Similar statistics can be cited for the nations of Africa, the Near East, and Asia. The deceptive thing about the statistics, though, is that the absence or low incidence of reported outbreaks does not necessarily mean that only a few or none have occurred. Many nations are lax in their reporting and it is very difficult, if not impossible, to get accurate figures. It will only be by definite, concerted regional and international efforts, though, that foot-and-mouth disease will ever be eradicated. Country A may make every effort to check the disease inside its boundaries, but so long as the disease exists in country B from which country A is separated by nothing but an imaginary line, A will be at the mercy of the disease.

FMD in the U.S.A.

To review briefly the history of the disease in the United States, there were outbreaks in 1870, 1880, 1884, 1902, 1908, 1914, 1924, (two separate outbreaks), and in 1929. The 1914 outbreak was the most damaging. Between October of that year and September 1915, it spread through 22 states and the District of Columbia after it gained entry into the Chicago Stockyards and other eastern stockyards. The eradication program required the slaughter of 77,000 cattle; 85,000 swine; 10,000 sheep; 100 goats; and 9 deer.

The appraised value of the livestock condemned in the six epidemics since 1900 has been placed at $11,500,000. Administrative costs in the outbreaks would represent a similar sum, making a total of $23 million in direct costs. The indirect costs, however, the loss of export trade, decrease in the value of hides and dairy products and the effect on allied industries is estimated to run 10 times direct costs. Total direct costs plus indirect losses could thus well be set at $253 million. At today's prices, and abetted by the present rapid shipment of livestock around the country, an outbreak in the United States could well become the Billion-Dollar Disease.

How can it be prevented? Largely by unceasing vigilance coupled with the ability of livestock producers to recognize the symptoms and report immediately. As Dr. Norvan Meyer, of USDA's Animal Health Division said recently, "The success of any attack on foot-and-mouth disease depends upon early detection. If we can recognize it, isolate it and hit immediately, we can lick it with a minimum of damage. Once it gets a good start, though, we're in trouble. We'd fight it with a slaughter program, of course. I hope, though, that we would never think of using vaccine until we had exhausted every hope of success by the slaughter method."

The aversion of livestock health officials to vaccination in this and other countries free of FMD is based upon several factors:

1) The cost would be prohibitive. It is estimated that the cost of vaccinating cattle in this country alone would be more than $100 million a year.

2) A vaccination program would give protection against only one or two types out of the scores of types and subtypes that cause the disease. People lose faith in a program when vaccinated animals break out with the disease.

3) There is no reliable vaccine for swine.

4) Immunization of sheep is largely an unexplored matter.

5) As pointed out above, no country has ever eradicated or effectively controlled the disease with vaccine alone.

6) The use of vaccine can help to perpetuate FMD in a country by masking the disease.

None of these factors, however, should close the door on an all-out program of continuous research for a really safe and fully potent vaccine. If such could be developed a tremendous advance would have been made in the war on FMD.

First line of defense for this country is strict enforcement of the import laws. The Tariff Act of 1930, passed soon after the last FMD outbreak in this country, prohibits the importation of animals and of fresh-chilled or frozen meats from countries where FMD exists. Entry of potentially contaminated products is also subject to strict regulation. But too often the regulations are not applied nearly as strictly as those responsible for protecting the nation's livestock would like to see them. The USDA would like to have more of its own inspectors working shoulder to shoulder with customs inspectors and public health officials at international ports of entry. Few travelers would then leave manure-caked boots around airports or enter the country without ever being asked if they are wearing or carrying in their luggage shoes and clothing in which they have roamed over foreign farms or visited stock shows. The USDA people are actually much more fearful of FMD virus being brought into this country by tourists than they are of its coming in with livestock, over which they have good control.

Regarding the Canadian importations of cattle through the Grosse Ile Quarantine Station, for example, Dr. Meyer says: "The Canadian procedures are so stringent the dangers are miniscule." He does not have the same feeling about the tourists stepping off planes at Kennedy International Airport.

Dr. Mulhern's advice to American livestock producers is to scream for protection, to learn to recognize the disease, and to report the appearance of any vesicular disease immediately to local and state authorities.

Such a program can squelch the Billion-Dollar Epidemic before it ever starts.

What is Happening to Our Great Lakes?

Andrew Robertson

Lake Erie is dying! This rather strange and frightening statement has received widespread notice in the past several years. What does it mean and what can be done about it? These questions are really part of a bigger question—what is happening to the water quality in all the Great Lakes? In this article an attempt will be made to assess our present knowledge as to the state of the lakes and further to forecast what the future changes in the lakes might be if man's interference continues along its present path.

All Lakes Temporary

Considered in terms of the geological time scale, all lakes are temporary features on the earth's crust. A lake forms when some agency, either natural or human, causes the formation of a depression or basin on the land surface. However, as soon as the basin forms, geological processes are set in motion that tend to destroy it. Erosion, especially at the point of outflow from the lake, acts to lower the surrounding walls of the basin thus lowering the water level. At the same time the lake starts to fill through the accumulation of materials carried into it by inflowing streams and by the wind.

Pass Through Stages

In small lakes the process of filling usually predominates, and the lakes pass through a series of stages leading to their eventual extinction. The first stage after formation is usually a clear and, compared to later stages, cool and deep lake. Immediately, however, materials start to accumulate on the bottom. At first this process is slow because much of the material brought into the lake stays in solution and much of the material that does settle out is organic matter that can be decomposed and returned to solution by bacterial action. As time goes on, more and more dissolved chemicals are brought into the lake from the surrounding drainage area. Those chemicals include vital nutrients for the growth of plants and animals, such as nitrogen and phosphorus. The increased

From *Limnos* 2:1 (Spring 1969). Reprinted by permission.

amounts of nutrients allow greater growth of the organisms which, in turn, contribute increasing amounts of dead organic matter to the bottom. In decomposing, these materials use up the oxygen in the water. When the amounts of organic matter falling to the bottom are relatively small, the decrease in oxygen caused by decomposition is relatively unimportant. However, as the amount of decomposition increases, it reaches a point where it uses up much or even all of the oxygen in the water near the bottom. The resulting deficiency of oxygen in the near-bottom layers has profound consequences. All the larger bottom organisms, which require oxygen for respiration, are eliminated, and even the types of bacteria present are altered to those that do not require oxygen. These bacteria are slower and less efficient in decomposing the organic matter, and so it accumulates on the bottom at an accelerating rate.

Inhabitants Change

This accumulating organic matter hastens the filling of the lake. The waters warm as the lake becomes shallower, and the types of organisms present change as the environment becomes warmer and more productive. The fish fauna shifts from forms that prefer cold water, such as trout and whitefish, to those that prefer warmer water, such as bass, sunfish, and perch.

Filling Hastened

These changes in environment hasten the filling even more. When the water gets very shallow, more and more of the bottom gets close enough to the surface that oxygen depletion is no longer a problem. Oxygen can now mix the short distance from the water surface faster than decomposition can use it up. This shallow water provides the conditions needed by aquatic plants that take root in the bottom. At first these plants are types that grow entirely below the water surface, but as filling continues types that are rooted at the bottom but have their leaves floating on the surface, such as water lilies, take over. Finally, even the floating types are displaced, and types that emerge from the water and have their stems and leaves in the air over the surface, such as cattails and reeds, predominate.

As the lake fills it also shrinks in size because the shallow, near-shore areas become completely filled in. By the time the submerged, rooted plants have taken over most of the bottom, the area has usually shrunk to that of a pond. Then, as the emergent plants take over, the pond changes to a marsh. Finally, even the marsh fills in, and the original lake basin completely disappears as terrestrial vegetation takes over the entire area.

This classical pattern of lake extinction for small lakes does not completely apply to the Great Lakes. These lakes are so large and deep that it would take many millions of years for their basins to completely fill. Long before this could happen other geological changes such as erosion of the outlets and changes in sea level plus, perhaps, a new glacial age would have transformed the lakes beyond recognition. However, certain parts of the pattern do still apply.

The Great Lakes assumed their present form only a few thousand years ago when the glaciers withdrew from the present lake basins. Thus, they are very young, considered in geological terms. When the European explorers first saw the lakes, they clearly showed their age through the characteristics of their waters. They contained cold, pure water inhabited by organisms that prefer a cold, unproductive environment. Unfortunately, man has been accelerating the aging of these lakes. Already there are many signs that they are taking on some of the characteristics of middle age or even old age lakes.

Erie Aging Noticeably

These signs of aging are especially noticeable in Lake Erie, and are what has led to the statements that this lake is dying. In fact, this is not really accurate for there is little chance that this lake will die or become extinct in the near future. What is happening is that the lake is experiencing a great increase in nutrient concentrations. This is due to the wastes poured into it by the human populations along its shores. These wastes, especially either treated or untreated sewage, contain large amounts of the plant nutrients and act to fertilize the waters for the growth of microscopic plants or algae. The production of algae has greatly increased, causing profound changes in the lake.

In the western end of Lake Erie, the changes have been especially noticeable because of the proximity to the large metropolitan center of Detroit and because this part of the lake is very shallow and so has a limited volume of water available for dilution of the wastes. The production of algae has been so great as to cause masses of material to appear on the beaches and decompose there, producing an unsightly appearance and obnoxious odors. Also, the amounts of dead organic material settling to the bottom have reached such a point that oxygen depletion in the bottom layers is a common phenomenon during the summer. One of the most obvious consequences of the oxygen depletion has been the destruction of the mayfly or fishfly populations in the west end of the lake. The adults of these insects occurred in vast numbers during late spring and early summer along the shores of the lake until the early fifties. Since then they have largely disappeared. The young of these animals lived on the bottom of the lake and were eliminated by the lack of oxygen.

Fish Catches Change

The effects of the changes caused by the increased fertility of the lake have also been very noticeable with regard to the fish. The catches of many of the more desirable species that prefer relatively pure, unproductive water such as the whitefish, walleye, lake herring or cisco, and blue pike have declined disastrously. For example, the commercial catch of blue pike decreased from almost 20,000,000 pounds in 1956 to 79,000 pounds in 1959 and practically none at all since. However, it should not be concluded that the total pounds of fish in the lake have decreased. Because the lake has been fertilized, it should still support as many fish as previously and probably even more. In fact, the total commercial catch has not shown the decline exhibited by the individual species. What has happened is that the dominant species have changed and now include less desirable fish such as carp, fresh-water drum or sheepshead, yellow perch, and smelt.

Ontario "Middle Aged"

The signs of aging in the other lakes are not as great as in Lake Erie. However, Lake Ontario is exhibiting many of the signs of middle age. It receives the fertilized water from Lake Erie and also is surrounded by a large population that contributes even more wastes. However, the volume of this lake is greater than Lake Erie, and conditions do not restrict dilution as severely as in the western end of that lake. Thus, Ontario has not proceeded quite as far along the aging process as its southern sister.

Of the three upper lakes only Lake Michigan has shown appreciable signs of aging. Lakes Huron and Superior contain tremendous volumes of water and have relatively small populations in their drainage basins. Thus, except for restricted areas such as Saginaw Bay, their waters seem to be little changed from the conditions present when the lakes were first discovered. Lake Huron has shown some signs of change, probably more because it receives the out-flow from Lake Michigan than because of materials brought in by its own streams. Although Lake Michigan is a very large lake, it has recently shown clear signs of aging. There seems good reason to believe that its organic production has increased to a considerable extent. Recent studies have indicated increased amounts of algae and of bottom organisms. There is even some evidence of oxygen depletion near bottom. The cause of these changes is probably the wastes contributed by the large population concentrated along the shores of the lake. Surprisingly, Chicago, the largest city, is not a major contributor because its wastes are discharged into the Mississippi River drainage system and not into the lake. Unfortunately however, many of the cities and industries around Chicago as well as elsewhere around the lake do send their wastes into its waters. The U.S. Public Health Service has recently reported high concentrations of both nutrients and toxic substances, such as ammonia and phenols, in the extreme southern end of the lake. These substances are concentrated here because of the large industrial complex crowded along the southern shore in Indiana and Illinois.

Trouble For Descendants

The aging in Lake Michigan is especially serious just because it is such a large lake and has a large volume of water. Although large size slows down the aging process by diluting wastes, it also slows down recovery of a lake when waste addition is decreased or stopped. In Lake Erie the volume is relatively small compared to the outflow rate down the Niagara River, and, if pollution were stopped today, it would take only about 6 years for 90 percent of the dissolved nutrients to be flushed into Lake Ontario. In Lake Michigan, however, the volume is so great compared to the outflow that the same process would take about 100 years, and in Lake Superior it would take more than 500 years. Thus, the wastes and nutrients we add to Lake Michigan today will still be causing problems for our descendants for hundreds of years.

Dissolved Solids Up

The changes in the Great Lakes can be illustrated by comparing the amounts of total dissolved solids in the different lakes now and sixty years ago. These total dissolved solids include the nutrients and have been increasing in all the lakes except Superior. Lake Huron has shown only a slight increase of less than 10 per cent, while Lake Michigan has shown an increase of about 20 per cent.

Lake Erie and Ontario have experienced by far the greatest change with an increase of from 30 to 35 per cent.

What will happen if this fertilization and pollution of our lakes continues unchecked? Their production of algae will continue to increase and oxygen depletion in the deeper waters will increase. These changes, in turn, will cause continued changes in the dominant organisms in the lakes and in the water quality.

If these processes continue to follow the paths taken by smaller lakes during aging, the Great Lakes will become less and less valuable as a natural resource. Their waters will be so full of algae, chemicals, and dangerous bacteria that it will become more and more expensive to conduct the treatment needed to provide water fit for household and industrial purposes. In spite of and because of the increased treatment, the water will have offensive smells and tastes at times. The beaches will become less and less desirable for recreation because of the piles of dead and decaying organic matter. The fish will change to types much less desirable for sport and commercial fishing, and these activities will decline. All in all the Great Lakes will lose a great part of their present value and become more and more an eyesore and a health hazard.

When presented with these facts, the natural reaction is to ask what can be done to stop the aging of our lakes. This question is both easy and hard to answer. The easy part is to state the obvious and say that we must stop or greatly decrease the addition of wastes and nutrients to the Great Lakes waters. The hard part is to formulate a plan to stop polluting these waters without ruining the economy of many of the industries and cities around the lakes.

One solution would be to divert the water taken from the lakes into other drainage areas rather than return it to the lakes. This would keep the pollution out of the lakes entirely. This is the solution Chicago has used to keep its wastes away from its lakeshore. There are several problems with this approach. For one thing it would be expensive to construct the pipelines and canals needed to carry the waste water to other drainage systems. Another problem is that the inhabitants of other drainage systems do not want the polluted water any more than the people in the Great Lakes area. A final problem would be that the lake levels would go down because a great deal of water would be taken out of the lakes without being replaced. This problem would force the placing of severe restrictions on the amount of water that could be removed for diversion. Unless these restrictions were imposed, the fall in water level would probably be so great as to severely restrict shipping and the production of hydro-electricity.

Another Solution

Another solution, and the one that will probably have to be used, is to develop methods of purifying the polluted water before it is put back in the lakes. For some of the pollutants the ways of doing this are already known and all that is needed is construction of the proper facilities. Such is the case with the removal of disease-causing bacteria from the water.

However, especially for the nutrients, the problem is more complex. These substances are not removed to any large extent by the present methods of treating waste water and sewage. These methods kill the dangerous microorganisms and cause the decomposition of solid organic wastes, but increase rather than decrease the concentrations of the nutrients. This increase is caused by the decomposition of the organic matter which frees the contained nutrients.

Obviously, methods are needed to strip the nutrients from the water, and a great deal of research is being devoted to this end. Already several promising avenues for further research have been found. One of the most promising encourages the growth of algae in waste water before it is returned to the lake. This algal growth locks up the nutrients in the algal cells and then, if the algae can be removed, the nutrients are removed as well. This method has been found to lower the nutrient concentrations during experiments. However, it is still too expensive to be used in a large-scale treatment program.

Money, Research Needed

This matter of expense seems to be the general stumbling block for nutrient removal. Hopefully, more research will get around this obstacle in the near future because time is running out. As pointed out earlier, Lake Erie has already been very seriously altered, and Lakes Ontario and Michigan are both showing clear evidence of aging. We must find a way at least to slow down, if not reverse, the aging of our lakes if we are going to leave our children this tremendous resource in useable condition. The development and installation of the facilities needed to retard aging will cost appreciable sums in taxes and in increased costs of consumer goods but will be well worth the cost in the long run. What better heritage can we leave our descendants than the opportunity to enjoy and utilize the same natural advantages that we have inherited?

Must Technology and Humanity Conflict?

Joseph Wood Krutch

The quarter century just past has seen advances in science and technology unprecedented in human history. Atomic fission, space travel and, most recently, the discoveries relating to the innermost secrets of life and heredity would hardly have been predicted even a generation ago except, perhaps, for some dim future as far ahead as thoughts can reach. They have come upon us almost unaware, and we hope, of course, that somehow good will be the result of all three. But even the most optimistic are bound to admit that each is also a potential threat. The growing question is: Does our nation need some central advisory body or criteria to judge whether advances in science and technology contribute to human welfare or create still other potential threats?

Atomic fission raises the possibility that civilization may be destroyed. A war of the worlds made possible by space travel is not so likely as the possibility that its appeal to the imagination may tempt us to spend the money, energy and brain power on it which might more profitably be employed in solving human problems here on earth. The threat from macromolecular biology may be more remote but is, ultimately, at least equally frightening. If we believe the claims of those in the best position to know, it promises ultimately the power to determine the intelligence, character and temperament of unborn generations. And that suggests the possibility of a totalitarianism more complete than we have previously dreamed of.

Up until now, there always seemed the possibility that human nature could not be completely controlled either for good or for ill. But what if human nature itself can be changed or abolished?

None of these threats will necessarily become a reality. And in the past, science has bestowed upon us enormous increases in comfort, health and affluence. Yet during the quarter century which gave us atomic fission, space travel and the achievements of biochemistry, some aspects of the human condition have deteriorated. Ours is much more conspicuously an age of anxiety than it was.

From *Bell Telephone Magazine* 48:2 (March-April 1969). Reprinted by permission.

Specifically, overpopulation, environmental pollution and epidemic violence are all new. They are the most pressing problems of today and are likely to continue to be for a long time to come despite atomic fission, trips to the moon and the sensational discoveries in biochemistry.

It is not necessary to believe that advances in science and technology are the cause of these deteriorations. But one has accompanied the other and the minimum conclusion to be drawn is that advances in science and technology alone are no guarantee of accompanying improvement in the human condition. What is new today is the fact that warnings are now beginning to be heard from within the very professions and organizations which have formerly been most likely to assume that progress is inevitable and that progress in technology inevitably means improvement in the human condition.

As Dr. Laurence Gould, former president of the American Association for the Advancement of Science, pointed out, most great civilizations of the past have succumbed to deterioration from within rather than to attacks from without.

Dr. Gould's thoughts caused the Institute of Life Insurance to take full-page advertisements in various publications to ask: "Could this happen to us? To our families? To our way of life? Could this happen to America the Beautiful? Well, look around. You can see signs of it at this very moment in every major city of this country. You can see it in the slums, in the jobless, in the crime rates, in our polluted air, in our fouled rivers and harbors and lakes. You can see it in our roads strangled with traffic. . . . We must all do something about it. While there is still time. Before our cities become unfit places in which to live."

Many scientists question fundamental assumptions

To be sure, there have always been mavericks (usually men of letters) who have expressed doubts about "progress." And there was also the philosopher in Samuel Johnson's moral romance *Rasselas* who had invented a flying machine but refused to reveal its secret because, so he said, men should not be permitted to fly until after they had become virtuous. But despite such grumblers, the generally accepted assumptions ever since the sixteenth century had been that every increase in knowledge, power or technical ingenuity would in the end contribute to the improvement of the human condition; that the extent to which science and technology had developed was indeed a measure of the extent to which a good life was being led in any community; and finally, that, as the Marxists said, all changes in the human condition are simply the inevitable consequences of evolving technology. From these propositions, and especially from the last, there was a tendency to conclude that one need not concern oneself with any other aspect of a good life for the simple reason that the propositions will all develop as by-products of the advancing knowledge, power and affluence.

Because technological changes have been so accelerated during the past quarter century, responsible scientists and technicians have begun to question fundamental assumptions. And they are suggesting that the time has come when we must realize that certain powers are dangerous, certain inventions are threats rather than promises, and that, in a word, we must begin to ask not simply *can* we do this or that but *should* we do this or that. We may not be able to wait for men to become virtuous before sending them to the moon, but we realize that sending them there will not necessarily make them more so.

Neither Anthony Weiner, formerly of the Massachusetts Institute of Technology, nor Herman Kahn, formerly of the Rand Corporation, are men whom we would expect to be enemies of science and technology, yet in their recent book *The Year 2000* they issue a solemn warning: "Practically all the major technological changes since the beginning of industrialization have resulted in unforeseen consequences. . . . Our very power over nature threatens to become itself a source of power that is out of control. . . . Choices are posed that are too large, too complex, too important and comprehensive to be safely left to fallible human beings."

New drugs put godlike powers in medical scientists' hands

Some threats are indirect in the sense that they affect the environment which in turn affects the human being. Those created by biochemistry threaten directly human intelligence, personality and character. They put into man's hands godlike powers he himself is not sufficiently godlike to be trusted with. In April 1968 the University of California psychologist, Dr. David Krech, told a Senate subcommittee that within the next decade medical scientists will be able to exert a significant degree of control over man's mind.

Different drugs, said Dr. Krech, affect different kinds of intellectual activity. Thus an antibiotic called Puromycin prevents long-time, but not short-time, memories. Injected into an animal, it "permits it to put in an ambitious day's work although it will not build up a permanent body of experiences or memories or abilities." It might be used to produce, for instance, a body of subhuman but docile workers much like those who compose one of

the biologically established social classes in Aldous Huxley's
Brave New World, considered wild fantasy only 37 years ago.
What humans will determine how new powers are used?
Dr. Krech's statement is cautious because it looks a mere decade
ahead. His colleague at the University of California, Prof.
Robert Sinsheimer, professor of biophysics, raises more alarming possibilities without setting a deadline: "Eventually we will surely
come to the time when man will have the power to alter, specifically and consciously, his very genes. This will be a new event in
the universe. No longer need nature wait for the chance mutation
and the slow process of selection. Intelligence can be applied to
evolution. How might we like to change his genes? Perhaps we
would like to alter the uneasy balance of our emotions. Should we
be less warlike, more self-confident, more serene? Perhaps. Perhaps we shall finally achieve these long-sought goals with techniques far superior to those which we have had to make do for
many centuries."

Is such a power too great to be trusted to "fallible human
beings"? Will it be used to make us more or less warlike, self-
confident and serene? The answer, no doubt, is that this will
depend upon whose hands the power falls into. And as things now
stand, we who already control so much have developed no way of
determining into whose hands any of our new powers will pass.

In its simplest form, the question of proper use arises in connection with what has come to be called "the responsibility of the
scientist." It is his duty, before giving a discovery or an invention
to the public, to ask the simple question, "Will this knowledge (or
indeed *can* this knowledge) be well used?" What would have been
the nearly unanimous reply until very recently was given a few
years ago by Edward Teller in connection with atomic fission and
its possible catastrophic effects: "I believe that we would be un-
faithful to the tradition of western civilization if we were to shy
away from exploring the limits of human achievement. It is our
specific duty as scientists to explore and explain. Beyond that our
responsibilities cannot be greater than those of any other citizen of
our democratic society." At an opposite extreme, Robert Oppen-
heimer has confessed to the feeling that he has "known sin" as a
result of his involvement in the creation of the bomb.

We can do more than hope!

One need not question the reasonableness of either one or the
other of these attitudes to see that, justifiable or not, neither is

really helpful. Neither washing the hands nor wringing the hands solves the problems created by the fact, now plainly evident for the first time in history, that we have begun to assume powers which need to be channeled and not simply turned loose upon the world to see what will happen. Knowledge is power, but it is not equally evident that power is always good. Science is knowledge; technology is doing. But it is no longer safe to say that whatever we can do we should do.

Prof. Sinsheimer is an optimist: "After two billion years, this is the end of the beginning. It would seem clear, to some achingly clear, that the world, the society, and the man of the future will be far different from that we know. . . . We must hope for the responsibility and the wisdom and the nobility of spirit to match this ultimate freedom."

There remains the question of whether we can indeed do nothing more than hope (and perhaps fear). Prof. Sinsheimer seems willing to propose no alternative, but neither Prof. Krech nor the Messrs. Weiner and Kahn are willing to leave to chance the use which will be made of powers still difficult for most of us to imagine. "The issues I raised," said Prof. Krech, "are much too pervasive and too profound to permit the physician to scribble the necessary social policy on his prescription pad," and he proposes a national commission to determine how the new drugs shall be used. Messrs. Weiner and Kahn go even a step further than that. For the future they suggest that neither science nor technology shall pursue new discoveries or develop new applications of scientific knowledge without first investigating their possible consequences for evil as well as for good.

In saying that, they go far beyond the mere rejection of Dr. Teller's contention that the scientist should assume no responsibility for the use made of his discovery. They propose the attitude that the philosopher in *Rasselas* assumed when he believed that an invention should not be given to the world until men had become virtuous enough to make only good use of it. It is not likely that Dr. Johnson himself would regard his philosopher's proposal as practicable, and one begins to wonder if any other really is.

It is very well to suggest "a national council to evaluate how mind-influencing drugs shall be used" or to say with Messrs. Weiner and Kahn that the choices are too fateful "to be safely left to fallible human beings." But where are we to find infallible human beings to whom we may safely trust the control of the uncontrollable? A committee invested with the powers to determine just how virtuous mankind had become, how the human mind and

character should be changed, or even what technological uses
should be made of our increased power over nature would be possible only in a totalitarian society so absolute that its decrees
would, in the end, probably be more stupid than those made today
by pure chance. The brave new world would already be here.

Criteria for decisions needed

Obviously we will have to make do with something less fruitful
than tight bureaucratic control of science and inventions. On the
other hand, there is a desperate need for something more effective
than now exists. We need some body or bodies which would at
least suggest, influence and direct the ends toward which research
and its applications are directed and encourage certain tendencies
even if the bodies did not go so far as to forbid others.

   The beginnings of the power to do at least this much already
exist to a significant extent by virtue of the fact that a large portion
of all scientific and technological projects now being actively pursued owe their existence to grants from the national government,
various foundations, or industry itself. To a considerable extent
these institutions determine what enterprises in either pure or
applied science will be undertaken. They must have certain criteria on which they make their decisions.

   In the case of the government, the criteria are largely those
relating to supposed military necessity. In the case of industry,
they relate largely to the possibility of ultimate profits. But neither
government nor industry follow rigidly these criteria. Both support
projects which seem to be simply "in the public interest."

Central group could advise on threats of technology

Nevertheless and insofar as one can judge, the enterprises which
government, industry and the foundations support are selected on
the basis of criteria usually not up to date. They are based upon
the nineteenth century assumptions: all knowledge is good; even
the most useless scientific fact may turn out to be important; every
technological advance is beneficial; progress is inevitable, and so
forth and so forth. But none of these things is true any longer.
There are by now so many things which could be found out and
so many things which could be done that we must pick and choose
whether we do them on the basis of conscious or unconscious
preferences. Unless everything quoted in this article from distinguished contemporary scientists is untrue, there is a crying need
for revised criteria to help those who support research and development decide which project should be supported.

Perhaps the time will come soon—perhaps it is already here—when some central advisory committee will both advise and, without exercising any absolute authority, be able to do something more than merely advise, since it will control a good many of the purse strings. But even without the existence of a central body, those existing bodies which control important purse strings and apply certain criteria could accomplish a great deal by revising the criteria.

The implications of the need for criteria or some controls are strong for the United States and the rest of the world because all mankind faces the same threats. But international controls are almost unthinkable in a time when nations squabble over matters much more petty than the destiny of man. So a start could best be made right here at home.

There are several steps to be taken before either the existing bodies come up with acceptable criteria or a national board is created. These steps consist in recognizing the following facts:

—That science and technology can be catastrophic as well as beneficial.

—That we cannot afford to wait and see what the effects of any specific application of new powers will be because once they have been acquired they cannot be eliminated. Whether atomic fission and the ability to control the mind are regarded as promises or threats, we are saddled with them, and they cannot be abolished now.

—That science for science's sake, the pursuit of knowledge without thought of how it may be applied, are no longer tenable aims.

—That knowledge and power are good only insofar as they contribute to human welfare.

In a sense Congress determines whether certain projects shall be undertaken. It votes money for the space program, the National Science Foundation and so forth. But it does not really establish any priorities except insofar as it votes or refuses to vote funds. Nobody in a position to exercise any real influence ever asks what is, for example, the relative importance of getting to the moon and abolishing pollution on earth. Is it more important to build supersonic transport planes than to clear the slums? Those are questions which should be examined in the light of meaningful criteria. The criteria, however, have never been formulated. A body charged with formulating them and composed of men in the humanistic and the physical sciences could at least make a beginning.

Is the Peace Corps Dead?

Walter P. Blass

"Has the Peace Corps done any good?"
"What do you think you've accomplished?"
"Isn't it running out of steam?"

These are questions asked of any American who has served the Peace Corps overseas. Although volunteers return wiser and enriched, some also come back embittered, just as much at loose ends as when they left. In some cases, they leave considerable damage behind. For some, a sense of obligation has developed that propels them to help solve America's most pressing problems; for others, two years abroad have left the impact of a ship cruise.

The Peace Corps today is on a plateau—a plateau that can lead to a new stage of growth, or one that is the sure sign of decline. For lack of a clear vision of its potentially far more significant role, it is perilously close to the downward edge.

This does not mean the Peace Corps has failed. But in most cases the single most important success has been the sheer presence of an American Volunteer living in the foreign village, speaking the language, buying at the local stores, sharing the extremes of climate. The very differences of culture and upbringing, of dress, behavior and attitude stand out in sharp contrast to the traditional society. In most Afghan towns, for example, no woman is seen shopping, least of all unveiled. The presence of an American girl without a *chaderi*, the tent-like garment worn outdoors by most Afghan women, is noticed by everyone.

Closely allied to this foreign influence is the interaction of volunteers at the person-to-person level. Volunteers do not work through impersonal media, the injection of money, or by hectoring from the American Embassy. They communicate without interpreters, face-to-face with students and principals, office workers, peasants, mothers and patients. They are there when babies are born, when the sick die, when students go on strike, or when the price of bread triples.

From *Bell Telephone Magazine,* 47:6 (November-December 1968). Reprinted by permission.

Ideally, they bring a specific skill, together with a sensitivity to the local culture, to bear on the problems of the people they work with.

By teaching in a different style—farming with fertilizer, nursing as a medical professional where "nursing" is equated with prostitution—volunteers cause change in host countries. They make it difficult for less effective traditional methods and attitudes to survive. Like a grain of sand in the oyster, response by the host environment is unavoidable.

Achievement in this context is not measurable. While the Peace Corps itself has tried to measure its impact in some sort of numbers, too little is understood about the process of attitudinal change to measure social and economic progress with certitude.

But it is true that volunteers make an impact on individuals and on small towns they touch directly. For example, a progressive Afghan governor requested Peace Corps volunteers to help build bridges, draw up plans and supervise construction of a school addition, and teach English. A short time later, a new governor reverted to established patterns of autocracy by jailing a teacher who flunked his nephew. But the town wouldn't stand for it; it had the teacher released, the governor sacked. Although the third governor transferred the volunteers, he couldn't get rid of the newfound spirit the townspeople had acquired.

In another example, Peace Corps nurses taught classes of auxiliary nurses in seven Afghan towns. The auxiliary nurses completed classes in four of the towns. In two of the remaining towns, the volunteers were forced to leave because the frustrations were too great. In the seventh town, the course fell apart for the lack of official support. In the four successful sites, however, not only did the auxiliary nurses finish with considerable formal knowledge but also with the beginnings of compassion for patients who were not relatives.

The impact of volunteers also was demonstrated by 16 girls who revitalized a smallpox eradication program. The girls vaccinated 2,000 persons a week each and were constantly pressed to advise on health programs. A World Health Organization official said there would have been no vaccination program worth the name were it not for the girls.

What about the volunteers themselves? Are they changed in the process of serving?

The vast majority of volunteers are 23 years old and have just graduated from college. They have never held a job for a period as long as a year. They crave the responsibility for their own future and seek an environment that demands all they have in the way of initiative, self-testing and learning.

The Peace Corps gives most of its volunteers just such a chance. It involves an individual in a real life situation: learning how to get along with supervisors, how to bring theory to the world of reality, how to refine one's objectives in terms of the means at hand. These are the valuable lessons that the Peace Corps offers. But the volunteer is often the last to realize the benefits.

The lessons are badly needed. Our educational system isolates college students from the mainstream of American life. The college graduate-to-be typically continues his studies, isolated from reality, kept from power, told "you are not yet ready" well into his twenties. The stresses the Peace Corps offers and the way in which America's young people respond are proof of the indestructibility of youth.

Too often, however, some volunteers find they can't take it. They quit and come home. In the first years of the Peace Corps an average of 11 percent of the volunteers came home early, but in recent years rates in the 50 percent range have occurred with increasing frequency. In part, these dropout rates reflect the lack of readiness for "reality" built into our educational system, part of what John W. Gardner of the Urban Coalition calls the "antileadership vaccine." In part, they result from poor Peace Corps planning and training.

The learning experienced by volunteers who stay, however, is significant. Volunteers have learned some 180 languages, most of them rare and hardly known, even by professional linguists. They have learned teaching skills to the point where several state departments of education have hired them sight unseen for teaching in inner city schools. Far from removing scarce, experienced teachers from the United States, the Peace Corps supplies many times their number in returned volunteers.

Still, the most important learning experience of volunteers lies not in the cold statistics of languages learned, or teaching skills acquired, but in their exposure to the human condition. Like veterans of World War II, volunteers return with insights and feelings about human relationships that differ markedly from those of the average American. Undoubtedly, the Peace Corps has brought about a better understanding of other nations to the U.S. than any other program the United States has yet devised. Even in indirection, the aim has been achieved. As a volunteer to Ethiopia said:

"This by-product of Peace Corps is the world awareness that is born in the family and friends of a Peace Corps volunteer. I am very aware of this in my home state where many times the isolationist attitude is seen at its genial best. The fact that there is a world 'out there' sometimes never dawns on them until they are emotionally involved with someone out there. Then the world takes on new dimensions; poverty and leprosy and a lack of education suddenly take on a new meaning for them because you are there."

This young woman's comment is the germ of an unforeseen benefit of sending 38,000 young Americans to five continents: the sharp awareness of deprivation and need.

At home we have moved from the self-satisfied 1950's to the tortured 1960's where shortcomings in the American way of life are becoming clear and visibly dangerous. What volunteers bring back is a realization that these shortcomings are no different from the problems faced by developing countries. Furthermore, the same techniques are needed to remedy them. The conflict of attitudes between black parents and white teachers is the same in Africa as in New York City.

Racial prejudice, the affluent's lack of concern for the problems of the poor, the plight of the uneducated and unemployed, urban sprawl—these problems are common to all continents. Their solution lies in developing a person-to-person relationship just like the Peace Corps volunteer worked out with students, townspeople, storekeepers and others with whom he worked. By necessity he learned a new "language" by which to communicate effectively.

The most precious gift that the volunteer can bring back to the United States is a commitment to do something about domestic problems. He has the skills. The Peace Corps was invented to help foreign nations, but its not-so-small by-product is the potential for helping to solve America's own problems.

Harris Wofford was associate director for planning in the Peace Corps in 1966 when he said:

"Behind the Peace Corps' back, a cold wind is blowing; a feeling that it is living off the past capital of Kennedy's memory or its own magic beginning; a feeling founded on a fact that the Peace Corps may be leveling off. . . . For the Peace Corps, which began as a quantum jump, this constitutes a crisis, a familiar crisis for movements and institutions. It is the turning point at which one course leads on toward the big vision; the other leads out to pasture."

Two and a half years later, these comments are even more true. Peace Corps volunteers have leveled off at 12,000 and are going down. In 14 of the 16 largest countries, the number of Peace Corps volunteers is dropping by more than 100 volunteers each; India, the largest, is cutting back from 1,133 to 770. The causes include disenchantment of young people with the Johnson Administration and what appears to some to be a miniscule Peace Corps compared to a vast War Corps. In part, host countries are requesting fewer and more highly qualified volunteers. But probably the single biggest factor is a quiet subsiding of the Peace Corps into just another routine government agency. The saddest comment about the Peace Corps is that it has fallen far short of what it could have accomplished.

Need that be the fate of what has been called the single best contribution of the Kennedy Administration? The Peace Corps can fight off such an ending and gain new life.

Four years ago at Wesleyan University, Sargent Shriver, then director of the Peace Corps, proposed that colleges and universities open their doors outward: "Let the bored, or confused, or 'burned-out' undergraduate have a short meaningful interlude . . .a sojourn . . . for a year, or even two years, so that he may come back revitalized, committed, concerned enough to finish both college and graduate school. And let these interludes be periods of service, whether in the Peace Corps, the poverty program, the American Friends, Papal volunteers, or any other service involving the reality of human needs.'

Actually, why should these comments be restricted to students in higher education? Business, government and universities have many individuals who are "bored, confused or burned out." Increasing numbers in all walks of life face the question of relevancy to the burning problems of our time.

Drastic changes would have to be made in the Peace Corps itself if it took on such a broader mandate. It would have to turn from being a quiet haven for college students in an interstitial period into a broadly based "mobilization in development." Taking people of all ages who are aware of the complexity of social and economic change and sense the need to be involved in such change, it would train and send them out to needed areas, whether domestic or foreign. Leaving the affluence of most Americans, they would work and live among the needy, the forsaken, the "undeveloped."

Recognizing that what is needed is an elite, the Peace Corps would develop an elite that could communicate with the man in the street, not just with the other "educated" few. It would further recognize that such intense periods of commitment need to be spelled by periods in other activities. The institutional mechanisms would be present to allow a young person to develop skills, say in community development in an urban ghetto, then come back 10 years later to work perhaps in a similar program overseas. Or he could come back as he became financially unencumbered in later life. The Peace Corps would, in effect, keep track of its alumni and offer them new opportunities to serve over their lifetime.

The present Peace Corps is running out of steam because it has turned into an accepted, not-too-daring program for young adults before they settle down to take on the tasks of earning a living at home. Such a development was not inevitable, nor is it yet. But if the Peace Corps doesn't reshape itself into an exciting forefront of development, it will only attract the sort of people who follow its current line of advertising, "Don't know what to do, lawyer, engineer, doctor, business? Join the Peace Corps!" Too many good volunteers and potentially good volunteers are turned off now because a sense of movement and inner development is lacking in the program.

The potential benefits of this transformed program would be far greater than current benefits. The Peace Corps would turn into an instrument that would help resolve the new diffuse frustrations of Americans with their own society's failures. It would engage the attention of many people to the critical problems at home and abroad. It would tap resources and skills that are desperately needed overseas but are available only in the over-25 age group that the Peace Corps doesn't tap today.

It would feed not a small fraction of its "graduates" but a substantial number of them into the business, governmental and non-profit organizations that deal with development. Perhaps it might even absorb them like a successful merger-oriented firm. It could go on to serve as an example bright enough to lead the "developing" nations into setting up their own versions to gain the same benefits, even by sending their volunteers to the United States.

In many small ways, current developments hint at such a move: an Exchange Peace Corps involving a few hundred foreign volunteers coming to the United States; a small Teacher Corps that hires returned Peace Corps volunteers; a VISTA associates program that moves domestic volunteers overseas after a year; a Career Information Center in Peace Corps/Washington that informs volunteers of opportunities for service here and abroad. But what is lacking is Wofford's "big vision"—a vision that will pull the disparate elements together into a critical mass that is self-sustaining.

Fulfilling the vision would mobilize the developed skills of America in the service of needs greater than those of affluence. By channeling the desire of man to find meaning in his work, the Peace Corps could move from being statistically inconsequential to becoming a major catalyst abroad and at home.

By exposing Americans to the problems of the world's majority who lack health, an assured food supply, or a future with hope, it has the potential to change our own ethic about the proper distribution of goods and services. If the Peace Corps could make some small steps in that direction, it would have grown in the way that President Kennedy had hoped, not in size alone, but in quality, not just for export but to improve America as well.

Industrial Arts and the Space Age

Harold E. Mehrens, Jr.

I feel that we in NASA and particularly the John F. Kennedy Space Center have many common interests and goals. You in the field of industrial arts, and we in the space program are both vitally interested in a continuing quest for excellence. And over the long pull, our success depends upon yours—how well you are training people for their responsibilities in the space age.

NASA began a program in 1962 to meet the needs of our manned and unmanned space activities for a continuing supply of scientifically and technically trained manpower. This program of university training grants has served to accelerate the production of Ph.D.'s in science and technology. It also serves to strengthen the universities' graduate capabilities. The ultimate goal of this program is to add a thousand new Ph.D.'s a year to the nation's pool of trained manpower.

Space related projects are under way on the campuses of more than 150 universities in every state of the union. Almost 10,000 scholars, researchers, students, and others are taking part.

Specific Overlapping Areas

There are more specific areas where our interests overlap. In any study of vocations, space exploration must be given a place of first importance. The aerospace industry, the missile industry, the university, and the government employ scientists, engineers, technicians, and skilled space workers of all kinds. More than 100 different kinds of skills are represented by these workers.

Today, the NASA manned space flight program is carried out by a team consisting of our Washington headquarters, three field centers, 12 prime contractors and some 17,000 subcontractors. We have arrived at a manpower peak of some 300,000 people; only 5 percent of these are government civil service workers.

Most of the skills utilized by these people are introduced to the youth of this nation in the industrial arts classroom. Consequently, we do not advocate courses in space industrial arts or space subjects in any discipline. What we do suggest, however, are space related activities in the sciences, math and industrial arts. These activities generally are those which are normally taught, but should introduce the relationship of these activities to aerospace industries.

In view of these facts, I think that an extremely broad field view of industry should consequently be considered in the industrial arts lab. We must keep in mind that mathematics, physics, chemistry, biology, and virtually all other disciplines are as much a part of industry today in the space age as is the machine shop, the woodworking shop, and the foundry.

Last year, the annual indexes of space related research listed over 55,000 published reports. Over 55,000 new contributions to knowledge in this one field, in one year! They represent an avalanche that began not too long ago, possibly with the International Geophysical Year of 1958; and it is increasing in magnitude.

Some Examples

I am aware of some of the forward looking broad-gauge efforts of your leaders to relate the industrial arts to the objectives of the total school program. One noteworthy example was carried on by the University of Maryland in an in-service program for Montgomery County industrial arts teachers. For the seventh grade it involved an anthropological approach to the study of certain basic elements common to all mankind—tools and machines, power and energy, communications and transportation. It involved the student in drawing, problem-solving, using hand tools, selecting materials, planning with others and collecting, organizing, and presenting his ideas. The student selected a tool or machine for study, researched his selection, presented his findings both orally and in writing, and constructed a model of the tool or machine.

At the eighth-grade level, the group project students organized and worked together to produce a project that would represent or depict a major American industry. Each student selected a specific topic to report on, and constructed a specific part of the project. The students of the eighth grade also undertook a line production project, which involved them in designing a product, assuming duties of a member of a company's personnel organization, working with others in planning for the production, constructing jigs and fixtures, and operating a job on the assembly line. Each ninth grade student undertook a program more individualized in terms of his interests. In this grade the emphasis was on contemporary units of study, increasing depth of study in industry, and greater understanding of problems of industry.

From Florida, a report of a program similar in nature, in which the writer says high school students undertook individual projects, requiring research, study, experimentation, construction, and reporting. The instructor's duty became that of making certain the students understood the steps they were to follow from initial investigation to final report of finding. Projects, in addition to those of the usual woodworking, printing, metalwork, and drafting, include, believe it or not, solid-state physics, prosthetics, science, and English skills.

Industrial Arts in Integrating Role

I recognize that these accounts of industrial arts activities may be idealized. The point is that there are teachers and leaders of the profession in other parts of the nation who, as do many of you, see the possibilities for the industrial arts taking an integrating role in education. The vast accumulation of knowledge resulting from the space program will help us to develop to human progress and welfare—to make new consumer goods, to keep building our standard of living.

The field of electronics provides many good illustrations of this. For example, heat-resistant electronic components, so vital in space vehicles and spacecraft, will find many uses in radio and television sets, where self-generated heat is a problem. In the field of materials the space program demands faster and more powerful vehicles and engines that are light, strong, and resistant to heat. We have developed engines which produce controlled power at operating temperatures 1500 degrees Fahrenheit above the melting point of steel.

Solid lubricants have been developed which are usable up to 2000 degrees Fahrenheit for a short period of time. We have developed steels twice as strong as those in use 20 years ago. Research on paint pigments aimed at reflecting the sun's heat away from fuel tanks of spacecraft will find application in paints for industrial use such as fuel and gas tank storage and refrigeration plants, and even for helping to keep our homes and buildings cooler in summer, warmer in winter.

As you know, a fuel cell is a device for converting chemical energy directly into electrical energy. The Gemini spacecraft utilized such a power source. Although some difficulties have been experienced, NASA continues to conduct research on many types of fuel cells. Some experts say they will be supplying 30 percent of the nation's power needs by 1990. By the year 2000 perhaps homes will be equipped with this source of power; surface vehicles using them may be provided with essentially trouble-free motive power —eliminating not only many moving parts, but the unwelcome exhaust fumes that now smog our cities.

These are a few examples of space-related developments with obvious applications for the industrial arts classroom. There are many others: materials that keep their strength at extremes of temperatures; microminiaturized electronic components of great ruggedness and reliability; instruments of extreme sensitivity and accuracy, medical devices stemming from the manned space flight research, and so on.

The Challenge

In regard to the last item, I note with considerable interest that NASA, as part of its telemetry research, has developed a small radio transmitter to be swallowed by an astronaut and suspended in the stomach without surgery. It will enable scientists to monitor his physical condition, especially thermal stresses, gaseous conditions, and tensions. The device is only the size of a large vitamin capsule.

Couple these fantastic achievements in space technology with the great accumulation of new knowledge in space-related science, and we have the ingredients for the profound effects of the space enterprise on patterns for living, and most certainly the industrial arts curriculum.

Because of these tremendous advances, the many achievements not considered in this very short article are the new techniques, new materials, and new processes that are just across the threshold. We in the profession of industrial arts education have a challenge. The challenge is to meet the needs of our youth in a general education program. A program designed for each and every youngster that enters our school, no matter what his ultimate role in life may be. This industrial arts program must be in tune with the age of space, an age when accomplishments are greater than we dare imagine. The challenge to the industrial arts is here—is the profession willing to accept this challenge? I think it is.

Inaugural Address, January 20, 1961

John F. Kennedy

Fellow citizens:

We observe today not a victory of party but a celebration of freedom—symbolizing an end as well as a beginning—signifying renewal as well as change. For I have sworn before you and Almighty God the same solemn oath our forebears prescribed nearly a century and three-quarters ago.

The world is very different now. For man holds in his mortal hands the power to abolish all forms of human poverty and all forms of human life. And yet the same revolutionary beliefs for which our forebears fought are still at issue around the globe—the belief that the rights of man come not from the generosity of the state but from the hand of God.

We dare not forget today that we are the heirs of that first revolution. Let the word go forth from this time and place, to friend and foe alike, that the torch has been passed to a new generation of Americans—born in this century, tempered by war, disciplined by a hard and bitter peace, proud of our ancient heritage—and unwilling to witness or permit the slow undoing of those human rights to which we are committed today at home and around the world.

Let every nation know, whether it wishes us well or ill, that we shall pay any price, bear any burden, meet any hardship, support any friend, oppose any foe to assure the survival and the success of liberty.

This much we pledge—and more.

To those old allies whose cultural and spiritual origins we share, we pledge the loyalty of faithful friends. United, there is little we cannot do in a host of cooperative ventures. Divided, there is little we can do—for we dare not meet a powerful challenge at odds and split asunder.

To those new states whom we welcome to the ranks of the free, we pledge our word that one form of colonial control shall not have passed away merely to be replaced by a far more iron tyranny. We shall not always expect to find them supporting our view. But we shall always hope to find them strongly supporting their own freedom—and to remember that, in the past, those who foolishly sought power by riding the back of the tiger ended up inside.

To those peoples in the huts and villages of half the globe struggling to break the bonds of mass misery, we pledge our best efforts to help them help themselves, for whatever period is required—not because the Communists may be doing it, not because we seek their votes, but because it is right. If a free society cannot help the many who are poor, it can not save the few who are rich.

To our sister republics south of the border, we offer a special pledge—to convert our good words into good deeds—in a new alliance for progress—to assist free men and free governments in casting off the chains of poverty. But this peaceful revolution of hope cannot become the prey of hostile powers. Let all our neighbors know that we shall join with them to oppose aggression or subversion anywhere in the Americas. And let every other power know that this hemisphere intends to remain the master of its own house.

To that world assembly of sovereign states, the United Nations, our last best hope in an age where the instruments of war have far outpaced the instruments of peace, we renew our pledge of support—to prevent it from becoming merely a forum for invective—to strengthen its shield of the new and the weak—and to enlarge the area in which its writ may run.

Finally, to those nations who would make themselves our adversary, we offer not a pledge but a request: that both sides begin anew the quest for peace, before the dark powers of destruction unleashed by science engulf all humanity in planned or accidental self-destruction.

We dare not tempt them with weakness. For only when our arms are sufficient beyond doubt can we be certain beyond doubt that they will never be employed.

But neither can two great and powerful groups of nations take comfort from our present course—both sides overburdened by the cost of modern weapons, both rightly alarmed by the steady spread of the deadly atom, yet both racing to alter that uncertain balance of terror that stays the hand of mankind's final war.

So let us begin anew—remembering on both sides that civility is not a sign of weakness, and sincerity is always subject to proof. Let us never negotiate out of fear. But let us never fear to negotiate.

Let both sides explore what problems unite us instead of belaboring those problems which divide us.

Let both sides, for the first time, formulate serious and precise proposals for the inspection and control of arms—and bring the absolute power to destroy other nations under the absolute control of all nations.

Let both sides seek to invoke the wonders of science instead of its terrors. Together let us explore the stars, conquer the deserts, eradicate disease, tap the ocean depths and encourage the arts and commerce.

Let both sides unite to heed in all corners of the earth the command of Isaiah—to "undo the heavy burdens . . . let the oppressed go free."

And if a beach-head of cooperation may push back the jungle of suspicion, let both sides join in creating a new endeavor, not a new balance of power, but a new world of law, where the strong are just and the weak secure and the peace preserved.

All this will not be finished in the first 100 days. Nor will it be finished in the first 1000, nor in the life of this Administration, nor even perhaps in our lifetime on this planet. But let us begin.

In your hands, my fellow citizens, more than mine, will rest the final success or failure of our course. Since this country was founded, each generation of Americans has been summoned to give testimony to its national loyalty. The graves of young Americans who answered the call to service surround the globe.

Now the trumpet summons us again—not as a call to battle, though embattled we are—but a call to bear the burden of a long twilight struggle year in and year out, "rejoicing in hope, patient in tribulation"—a struggle against the common enemies of man: tyranny, poverty, disease and war itself.

Can we forge against these enemies a grand and global alliance, north and south, east and west, that can assure a more fruitful life for all mankind? Will you join in that historic effort?

In the long history of the world, only a few generations have been granted the role of defending freedom in its hour of maximum danger. I do not shrink from this responsibility—I welcome it. I do not believe that any of us would exchange places with any other people or any other generation. The energy, the faith, the devotion which we bring to this endeavor will light our country and all who serve it—and the glow from that fire can truly light the world.

And so, my fellow Americans: ask not what your country can do for you—ask what you can do for your country.

My fellow citizens of the world: ask not what America will do for you, but what together we can do for the freedom of man.

Finally, whether you are citizens of America or citizens of the world, ask of us here the same high standards of strength and sacrifice which we ask of you. With a good conscience our only sure reward, with history the final judge of our deeds, let us go forth to lead the land we love, asking His blessing and asking His help, but knowing that here on earth God's work must truly be our own.

The Valley of Tomorrow

When seven men in two birch-bark canoes swept down the Wisconsin River and entered the "Father of Waters" one June day in 1673, an important chapter in American history was being written.

That small group, led by Father Jacques Marquette and Louis Jolliet, are credited with reporting the first accurate data on the course of the Mississippi River.

Today, almost 300 years later, another exploration has taken place and another important chapter in history is being written.

This time, instead of seven men, the modern exploring party consisted of about 1,200 men.

The scope and the comprehensiveness of the modern exploration would have staggered the imagination of Marquette and Jolliet. Indeed, it may well stagger your imagination, too.

A modern study of the Upper Mississippi River Valley was authorized to inventory the 121 million acres of land and water and what course man will follow in using and conserving these resources during the next 50 years.

To do this job the U.S. Department of Agriculture combined forces with 14 Federal agencies and seven States.

Some of the questions facing the explorers were:

How can we use this huge valley best?

In what condition will we leave it for our sons and daughters?

What actions can we take now to prevent problems in the valley for our grandchildren?

This vast region extends from Cairo, Illinois, on the south to Bemidji, Minnesota, on the north—a distance of 700 airline miles. It extends from South Bend, Indiana, on the east to Big Stone Lake, South Dakota, on the west—a distance of 500 airline miles.

The basin includes parts of Missouri, Iowa, Minnesota, South Dakota, Illinois, Indiana, and Wisconsin.

The investigation dealt with much more than the Mississippi River itself. It also included all the tributaries and creeks that flow into the Mississippi and all the land draining into them.

The modern army of explorers were a quiet group. Few of "the natives" knew anything about their work. They fanned out

From "The Valley of Tomorrow," United States Department of Agriculture, Soil Conservation Service (Lincoln, Nebr.: 1969).

through the seven-state area by automobiles, jeeps, motor boats, airplanes and helicopters.

Their purpose was to discover the condition of our water and land resources today, and what the condition these resources will be in in 1980 . . . in 2000 . . . in 2020.

The explorers made comprehensive studies of the area's climate, mineral resources, ground water and geology, water supply and quality, navigation, recreation, fish and wildlife, and economic development. But since the highly productive "Corn Belt" runs through each state in the basin and some of the nation's major forest areas are concentrated in the northern and southern portions of the basin, the agricultural and forestry phases of the study deserve special attention.

What Has Happened?

Before the pioneers started to settle in the Upper Mississippi River Valley, there seemed to be no limit to the vast forests and grasslands, productive soils, clear streams and lakes, and wildlife. These were the riches that attracted the pioneers.

They cleared the forests and plowed the prairies. They established trade centers and a thriving society developed. By the turn of the century, the end of the "unlimited" water and land resources was in sight.

By the thirties, man's demands on water and land resources had become greatly intensified.

By the sixties, the landowners in the Upper Mississippi River Valley had entered an era marked by bigger farms, bigger machinery, row crops grown continuously in fields year after year, narrower rows, heavier applications of commercial fertilizer, wider use of herbicides and pesticides . . . and far too little effort in conserving the soil.

Their demands on water and land resources were becoming "exploitative"—with eroding hillsides, burning and grazing of forest land, sediment laden streams.

Man's lack of understanding regarding the capabilities of the resources and the consequences of his exploitative actions have been and remain the basic land and water resource problem within the Upper Mississippi River basin.

Problems in the Valley

Conservation practices of one kind or another are needed on 93 percent of the land in order to preserve or develop the resources.

The chief problems to agricultural and urban areas in the basin are erosion, sediment and flood-water damage, and inadequate drainage of the land.

Gully erosion and floodwater damage in the valley amounts to nearly $70 million a year, and by 2020, the cost may reach approximately $200 million.

Water and wind erosion are now depleting over 25 million acres of the basin's land, reducing the land's ability to produce crops and adding to sediment pollution of surface waters.

Gully erosion alone causes $14 million worth of damage annually to an estimated 93,000 acres of land and to roads, bridges and other improvements. Sheet erosion is a problem on 25 million acres of land.

Topsoil washing from the farmland in the Upper Mississippi River Valley becomes sediment in the navigation channel of the river itself. About 8 million cubic yards of sediment must be dredged from the Upper Mississippi River annually at a cost of $2 million.

This amount of sediment is enough to cover the city of St. Louis to a depth of 1.4 inches.

Floodwaters damage 7.9 million acres of floodplain crop and pasture land each year. Damages to this land and to other agricultural property, urban areas, roads, and rural nonagricultural areas amount to $119 million annually.

Pollution of water by sediment, fertilizers, pulp and paper mill effluents, manure, pesticides, and herbicides can cause water problems for recreation, fish and wildlife, and municipal and industrial water supply development. Livestock numbers are expected to double in the Upper Mississippi River Valley by 2020 and fertilizer use is expected to increase more than threefold.

Excess water, or inadequate drainage, is a problem on 48.8 million acres of crop and pasture land in the basin. The wetness problem has been corrected on about 28.2 million acres, but 20.2 million acres still need drainage development to reach full production. Individual farmers or small groups of farmers acting collectively could treat 9.2 million acres of this land, but community action developments are needed to correct the problem on the remaining 11 million acres. There are 400,000 acres that are not practical to drain because of soil conditions or lack of adequate outlets.

In the forested areas of the basin, there have been numerous fires over the years, caused chiefly by debris burning. Until controlled by natural barriers, fires often spread unchecked because of carelessness, disinterest, or shortages of local fire control personnel.

In 1958, over 5 million acres were not receiving adequate fire protection.

Forest lands have been damaged where livestock are permitted to graze. Good forest land and good pasture cannot be found on the same ground at the same time. The trampling of livestock kills tree seedlings, packs forest soils, and reduces soil water holding capacity on nearly six million acres of forest land.

Since private owners control over 18 million acres of forest land, it is essential that they realize the importance of good forestry management.

What Has Been Done?

Although the Upper Mississippi River Valley has changed greatly since Marquette and Jolliet first explored this fertile land, it cannot be said that the valley has been plundered nor that only a vast wasteland remains.

Many far-sighted and dedicated men have worked diligently to conserve the basin's rich soil, keep the streams and lakes clear of sediment, and preserve and manage the forests.

Contributing to this effort has been the Soil and Water Conservation Districts that cover 97 percent of the agricultural land in the basin. Each district has a conservation program oriented to solve its local problems. Each uses a combination of local, state, and federal services in helping farmers with their individual conservation problems.

Rehabilitation and improvement of the forest land has been the charge of the various State Forestry Programs. Federal foresters cooperating with State agencies and private forest owners encourage better forest practices, for conservation and profit on the basin's 20 million acres of private forest land, secure protection of the forest land and critical watersheds against fire, insects, and diseases, and stimulate development and proper management of over 4 million acres of state, county, and community forests.

The Watershed Protection and Flood Prevention Act (Public Law 566), which was passed by Congress in 1954, provides a "partnership" approach by federal and state governments and local communities to deal with water resource problems.

The original purpose of the Act was to carry out works of improvement pertaining to soil and water conservation and flood prevention. However, the scope of the act has been greatly expanded and now includes assistance in nearly all water and land resource problems.

Some of these are provisions for assistance for recreation or fish and wildlife development; municipal or industrial water supply; and water-management measures such as those designed to reduce water pollution.

The upstream watershed protection and flood prevention activities of the Department of Agriculture are an integral part of the total soil and water conservation job. The job involves working with local organizations that sponsor watershed projects and with individual landowners and operators in watershed project areas.

As of January 1, 1967, 53 USDA watershed projects had been authorized for construction in the basin, primarily for flood prevention. These projects include 356 miles of channel improvement and 185 dams and reservoirs which can store 94,000 acre feet of floodwater and 20,300 acre feet of sediment.

These and associated conservation measures provide protection to 105,000 acres of upstream floodplain and reduce damage $1.1 million annually.

Twelve of these 53 projects include drainage as well as flood prevention. A total of 28 million acres have now been drained through local drainage districts and by individual farmers.

Ten of the projects include additional water storage and development of recreational areas. These recreational developments include 4200 surface acres of water and 16,900 acres of land for hiking trails, beaches, bathhouses, etc. They can provide 630,000 people with a day of recreation each year.

There are 48,000 farm ponds and other non-project reservoirs in the basin that can supply a million people with a day of recreation each year. There are 3800 acres of water project reservoirs that can supply an additional 80,000 people with a day of recreation.

The farm ponds and thousands of natural lakes and streams provide favorable habitat for beaver and muskrat and are also suitable for many species of fish. Farm ponds provide many opportunities for the production of bass, bluegill and channel catfish and, in some areas, trout.

The public has chosen to acquire forest ownerships in certain areas of the basin for the purpose of insuring a sustained timber production, protecting the quality of water supplies, providing wildlife habitat, or developing public outdoor recreational opportunities. These ownerships involve approximately 23 percent of the forest land area of the basin. They are managed as National Forests or State and County forests.

Small wildlife species found in forested or wooded areas include chipmunk, opossum, raccoon, porcupine, skunk, marten, and squirrel. The forests also provide habitat for bear and moose. The grasslands and forest land interspersed with cropland in the northern part of the basin provide habitat for prairie chicken and sharp-tailed grouse.

Deer are distributed throughout the basin and their numbers have increased in recent years.

Where Are We Heading?

The population of the United States is expected to increase from 200 to 460 million between 1967 and 2020. The basin's population is also expected to double.

This increase in population combined with rising incomes (5 times by 2020) can be expected to exert ever increasing pressures on the land and water resources of the Upper Mississippi River Basin. Increased demands for foreign and domestic exports are expected to exert further pressures for production of food and fiber in the basin.

These population and income projections have been translated into demands for food, feed, and fiber and needs for changes in the land use patterns of the basin.

These projections show that during the next 50 years, the demand for agriculture and forest products will increase as follows:

Fourfold for soybeans.

Somewhat less than fourfold for vegetables.

Greater than threefold for beef and veal.

Threefold for wheat.

Somewhat less than threefold for feed grains, milk and milk products.

Over twofold for pork.

Somewhat less than threefold for wood products.

Substantial technological improvements in production efficiency can be expected over the next several decades. Nevertheless, an increasing number of acres of land will be required to meet needs for production.

The demand for land for urban areas is expected to almost double. In 1960, 6 million acres were in urban and built-up areas; by 2020 this will be about 11 million acres.

By 2020, the pressure for land can be expected to increase to such an extent that water resource development projects will be essential in order to supply all of our needs.

The decline in availability of some wood products such as veneer has already caused financial difficulties in some wood industries and discouraged growth in others. The hardwood market previously held by the best grades of American hardwood timber is declining.

The increase in leisure time since the early 1940's together with increased income has moved recreation from a minor position to one of major importance for most of the basin's population. The present supply of recreational land is concentrated in approximately 11,000 recreational areas. Nearly 80 percent of the outdoor recreation activities are located in the major forest areas. A great demand exists for areas which would provide local hunting, fishing, camping, and hiking opportunities. Much of this area could be supplied by private landowners.

Landowners and others have been gradually accepting the concept and its application within the bounds of physical capabilities of land and water areas. These changes have come slowly. Restoration, conservation, treatment and wise use of the basin's water, soil, forest and grassland is a "real" concern. There is an underlying problem of individual indifference. It remains.

What Must Be Done?

One of the most important conclusions reached by the army of modern explorers is that a resource development plan is essential to make the most efficient use of the basin's water and land resources.

Watershed projects, which include flood prevention dams and land treatment measures, will provide water and recreation benefits for the population and offer opportunity to improve the quality of forest acreages. They can also provide better habitat for fish and wildlife.

The modern explorers identified 1189 potentially feasible watershed projects in the upstream areas which would conserve and develop the land and forest resources.

In most areas of the basin, resources can be developed to fulfill the water needs for recreation, fish and wildlife, rural community, municipal and industrial water supply, and water quality control. These water needs could be stored in flood prevention reservoirs, in single purpose dams and reservoirs, or in multiple-purpose dams.

Effective shifting of land uses and the adoption of better farming methods will be necessary in the years ahead for efficient use of the land base. Good land use will not only protect the land's ability to produce food, fiber, and the other basic resources for the present, but for the future as well.

A more effective pollution control program is needed to insure an adequate supply of uncontaminated water and to reduce the costs of treatment for municipal and industrial water supplies.

The management of areas, such as the National and State Forests, can be intensified and improved by additional public land purchase to unite present holdings. It would insure a continuing supply of wood fiber, quality water, wildlife habitat, and a source of outdoor recreation.

When Marquette and Jolliet made their explorations, they found wide variations in the quality of water in various parts of the river, in the soils along the banks, in the trees and other vegetation that sprang from the prairies and even in the Indian tribes they met along the way.

So too, the modern explorers found wide variety in the degrees of problems, from geographical and topographical differences to the personal differences of people using the land area. Recognizing these differences, they are aware that major resource planning cannot be done on an individualized basis for as large an area as the Upper Mississippi River Basin. So, their studies have provided a general over-all appraisal of local soil and water problems. These studies offer an inventory and discussion of these problems, and suggest means of alleviating many of them.

Conclusions and Recommendations

Each citizen in the Upper Mississippi River Valley—whether he be a farmer or city dweller, housewife or professional man, lawmaker or tax payer, youngster or senior citizen—has a responsibility concerning the future of the valley.

For some, such as teachers and the locally-elected Soil Conservation District Commissioners, the opportunities to influence the future of the valley are greater than for others. But no one can say that wise use and management of our natural resources has nothing to do with him—or his children—or his grandchildren.

The co-ordinators of the modern study of the Upper Mississippi River Basin offer these conclusions and recommendations:

1. Since watershed protection by land treatment measures is needed on 70 million acres in the basin, it is recommended that the application of watershed protection by land treatment measures be accelerated through the motivation of private landowners and that a goal be established calling for adequate land treatment of the entire basin by the year 2000.

2. Inasmuch as upstream watershed developments are an effective means of developing water and related land resources, it is recommended that project development be accelerated in the 1189 potential upstream watershed projects; and that provisions be made for federal assistance for water pollution control measures.

3. Since opportunities exist for reducing the cost of producing agricultural and forest products and for increasing output when required, it is recommended that more emphasis be placed on resource development programs.

4. Since the scattered pattern of public ownership within the boundaries of public forest areas causes serious land and water management problems, it is recommended that public ownership for multiple forest uses be increased rapidly within the boundaries of national, state and county forest areas, particularly where special situations exist, such as sites of unique or historic interest.

The Message Carriers

The spring following the great Marquette-Jolliet exploration of the Upper Mississippi River Valley, Louis Jolliet's canoe capsized in the turbulent waters of Lachine Rapids near Montreal. All of his maps, records and other reports of the expedition were lost.

Fortunately, Father Marquette's simple narration of the exploration was delivered by friendly Indians to his headquarters in Quebec, but this constitutes almost the entire stock of information concerning their expedition.

It seems apparent that our modern day explorers have completed an expedition that is even more important than Marquette's and Jolliet's.

But the modern explorers' message could well be lost in the turbulent currents of our busy world—just as Jolliet's was lost in the Lachine Rapids.

A more optimistic parallel can be drawn, however:

Just as Marquette depended on his friends, the Indians, to get his message through, the modern explorers are depending on such friends as conservationists, teachers, clergymen, lawmakers, students, farmers, and editors to spread their message throughout the valley.

You, too, can carry the message. It may help shape the history of the valley for years to come.

Less Peace Corps, More James Bond

John Rothchild

Most Americans, whether students, Peace Corps Volunteers, diplomats, or tourists, arrive in Latin America as equals. Our political knowledge and our Spanish proficiency may vary. But emotionally, we have all had fairly similar exposures to Cantinflas, Pancho Villa, Che Guevara, the immigrant elf-shoed pickpockets of the U. S. cities, and the fat Cisco Kid's Pancho. These are the characters that populate our emotional Latin America.

On the way home, we are no longer equals. Of all groups, the most likely to arrive back with a positive emotional attitude about what they have experienced are the tourists. After all, Latin America after 9 capital cities in 14 days can still be quaint and daring. Its frequent hot-blooded, irrational revolutions, as reflected in the eyes of an unshaven man who appears in a slyly-taken photograph, can still be exciting. An original drawing of a barefoot man walking down a dusty road with a donkey trailing behind bought from a genuine starving artist, is real enough to be almost like fiction. Memories of the frequent fiestas and siestas on humid afternoons will always fill the homeland coffee breaks.

On the other hand, for Peace Corps Volunteers who have been in country at least two years, understanding the culture more in many cases means loving it less. Like honeymooners in their second week, we learn that romantic qualities can quickly become maddening frivolities. Quaintness easily becomes dirtiness, hot-blooded men turn into children, and frequent restful parties are just lazy escapes.

Such distinctions between tourists and Peace Corps men are obvious to any Volunteer who has been visited in the host country capital by his untravelled mother. Anti-host culture emotions have to be dealt with by all of us, and some of us resolve the conflicts by ending up hating the foreigners, while most end up half compromising, arriving home with an image of the old Cisco Kid transposed lightly onto the recently abandoned counterpart. Most of us, to some degree, end up disliking in the real what we loved in the abstract.

From Peace Corps *Volunteer* (May 1969). Reprinted by permission.

The extensions of this observation are rarely treated in articles or analyses of the Peace Corps by its staff members. Most reps and staff, intent on investigating why the Peace Corps has not accomplished social change, physical or attitudinal, to the degree formerly hoped, do not often question the basic premise that may provide an answer to the secondary one. That basic premise is that personal communication, carried out in good faith, somehow leads to increased emotional closeness and understanding between peoples. It is not enough that the premise does not hold because a "dear John" letter is safer than a visit to the betrayed, or that a time clock is easier to accept than a nosy boss. More important, between societies, especially between those which have already built up well-defined images of their neighbors, images which are important to their own psychological security, it may be true that increased personal communication on a real level may be more painful than delightful, more harmful than good, more misunderstood than understood.

The Volunteer, for instance, often finds his greatest problem not in adapting to the host people, but in adapting to their perceptions of him. All of us who are somewhat like Lord Jim have a vested interest in escaping from the Great Mistake, in finding a brief respite from the World Movers and the Power Brokers back home. Most of us, conscious of our inequality with the world, want to enjoy, at least for 24 months, the myth that we can be equal with humanity. When a *campesino* called me "patron," I carefully explained to him that I did not want to be a *patron* (master). He gave me a painful look and then shrugged his shoulders and said: "Si, patron."

Continued questions about how much my camera costs, why Jackie married Onassis, whether the astronauts brought back the Hong Kong flu, or why I tried to find a comfortable mud hut instead of living in the richest apartment in Riobamba (which I could well afford), are the most painful. It is much easier to suffer poverty than to be told that I am unsuited to live in poverty because I am a rich man. My desire to pay for a two-year indulgence with discomfort, to identify with the powerless, is unattained. And only after this failure did I begin to criticize the society of my hosts, and return to my storybook images of "how things should be in Latin America."

Likewise, the semi-permanent arrival of a *gringo* into a Latin American town can be a most disquieting thing. After Kirk Douglas in the *Last Sundown*, Marlon Brando in *On the Waterfront*, the

Beatles on radio, and Jackie and the astronauts in the papers, seeing an ordinary *gringo* can be very disillusioning. A study has never been done on Volunteers' effectiveness as dependent on their physical size and beauty, and how they looked compared to movie stars; but in Ecuador, many of the Volunteers most successful in integrating themselves are not those who reject the role of the soft-spoken, physically indestructible Gringo God, but those who best conform to the image.

A good illustration of what people want to see in us (if only as a way of rejecting us) is in the images they themselves create of us. In Ecuador, this image has increasingly changed from the blurred incredulity to seeing us as threats: spies or imperialists in revolutionary clothing.

People here have a need to see us as CIA agents, just as we have a need to see them as in need of development. If we are CIA agents, then they will be reassured that there really is something about them worth spying on, and also that the beautiful, destructive world of the movies is really real. They also have a need to see us as imperialists. Then we can be blamed for their own "underdevelopment" and it can be explained why we are here, without having to refer to our painful (for them) altruism. They have a need to see us as elitists. If we are elitists, then by choosing to live here, we are bringing them into our elitism.

The idea that we are here to help is as distasteful as was Lyndon Johnson. Benevolence in Latin America always arrives on a Big White Horse, and the heroes, from Cortes to Kennedy, have always doled out graces from wistful myths like Quetzalcoatl or the Alliance for Progress. Kennedy was loved in Latin America, not primarily because he loved the poor, but because he was rich and beautiful, and secondarily worked for the poor. The idea of *caballero* (dashing gentleman) is central to the way of giving in Latin America.

If the Peace Corps has served any function here, it has been in perpetrating these myths, despite the fact that every Volunteer fights them in some way. Just as our dream of being accepted by the Third World as equals in humanity is shattered every day, and yet we still hold on to it tenaciously, so the movie-picture image of a *gringo* as *caballero* is also broken by the presence of a Volunteer. But the nationals here, like us, cling to the fiction because the idea of an American living as a poor man (Poor Like Me) is repugnant both to the aristocracy of the rich, who want to feel their society is already equal to that of the United States, and the aristocracy of the poor, who want to believe that there is nothing about their lives that should necessarily be changed.

In Ecuador, after six years of Peace Corps, the images seem to be getting stronger on both sides, and the "real understanding" is diminishing. It has been argued that with increased contact, our international rapport will be greater. In some places this may be true. Here, it may be the opposite: the more contact we have, the more misunderstanding and clash will erupt. Part of the problem is that the honeymoon is over. Part can be attributed to the short time we have been here. But staff is finding it harder and harder to communicate with national institutions, and the country itself is becoming every day more skeptical about our presence.

Such difficulties are not all new. The Peace Corps has always encountered problems in working with Ecuadorian institutions, which are often poorly funded and poorly managed, thus offending Volunteers who cannot accept inefficiency and ineffectiveness. However, lately there has also been a visible worsening of personal relationships between Volunteers and Ecuadorians, and the misrepresentations of our role here have become more rather than less widespread as our contact has increased. In the Sierra town of Ambato a group of businessmen and students have started a cafe, El Psiqué, where *gringos* are not welcome, as a reaction to the presence of American Volunteers in the other city cafes. In Quito and Guayaquil, the Peace Corps offices, once immune from the anti-American wrath of students, are now popular targets. During the last year the Quito office weathered a bomb-throwing, while in Guayaquil the secretary suffered severe acid burns after a student attack on the building.

On a less colorful level, day-to-day relations between nationals and Volunteers are being described in the same terms the Ecuadorians have always used to describe the stereotyped American diplomat. Volunteers were once the exception to such characterizations, but this is less true today. In the latest *El Ecuador,* the in-country Peace Corps magazine, an Ecuadorian law student characterizes Volunteers as cold, in-groupish, unwilling to mix with Ecuadorians, and disdainful, and concludes that therefore, we must be spies or at least here to accomplish some task other than friendship. Image problems have prompted the country's director, Joseph Haratani, to think in terms of publicity campaigns to improve our relations with Ecuadorians. As one Volunteer told me, "Once, the best thing an American could do to find acceptance was to say he was a Volunteer. I'm finding it difficult when asked the question, and I would be more comfortable by answering that I was a tourist."

On staff level, programming problems result not from a lack of good ideas, or of available Volunteers, but in finding institutions which can forge a cordial, workable entente with Volunteers, and vice versa. Many of the larger programs no longer work directly with Ecuadorian institutions, such as *campesino* leadership training and, in some instances, the heifer project—which distributes animals to farmers in various areas. Peace Corps officials usually point to CREA, a regional development organization, as the shining example of good Volunteer-host national relations, but even in CREA, criticisms of Volunteers as being clannish, unconcerned and disturbingly informal are just below the surface and are becoming more visible every day. A six-year relationship with Ecuador has not strengthened Volunteers' contact with Ecuadorian institutions and people, but has rather increased isolation in daily discourse, in Peace Corps programs, and in people's understanding of the Peace Corps program and its purposes.

One Volunteer in Santo Domingo (Ecuador), who worked here almost four years, had a long-time friend with whom he had had contact for his whole stay in Ecuador. A few days before he left, the friend asked him: "Tell me, what really is your purpose here?" Trying to be honest, the Volunteer said: "At times I don't even know." That convinced the long-time friend that the Volunteer was a member of some international spy network. The opportunities to understand were great, but the need to understand was something different. The Ecuadorian in many cases protects his need to understand the *gringo* as an imperialist spy.

It is hard to condemn this while the world continues to be a stage for our own domestic hang-ups. Only when we are worried about political amorality at home does Latin America's "problem" become seen in the same terms. When we are expanding economically (as in the post-War), the sister nations' problems become economic. And currently, while we are worried about how to get along together at home, we are working toward a non-directive methodology, toward mental and attitudinal change abroad. Our world is a stage, but the host country nationals are lousing up the acting.

After six years of an attempt at being friends, it sometimes seems that Ecuador would like less of the Peace Corps and more of James Bond. It is not just on the intellectual level, where such thinkers as Albert Memmi criticize the "left-wing colonists" and

Mon. Ivan Illich of Mexico asks that all American "do-gooders" get out of his country. On the level of the masses, Volunteers trying to shake the international world-mover syndrome have clashed with people who have tried valiantly to remind him of it. While we have not tried to wield power, the people have asked why the country which made it to the moon couldn't save their village. The Volunteer feels a lack of effectiveness. The people do not. They view the problem as a Volunteer's lack of interest (he is really a spy) or lack of drive (he is lazy, doesn't think we are worth it). Increasingly, the Peace Corps is called "Cuerpo de Paseo" (Vacation Corps).

These problems will not be solved by sending more technically-qualified people, or by changing recruiting or training. They may be solved by honest dialogue about our images of each other, and why they don't reach. But most likely, it will probably be that we and they will continue to protect and perfect the image we personally need, by isolating ourselves, by rejecting social realities, by disliking the people's attitudes. There is no doubt that we change in our view of the host country much more than they change their movie view of *gringos*. But for both Ecuadorians and Volunteers, the process of personal communication and contact is painful and often futile. To paraphrase a Bob Dylan idea: We do not let them live in their dream, and they do not let us live in ours.

The Usefulness of Scientists

Howard Reiss
Jack Balderston

Many research laboratories have been established by American industry in recent years, and many of these laboratories have failed within an average lifetime of five years. Such wasteful occurrences indicate a serious lack of understanding of the roles and missions of a research laboratory.

Not every business requires a research organization. Some can get along very well without one. But management ought to know, first of all, whether it needs research or not. And when it knows that it does need research, it should have an explicit and credible conception of what research ought to contribute to the business.

What is a laboratory for?

A scientific research laboratory within an industrial organization may serve a variety of functions. We will discuss just two of these in this article, but for the record let us list some of the others as well, beginning with the two functions that are most frequently mentioned in the literature of research management:

—Evolve and prove the feasibility of some application the company wishes to exploit.

—Solve scientific problems in support of engineering or development problems.

We want to emphasize that there are other functions of the research laboratory—functions which are advisory and service, for the purpose of improving the company's business position:

—Be a source of the latest in scientific information and techniques.

—Use combinations of scientific backgrounds to synthesize new technological capabilities.

(These two functions are the principal focus of this article.)

—Advise corporate management in planning for the technological future.

—Train selected scientists towards eventual technical managerial positions.

Reprinted by permission from *Science and Technology*. Copyright © 1966 by International Communications, Inc.

—Stimulate research in outside laboratories to the eventual benefit of the company.

Who should perform the advisory and service functions? In most industrial laboratories, these functions are performed by scientists whose professional interests are in areas of *applied* research. It is our belief that this is a mistake. We believe the advisory and service functions of an industrial research department are best performed by scientists who are "phenomena-oriented," rather than "applications-oriented."

What do we mean by this? What is the difference between an applied scientist and a "phenomena-oriented" scientist? It is a difference in professional goals. The applied scientist has as his ultimate goal the development of a device, a process, or a system. He may perform a great deal of research concerned with the elucidation of fundamental natural mechanisms in the course of his work, but it is necessary for him to keep his attention focused on the achievement of that ultimate goal. This is a full-time job requiring a great deal of creative synthesis. It cannot be pursued efficiently if the man must turn his attention from one problem to another in intermittent fashion.

The phenomena-oriented scientist, on the other hand, has as his goal the elucidation of natural phenomena. This is usually what is implied by the conventional use of the term "fundamental research," but we prefer to describe this scientist as "phenomena-oriented," rather than as a "fundamental scientist" or a "basic scientist," because the applied scientist may *also* do fundamental research or basic research. The difference between these men, then, is *not* that one does applied research while the other does fundamental research—since both may do fundamental research. The difference, as we said a moment ago, is that the applied scientist is seeking after a technological artifact while the phenomena-oriented scientist seeks the elucidation of natural phenomena.

And this important distinction leads us to the logic underlying our paradoxical-sounding thesis: The advisory and service functions of an industrial laboratory are best done by scientists who are phenomena-oriented. The research performed by these scientists may *never* yield results which are of business interest to the company. You do not have these people in your organization because you expect to apply the results of their research. You have them for their *expertness*, for their ability to perform the advisory and service functions. You support their research, not as an end in itself, but as a means of keeping them expert, by having them solve problems at the scientific frontiers.

In such a phenomena-oriented group, both the profit motives of the company and the professional interests of the scientists can be served. From the point of view of the scientist, he can have a great deal of research freedom within the domain of his field— since the results of his research are not expected to be of immediate use. From the company's viewpoint, it is establishing its goal by maintaining the man's expertness.

Phenomena-oriented research should never be viewed by the company as a reward, granted because a man has contributed in some way to the business objectives of the company. Rather, it is a planned part of the company's program and it is incumbent upon the individual scientist to maintain his expertness in this way. In an applied research group, there is little time for such training experience.

Monitoring the world of science

Let us look at two roles—at monitoring the world of science and at capability synthesis. You will see as our discussion unfolds that these are not research roles in the strict sense of the term, yet they may be very important, and we believe these roles are better performed in a department staffed by phenomena-oriented scientists than in one staffed by people whose principal interests lie in applications.

Companies always have need for advance warning of events occurring at the frontiers of the technologies on which their businesses are based. Such events may threaten a company, but warnings of such events will also offer the company new opportunities.

The accumulation of modern scientific knowledge grows exponentially with time. Insofar as technological innovation is concerned, the interval between the discovery and elucidation of a new scientific phenomenon and its technological exploitation has been reduced from years to months. Actually, this interval is now comparable to the period of time which elapses between the submission of a scientific paper to a journal and its subsequent publication. This means that a company frequently cannot wait for publication of new scientific information. To take advantage of new information, it must have means for learning of the event immediately. The company possessing a direct communication link with the source of discovery enjoys a concrete advantage.

Scientific information moves with great velocity through a grapevine which threads its way through various strata of the scientific community. We have all heard it said that there exists a society of scientific elite—as indeed there does. In fact, the scientific community, like society at large, is stratified into many classes, involving various degrees of the sub-elite. The key to early notice of scientific information involves membership in the society. The entrance requirements are not simple, particularly for the industrial scientist. Such requirements involve recognized scientific contribution; full knowledge of the mores of the members; association, both social and professional, with the inner circle; and even the ability to engage emotionally in what should be an objective scientific dispute.

Whatever the means of entrance to this community, it is clear that membership has practical value. And scientists from industry are infrequent members. To be accepted, the industrial scientist must be able to contribute as much as he receives. Generally, industrial "scientists" do not publish as significantly as their academic counterparts. Such people may be viewed by the elite as parasites.

But scientists from those few industrial laboratories which perform phenomena-oriented research with the same degree of excellence found at the better universities are in a different position. When they visit universities, these men are usually not regarded as visiting industrialists. They may be invited to present seminars. They are able to speak to students—and not as recruiters, but as professional people from whom the students can learn. At scientific meetings, such members of industrial laboratories play the same role as members of academia.

Putting information to work

The industrial enterprise must do more than *have access to* the latest events in the scientific world. It must do something with that information. It must use the information which is finally published in the scientific literature. But how does it interpret this material? Here again, the phenomena-oriented scientist is useful.

But why should not an applied scientist be as capable of interpreting the literature as the phenomena-oriented scientist? Are we implying that he isn't as "good" as the phenomena-oriented scientist? Not at all. In the best industrial laboratories, the applied scientists are just as able as the others. But the problem is this: the applied scientist, because of the nature of his function, must communicate not only with the world of fundamental science but also with the technological community. Also, he must devote much attention and time to his principal job—the reduction of natural phenomena to devices and systems. With these many demands upon him, it is hardly possible for him to give full attention to the voluminous literature. And for this reason he may not be able to fulfill this function as well as a member of the phenomena-oriented group.

The solid-state maser

An example will illustrate the scientific information function we have been discussing. The solid-state maser was first reduced to practice at Bell Telephone Laboratories. Its functioning is related to the nuclear magnetic-resonance phenomena associated with the nucleus of silicon-29. The theoretical principles underlying this device were first elucidated by Nicholas Bloembergen at Harvard University. Even during the formative stages of Bloembergen's theoretical considerations, several scientists at Bell Labs were in intimate professional communication with him. When his ideas were relatively complete and a paper was about to be published on the theory, Bloembergen welcomed George Feher's successful attempt (at Bell Labs) to produce an experimental maser. Feher accomplished this in almost record time and this application—although it involved a somewhat different phenomenon—played an important part in triggering the drive which culminated in the development of the optical maser.

The subsequent history of the optical maser program at Bell Labs deserves comment, because it illustrates several other points concerning the role of the phenomena-oriented research group. Although Bell had been interested in the optical maser from the outset, the first (even if only partial) reduction to practice took place at the Hughes Research Laboratories. Within days of the announcement of the Hughes accomplishment, Bell had mobilized such an effective research program that practically all further reduction to practice took place at Bell Labs. Furthermore, the bulk of the new science associated with the optical maser issued from Bell Labs. So completely did Bell blanket the field that if one reads the section on solid-state physics in the 1962 *Encyclopaedia Britannica Yearbook* one finds it stated that the optical maser was developed at Bell. There is no mention of Hughes at all! This was an unfortunate error on the part of the *Britannica,* but it shows how quickly a phenomena-oriented group, properly motivated, can climb onto a new problem and dominate it. Not all the people who were ultimately involved in Bell's program were working on masers when the program was started, but these people possessed the broad knowledge which enabled them to move in quickly and work effectively in this new field.

The example of the optical maser refers to the conduct of a large program. More frequently, the function of monitoring the world of science involves less dramatic situations. For example: A company has need for a material consisting of magnetic particles imbedded in a dielectric medium. These particles were to be distributed densely and each was to be small enough so that it encompassed but a single magnetic domain. Under these circumstances, one would be dealing with a super-paramagnetic material which could be alternately polarized in one or another direction at very high frequency (since domain wall movement was not involved).

At the time this need arose, one of the company's phenomena-oriented scientists was just returning from a visit to Northwestern, where he and Professor Morris Fine had spent an afternoon discussing scientific problems of mutual interest. In the course of that afternoon, Fine had mentioned that he and several students were engaged in a series of experiments concerning the mechanism of precipitation of one solid within another. Indeed, they had discovered a fine system for this purpose, involving a precipitate of iron oxide within magnesium oxide. Although the system was appropriate as a medium in which to study the scientific questions under consideration, no real technological use had been found. Fine went on to speculate that the system might find use in computer memories, because the precipitated particles were all single crystals, oriented in the same direction, distributed at very high densities but not in contact with one another. Further, both the size and number density of particles could be carefully controlled.

When the scientist returned to his company, he heard about the new material requirement—for magnetic particles imbedded in a dielectric medium—and he immediately thought of Fine's discovery. (Incidentally, the new requirement had nothing to do with computers.) He phoned Fine, got the recipe for preparing the precipitate, prepared some, and found it effective for the use at hand. And here we have an instance of the monitoring function wherein it is nothing more than an informal transmission of information between two scientists.

One further remark about the monitoring function: phenomena-oriented scientists should also serve as intermediaries communicating information and ideas among the various *technologies* of their companies. As an example, James McCalden of our phenomena-oriented group at North American Aviation was visiting our Propulsion Division one day. He saw a small ion engine, designed for propulsion in outer space, and he realized that he could use this engine to bombard a silicon crystal with cesium ions. When he experimented with the idea, it turned out that the cesium ions lodged in the crystal and proved to be electrically active in a manner that would be valuable for semiconductor-device applications. So an ion bombardment program was initiated —this time using a more sophisticated accelerator than an ion engine! And eventually the applications group also had a program.

Capability synthesis

Today's companies run the gamut of diversification with respect to technological commitment. At one extreme are those which specialize in one technology, or in a few technologies. Most small companies fit this description, as do many consumer-product firms. At the other extreme are those companies with commitments to an enormous number of technologies. The chances are your own company belongs in this second group. But with most companies, whether large or small, it is necessary to enter a new technology at least once during a lifetime. With some, especially the highly diversified companies, it is necessary to do this frequently. And when a company does decide to enter a new technology, it usually must mount a significant program quickly. How does it solve this difficult problem?

Perhaps it makes an attempt to hire experts in the new field. But this is an extremely time-consuming procedure. Further, if the field is one of the newer technologies, it may find that no such experts are available.

We believe the company's first step should be to determine precisely what that new technology *is*. What are the scientific disciplines that make it up? And here we need to think about the word *technology* itself: In its broadest sense, technology connotes a body of human skills aimed at accomplishing certain practical objectives. More specifically, a technology is composed of a limited number of building blocks—in much the same way as a word is constructed from a few letters of the alphabet. A particular body of skills *is* a technology because it is a combination of such building blocks, assembled for the purpose of achieving some practical end. The building blocks are the scientific disciplines—narrow, fairly homogeneous areas of science. In the matrix, we show

Thousands of Technologies from a Handful of Disciplines

some examples of both disciplines and technologies. The artist has pictured the technologies as appearing on an endless scroll, with only nine technologies appearing at a time. Taking any one of these technologies, we see those disciplines which make it up. With propulsion, for example, six of the disciplines shown here can be considered as contributing disciplines: thermodynamics, organic chemistry, mathematical analysis, kinetic theory, continuum mechanics, and spectroscopy.

Note that our definition of a discipline is somewhat different from the conventional. Usually, fields like chemistry, physics, and metallurgy are referred to as disciplines. But this scheme of classification is a bit too broad, so instead of looking upon all of chemistry as a single discipline, we divide chemistry into subcategories —such as electrochemistry, organic chemistry, and so on. The purpose of the matrix is to show the manner in which disciplines contribute to technologies. Actually, we could extend our list of technologies for pages and pages, since there are literally thousands of possible technologies—some dating back to the Middle Ages and some in the process of being formed this very minute. But the disciplines, on the other hand, number only a few dozen— some old and some new—and they reoccur again and again as the underlying structure of the technologies.

What has this to do with the phenomena-oriented scientist? Remember that we were talking about a company's entering a new technology, and how this difficult task can be accomplished quickly and effectively. The composite nature of any technology—based as it is on some few disciplines—can provide a means of accomplishing this task. And here is where the phenomena-oriented scientist enters the picture.

Let us assume that you must synthesize an effective, although temporary, technological capability. You accomplish this by bringing together phenomena-oriented experts in just those disciplines whch happen to compose that technology. Among its members, your task force of experts may possess so much of the basic knowledge of the technology in question that it will be able to draw abreast of the frontier with some mutual discussion and several days perusal of the literature. What the members of the task force do not know at the outset they can read, understand, and interpret in the course of a few days.

An example from our own experience: some time ago, stimulated by customer interest, our company became interested in the use of lasers in the transmission of enormous quantities of power. We had no people who were expert in the field of laser technology. But because the company had other technical capabilities, it was asked to propose on a conceptual study. Ultimately, the study would lead to a large systems program, so the company was anxious to present an outstanding proposal.

The company looked to the Science Center for help. (The Science Center is the home of our phenomena-oriented scientists.) But when the center first became aware of the problem, only one week remained before the proposal had to be submitted. And just as there were no laser experts in the corporate organization, there were none in the center either.

On a Saturday afternoon, a team was established involving four scientists—an expert in quantum mechanics, another in spectroscopy, another in solid-state physics, and a fourth in mechanical physics. These are the four disciplines underlying laser technology. On Sunday, the four scientists assembled in the library and spent the day reading and discussing a cross section of the literature. (At the time, the literature in the field was so sparse that a single day sufficed for self-education.) On Monday, they met with others from the company who represented other technologies—beyond laser technology—who were also involved in the forthcoming proposal. The next two days saw more discussion and the actual solution of problems. These were problems of pumping and the avoidance of spontaneous emission, problems of orienting the transmitting device, materials problems, and mathematical problems involved with the transport of energy along a laser rod.

Some of the problems solved that week were currently on the technological frontier. The scientists had overtaken the frontier in three days!

For example, the phenomenon known today as Q-spoiling (for the avoidance of inadvertent emission) was discussed on a theoretical basis. Eventually, this phenomenon was reduced to practice (by research people outside North American), but at the time of our discussion there was nothing available in the literature on Q-spoiling. Another problem concerned *super-radiance* associated with the transport of energy down a laser rod. Its mathematical aspects required the solution of certain nonlinear boundary value problems. Analytical solutions were actually accomplished and incorporated in our proposal. (Later, it turned out that North American was the only proposer to have solved this problem, though competing proposers did have experts in laser technology within their ranks.)

On the fourth day, the scientists and engineers began to write the proposal and by the fifth day, Thursday, it was completed in rough draft. It was ready for submission on Friday and on the following Tuesday we were notified that we had won the study contract.

Here, then, was an organization that started out with no experts in laser technology. One week later it could state with some confidence that it possessed a workable if not outstanding capability in this field.

More often than not, the special task force will be dissolved when the problem has been solved. This was the case with the laser-technology group, who simply went back to doing what they had been doing before. But the benefit of such an activity outlasts by far the brief period of the group's active work. Not only does the group map out the most fruitful path for future growth in a new technology; through its newly acquired knowledge of the literature and of the whereabouts of the experts, it can also assist in acquiring a permanent staff in the new technology.

There are times when the special task force is not dissolved, when the process of capability synthesis leads to the establishment of a permanent group, built around the phenomena-oriented scientists who made up the task force. For example, several years ago, at a time when semiconductor electronics had been well established, a communications company laboratory began to recognize that semiconductor circuitry was sensitive to the effects of radiation. The company had no experts in the technology surrounding the interaction of radiation with solids, but it did have a large and diverse staff of phenomena-oriented scientists. It induced a group of these people, including physicists and chemists expert in the field of atom movements and electrical properties, to turn their attention to radiation effects. As with the laser technology experts mentioned above, these people quickly educated themselves and soon were contributing to the relevant technology. But because of the importance of the field and the large number of significant phenomena-oriented problems within it, this group continued an independent and permanent existence.

The problem from out of nowhere

How frequently is a company likely to need this capability to synthesize a new technology? It is difficult to guess at frequency, even given the specifics of the company. Also, the specific questions to which a task group will address itself are seldom foreseen. More often it is a case of the problem that comes at you from out of nowhere. Nobody anticipated it. No individual can solve it. But you must have a solution next week.

This overstates the case just a bit. The need for monitoring the world of science predates this need for the synthesizing function. New technologies do not arise so fast, nor does a company find itself involved in new technologies so often that the need to synthesize capabilities occurs before the need to learn of discoveries in the world of science. However, it does not overstate the case to say that the two may occur almost simultaneously.

Does your company need these capabilities? Certainly if you have need for the synthesis function you have long since felt the need for people who are monitoring the world of science. (And conversely, if your company has no need to monitor the world of science it has no need for people who can perform the synthesis function.) Similarly, when a company's management considers the need to anticipate a synthesis requirement, it will already have recognized the necessity of employing phenomena-oriented scientists.

Let us suppose, then, that you are already performing the first of these functions. You are monitoring the world of science. You have a high-caliber, phenomena-oriented group and this is its principal task. What must you do if you wish to extend your capability, to include the synthesis function? We believe you will find that your group is already able to provide much of the coverage that capability synthesis will require. We are *not* suggesting that this can be done with just three or four outstanding individuals. When we say "phenomena-oriented group" we are thinking of perhaps two *dozen* outstanding people. Indeed, this number would constitute a small group. When the group is to perform both functions we have been discussing here—monitoring and capability synthesis—its size will likely range from 25 to 30 people on up to several dozen.

But there is one factor which tends to hold down the number of scientists you need to perform these functions in your organization. If you truly *have* phenomena-oriented research people, they will be able to work sequentially in several allied disciplines. A phenomena-oriented scientist is rarely a one-discipline man. Also —and this perhaps is the single most important thing of all about the phenomena-oriented scientist—he cannot be just a competent scientist, he must be an *outstanding* one. One does not have such people in an organization simply by instructing a dozen members of the staff: "Beginning tomorrow, we want you fellows to be phenomena-oriented."

We cannot overemphasize the importance of this—of seeking only outstanding people. Creative ability is distributed very unsymmetrically among human beings. The most creative scientist, by any one of several measures, may be a thousand times as creative as the least.

Within a phenomena-oriented group, the selection of which fields of science are of importance to the company—and hence which scientists should be on the company staff—is a choice which management must make. But the specific choice of *what* to research must be left to the scientists exclusively. Clearly, because the man himself is the expert in a particular discipline, and is trying to remain expert, he is the best judge of what problem will help him be so. Thus is the professional goal of the phenomena-oriented scientist achieved, while the company also satisfies its needs for monitoring and for synthesis. Does this suggest that management abdicates its authority? Not at all. There is *great* need for management direction in *motivating* the phenomena-oriented scientist to perform the advisory and service roles. But that is a subject unto itself.

The Sons of Martha

Richard McKenna

On that ship they did not have bunks and the sailors slept on brown canvas Army cots. In the tropics it was too hot to sleep in the crew's compartment amidships, so they set up their cots on the well decks. Every day at one o'clock they would go to the cot locker in the glory hole and bring up their cots and lay them, still folded, to claim a place. They all tried to find sheltered places, but there were not enough sheltered places to go around. The rule of the ship was that a place belonged to the man who got there first on that day. No man could know in the morning where he would sleep that night or whether or not he would be rained upon in his sleep.

In his first days aboard, Reed Kinburn did not try very hard for one of the sheltered places. He did not talk very much to anyone.

In Port Valdez it rained once or twice every night in gentle, wandering showers that sometimes fell upon one end of the ship and not upon the other. Green hills and darker green mangrove swamps ringed half of Port Valdez, with no buildings or any other sign of man visible. Kinburn liked that. The other half was a curving reef upon which the great Pacific swells broke all day and all night in a crested, tumbling line of white water athwart the blue vastness. The reef was a living thing of coral and on the darkest nights the line of breakers along it was still a ghostly white from living phosphorescence in the broken water. The rolling, washing sound of it came gentled by distance to be a part of all the sailors' talking and also of their silences.

In his first days Kinburn spent much time looking at the reef and at the calm water on the hither side of it. No other ship rode at anchor there. The water was blue shading into green dappled with lighter greens that became almost a milkiness where coral heads neared the surface. The color pattern changed constantly with the tides and sun angles but it was always a pattern and always beautiful. Beyond the reef were only and always the blue swells like titanic muscles working blindly, lifting and coming, endlessly from over the world's edge.

"You ought to see it in a typhoon sometime, kid," an older sailor told him once sardonically.

The ship was painted gray, or *war color,* as the sailors called it, in unconscious memory of a time long past when white had been *peace color.* The sides were waist-high steel bulwarks pierced here and there with hawse and scupper holes and square freeing ports with bars across them. There were no guns mounted anywhere about the decks. There was no strain and no pain and it was all somehow connected with the fact that she was station ship for the Navy island of Levanoa.

The island was larger and more populous than the solitude of Port Valdez seemed to indicate. During the lazy afternoons the ship's boats took liberty parties up a hidden channel to a village where there was a drinking place called Mama Lottie's. From there a road led to a much larger village where there were supposed to be several drinking places. Few of the sailors bothered to go ashore and Kinburn did not go at all, for a certain familiar old reason.

To him still the most special thing about the ship was that she was his first ship and that he had fallen in love with her name before he had ever seen her. As with all Navy supply ships, she was named after a star, and all those names were good ones, but *Stella Maris* had seemed to Kinburn the finest one of all from the first time he read it, typed opposite his name on a transfer list at Goat Island. He did not yet know what he thought about the ship herself.

The movie that night was Janet Gaynor in something very sentimental that made the sailors jeer at intervals. Kinburn watched it lying on his back on No. 4 cargo hatch, his head pillowed on his folded-up cot. After the movie he did not join the drift back to the poop deck. Instead he unfolded his cot and sat on it. He was fighting a small, familiar old battle with himself.

"Come on back and have a soda pop, Kinburn," Thorpe said, passing. "Evergreen's buying for the gang."

"No, thanks. Don't feel like one," Kinburn said.

On the poop deck light gleamed through the window of the ship's service store, which was always opened right after the movies. Inside, a swarthy little seaman was selling ice cream and soda pop and candy bars. The sailors moving by him, going back there, were still mostly without names or faces for Kinburn. They were just men in dungarees and Asiatic undershirts and tattoos and all knowing each other but not him. He knew only a few of them to speak to, Thorpe and Evergreen, and the big fireman Roach, who had been assigned to break him in to his fireroom duties. Kinburn had not reached out very far for friendship.

Some of the sailors in passing glanced curiously at Kinburn. He had come aboard all by himself rather than with a draft of other new men and word had spread from the ship's office that he had been a hospital apprentice before his rating was changed to fire-man third class. Both facts were enough to single him out sharply. They did not know yet where he would shake down to in their tight little universe. But all they saw when they glanced at him was a slender, wiry, brown-haired young man in regulation undershirt and dungarees sitting quietly on his cot. Nothing of the struggle within him showed on his smooth boy's face, unless it was a tense look of his mouth or the bunched muscle along the clean lines of his jaw.

He felt ashamed to have to fight himself over such a small thing as a candy bar. His rule was that he would have one every third night, and this was the third night, but the last time he had gone up there the devil of his yearning had overcome him and he had bought and eaten two candy bars. It was easy to slip. You could only buy with paper tickets which came in booklets, and the swarthy seaman had to tear them out of your book himself or they were no good. It was very easy in the sight and smell of it all to blurt out, "Make that two," and then be ashamed to counter-mand the order.

Voices and laughter came from the poop deck. *Gyp Joint,* the sailors called that shack, and *Gyp Joint* was the nickname of the swarthy sailor who ran it. "Hey, Gyp Joint, open up!" they would yell at him sometimes during the lazy afternoons. Finally the lights went out back there and Kinburn relaxed his jaw.

Men spread cots roundabout, rolled out bedding, and turned in. Kinburn thought on into the darkness, under the large stars. If only the *Stella Maris* did not have that gyp joint, he thought, it would be all right. It was far better than Mare Island, which was loaded with gyp joints and where you had to pay a dime to see the movies. Not yet had he escaped that thing which had always been an ache and later had become a shame to him as well. Once he had thought to escape at sixteen, when he became strong enough to do a man's work. Tomorrow he would be twenty, and he was very strong and enduring, but he still had not escaped. . . .

"Kinburn. That you, Kinburn?"

It was Roach. His thick fingers masked the beam of his flashlight.

"Something to tell you, Kinburn. Come below. I got the watch."

"What is it?"

"Come on down. There's coffee. I got some sugar."

They had to go through the engine room, down two ladders, and into a tunnel between the boilers. It was hot and steamy in the engine room. A clatter and groaning of pumps and the hum of the generator drowned out the sound of the reef. The fireroom was more open and clear of jumbled metal and the smell there was clean and sharp of fuel oil.

"Pour me a cup, too," Roach said. "I'll be right over."

The coffee was in an aluminum pitcher on the steel workbench. The cups were really thick white porcelain soup bowls from the crew's mess and they always had oily fingermarks on them. Kinburn stirred three spoons of sugar into his own coffee.

Roach was at the other end of the long, narrow space adjusting the fire in the middle furnace of the steaming boiler. A single furnace on one of the big boilers could make enough steam for port use. Roach was bent and squinting through the peephole while he jiggled the diffuser to make the flame as clean as he could. The three big Scotch boilers side by side looked to Kinburn like three huge and menacing faces. That was because their upper portions beetled forward to overhang the floor plates. Three cleanout doors on each one, painted aluminum, made two eyes and a longer, narrower nose beaking down between them. Beneath each door a circular furnace front, the middle one lower than those on either side, made an upward-curving mouth. To Kinburn it looked like the smirk on the face of a cannibal.

Roach came over and took his coffee. He was big and hearty, with coarse features and coarse black hair, and something was on his mind that he could not say easily.

"We clean firesides on number three tomorrow," he began. "You and me and Rothrock got to do it. Flangeface told me, right after the movies."

Kinburn nodded. Flangeface Hogan was the water tender first class in charge of the fireroom. He was an older man with a face very like the boiler faces and he seldom spoke. Kinburn feared and disliked him and he had vowed silently that he would never wait on Flangeface and bring him coffee, as the other firemen did. Yet Flangeface had never once spoken to him and hardly seemed to see him. Roach was watching Kinburn for a reaction. Kinburn did not reveal any.

"How far you been in school, did you say?" Roach asked.

"Finished high school."

"No college?"

"Me college? Hell, no!"

"What it takes down here in the stokehole is a strong back and a weak mind."

Roach was nodding approvingly, but they had been through that before. Something else was on Roach's mind.

"I hear scuttlebutt you just changed your rate over from hosapp," Roach said bluntly.

"That's right."

Hospital corpsmen learned early that ordinary sailors resented them. The sailors called them *pecker checkers* and *chancre mechanics* and pretended to doubt that they were really men. In the short time that he had been a common sailor himself Kinburn had already begun to sympathize with their attitude.

"I didn't change my rate," Kinburn said with difficulty. "They changed it for me."

"I didn't mean nothing, only wondering was it true. And how come they done it to you."

"Roosevelt done it, same time he cut the pay," Kinburn said. "He kicked the veterans out of Navy hospitals. Then all hosapps second had to change over to seaman or fireman or else take a special order discharge."

"You didn't want a discharge, huh?"

"Christ, no!" Kinburn slopped coffee and Roach laughed. "In Frisco I seen 'em sleeping in doorways and eating out of garbage cans," Kinburn said. "Roach, you guys out here just don't know."

"We hear. Guys get letters," Roach grinned. "We know, all right."

It made a sudden bond between them. They talked about the pay cut. It was really harder on the petty officers, Roach said. They lost all their longevity too, and 15 percent of their base pay was a bigger bite. Flangeface was losing $34 a month. But of course he still has $71 a month left. Kinburn was only losing $5.40 a month, but he felt a twinge of envy for Flangeface.

"Well, us third-class snipes still get our dollar a day," Roach said. "One day, one dollar, what the hell?" he shrugged.

"Dollar a day, jolly good pay, lucky to touch it—" Kinburn broke off the quote. "I just wish I did have a dollar a day," he finished bitterly.

"Got an allotment, huh?"

"Yeah."

He did not say how much, but when the first pay list was posted all hands would know that he had only $13 a month to keep himself decent in the world. He could no longer buy used clothing cheaply from sailors being medically surveyed, as he had done at Mare Island. On the other hand, in Port Valdez he did not have to fight the constant lure of liberty. He did not know yet how he was going to make out with it.

"Sometimes I help my old man out with a fin. I got a big brother on the railroad helps too," Roach said. "I don't believe in allotments. Once you start one, they say the paymaster won't let you stop it without you got permission from the other end."

"I ain't got an old man. All I got is a mother and some little brothers."

"Geez, that *is* tough!" Roach shook his head. "I heard about guys, their mothers wrote to their skippers, and their skippers ordered them to make out allotments."

"I seen it happen at Mare Island. For a fact."

"Maybe they'll open up rates next quarter. This guy Roosevelt—"

"He's the son of a bitch *closed* 'em!" Kinburn broke in. He scowled. Roach was scowling too.

"If they do open up rates, them college bastards will get 'em all," he said bitterly. "Them brain trusters down in the ice plant."

They poured themselves more coffee. Roach sighed deeply. "Well, hell!" he said. "Well, about firesides tomorrow. Come down in your oldest suit of whites and white hat. After tomorrow they won't be no good for anything else."

"Pretty dirty job, eh?"

"Hah! You got no idea! But it's more than the dirt and it's more than the work. It gets you another way the first time. That's what I wanted to tell you. You're kind of high-strung, I thought . . . well . . ."

"How do you mean?"

Roach screwed up his face in the effort to say it. "It gets inside of you and underneath of you someway," he said. "The first time I cleaned firesides I thought I was gonna die in there." He shook his head and grimaced. "Might be easier if you're braced for it. So I wanted to tell you."

"Well, thanks." Kinburn was wondering if it might not be a joke buildup, the way hospital corpsmen scared recruits with references to the square needle and the shot in the left testicle. He decided that it was not. "Well, thanks," he repeated. "I'll make out."

"Soon as we finish and clean up we always go over to Mama Lottie's and drink beer till midnight," Roach said. "It goes on Flangeface's bill, that's how he wants it. So we always work like hell. We try to get over there early and cost Flangeface all the beer we can, for making us clean firesides."

"I'll drink his beer," Kinburn said. He was finishing the last of his coffee, rolling it with his tongue, tasting the sugar. "Well, maybe I better go turn in," he said.

"First tell me how come you picked being a snipe instead of a deck ape."

"I had a chance to buy a dress white jumper for half a buck from a guy getting surveyed," Kinburn said. "It already had a red watch mark on it. So . . ." He shrugged and grinned.

Roach laughed heartily. "Tomorrow you gonna really gut-hate that guy for not having a blue watch mark," he said. "You gonna figure that half a dollar bought you the worst deal in your whole life."

"Listen, Roach. I want to tell *you* something," Kinburn said. "You don't have to believe it, but I want to tell you." Roach sobered. "I made out my allotment of my own free will," Kinburn said. "And twice before they changed my rate I put in myself to have it changed to seaman and they turned me down. I wanted to go to sea, to get the hell away from here."

"I believe you."

"Well, good night, then."

"Good night. Hope it don't rain.'

Kinburn ate breakfast in undress whites spotless and smoothly ironed, just as they had come last from the hospital laundry. He had cut the red-cross striker's badge off his sleeve, but much laundering had left two pink impressions of it stained indelibly into the fabric. He was not wearing underwear or socks, because he did not want to ruin any more clothing than he could help. Roach and Rothrock, at the same table, wore undress whites mottled yellow and brown and with dungaree-cloth patches on knees and elbows.

There was much joking talk about how rough it was cleaning firesides, none of it addressed directly to Kinburn, but he could feel their glances touch him. They were all watching him covertly except Flangeface Hogan, sitting at the head of the table.

Hogan was a big, dark, slow-moving man with absolutely no play of expression across his heavy face. His deep, slow voice seemed to come out of his barrel chest and there was never any tonal expression in it. He would probably announce that the ship was sinking in the same way that he asked for the salt. As always, he wore bleached dungarees and a blue-piped Asiatic undershirt and polished black shoes. Flangeface Hogan seemed not to know that Kinburn existed.

In the fireroom Roach was aloof again, as if the friendly talk of the night before had not taken place. The three fireside cleaners stood back against the workbench while the rest of the gang rigged a scaffold in front of No. 3 boiler. Some of them handed the rough, blackened planks down a trunked hatchway from the starboard bunker. Others took the small register doors off the three furnace fronts and pulled out the cone-shaped diffusers. Still others were unbolting the cleanout doors that overhung the furnace fronts. They worked with a jump and a drive unlike anything Kinburn had seen on the ship before. Skip Lea, the nervous little second class who straw-bossed the gang work, kept shouting at them.

"Higher! Pull them doors level, now!"

The cleanout doors were hinged at the top and they swung out like three canopies above the scaffold. They revealed vertical tube sheets, three solid arrays of two-inch tube ends, all clustery black with soot. A haze of dislodged soot seemed to hang in the air above the scaffold. In the clean distance beside the fuel-oil heaters Flangeface Hogan stood watching.

Skip Lea jumped up and down on the scaffold to test its solidity. He was a gingery, redheaded, sharp-featured little man in dungarees and he already had a powdering of soot on him. He jumped down with a clatter.

"Now, then, you firesiders! Over the top!" he yelled.

Roach and Rothrock jumped for the scaffold. Kinburn climbed up more slowly. Someone behind him said pensively, in a mock-cockney accent, "Eyen't it a shyme! Eyen't it a shyme!"

The center tube sheet had fallen to Kinburn. His array was longer than those on the sides, but not as wide, and it had the same number of tubes. The work itself was easy at first. Their brooms brought the soot down in soundless slithers and fine clouds that made Kinburn cough. The soot lay so lightly on his white jumper that he could blow a spot perfectly clean with his breath but wherever he touched it, however lightly, it would smear an inky black. The metal under the soot was a reddish-orange.

"That's corrosion, from the sulfuric acid," Rothrock told Kinburn. "You want to wire-brush good around them tube ends."

The corrosion came off in reddish dust. Kinburn finished his tube sheet at the same time as the others. He kept coughing.

Punching tubes was harder work. Each tube was furred thickly inside with soot and half-full of soot along the bottom. The tube brushes were larger than the tubes and had to be forced into them by pushing and turning to compress the springy coils. The brushes were mounted on heavy steel rods about ten feet long and they had to be pushed all the way through until they came out the other end, inside the combustion chamber, where the soot fell. It was very hard work pushing the brush in but it came back quite easily and came out with a puff of fine soot.

Kinburn found that he could not punch a tube as fast as the other two men. His brush would scrape along a few inches under a hard push, sending a vibration thrilling back to his hands through the steel rod. Roach and Rothrock sent their brushes through with long, easy-looking heaves and they had breath enough to spare for joking with each other past Kinburn working silently and with set teeth between them. They joked about how much beer they were going to drink on Flangeface. Under their turned-down white hats their faces were black with soot, as Kinburn knew his own must be. Rothrock's first name was Ezra, and Roach was making a joke of it.

"*Izz-rah!*" he would roar, grimacing his whole black face and baring all his teeth on the *Izz*, gaping his mouth cavernously on the *rah*. "*Izz-rah!*"

"All right, Cocky Roach. All right, Bugfeller," Rothrock would say. "Punch tubes, you ridge-runner!"

And they did punch tubes, drawing steadily ahead of Kinburn. He poured in all the strength he had, panting and coughing and feeling sweat trickle down his back and legs. It was no use. He had about thirty tubes to go when the others finished.

"Let's take a blow and have some coffee," Rothrock told Roach. "We can still sweep out combustion chambers before chow."

"Sure enough, we gonna make that three o'clock boat, *Izz-rah.*"

Kinburn drove himself on. When his arms became too heavy and numb he would let them hang and jerk and turn them until the feeling came back. As soon as he could close his fists all the way he would seize the rod and drive the brush with angry lunges through another two or three tubes. He saw Roach and Rothrock crawl into their respective furnaces through the small access holes. Then helpers pulled burlap sack after sack of soot out of those holes and took them away somewhere. The soot came right through the mesh of the burlap, each sack trailing a cloud, and the powdery soot haze filled the fireroom even to where Flangeface Hogan stood silently watching.

Kinburn was groggy and he almost fell when he climbed down at last from the scaffold. He took a drink of water from the bucket on the workbench. A scum of soot floated on the water. His hands were a shiny black. He blew his nose on a piece of cleaning rag and the stuff was jet black. Kinburn wished that he had not learned so much, as a hospital corpsman, about the structure of the human lung. He could not keep his mind off the thousandfold branching passages and the myriad tiny pockets where air touched blood.

"Take five," Skip Lea told him. "Have a cup of joe."

"No. I'm rested and I want to catch up," Kinburn said. "What do I do next, inside there?"

Lea squinted an eye. "*Maskee*, if you want to," he said. "I'll tell you what you do."

The furnace proper was a steel tube about thirty inches in diameter and eight feet long. It was shallowly corrugated, like a bellows tube, and the name for it was *corrugation*. Kinburn felt carbon grit and crunch beneath him as he crawled through it trailing the cord of a portable electric light. The outside men were pushing his other gear in behind him and he reached back for the broom.

A massively rounded steel collar made an orifice into the combustion chamber. Soot was banked high in there and spilling out into the corrugation. It would be thigh-deep.

It was so soft and light that he could not feel it with his fingers. He could not feel his feet sink in. It moved in a sluggish cloud rising that he could not feel. He thrust a wire-brush handle into one of the tube ends above his head and hung his light from it but the light did not illuminate anything. It did not reveal any form or outline. Blackness soaked up the light and did not let it come back. Very faintly he could see blobs and masses of soot hanging all around above him. His motions had stirred the soot and the tide was rising above his shoulders.

It had no substance. It was just blackness. It was just air stained black and choking, and the blackness was thicker at the bottom but it was rising to stop his breath and dim his eyes, and his heart was sledging away like a steam pump. Then a clear, certain little voice inside his head spoke with the authority of God Almighty:

Get out of here. Fast. Now.

His legs tried to obey but his arms fought it madly with the broom, swiping and thrusting with the broom, he choking and cursing in panic torn between them, and the blackness swirled about his face until his light was a lost red spark. Slithering, whispering, patting gently his face and hands, blackness descended upon him, and he bit his curses into its sour nothingness until his frantic broom swept light back into that place in reddish-brown walls and angles and rows of rivet heads that gave the light back to his clamoring eyes.

He dropped his broom. He was all right now. He knew what Roach had meant. His stomach rose up, and he retched and heaved. Nothing came up but a little sour water. It left him weak and shaky, but he knew that he was all right. He knew the blackness had reached and stained indelibly the least, last, tiniest, most hidden remote alveolar pocket within him. He had nothing left him to protect against the blackness, and he would be all right now.

He filled the sacks with a dustpan. The soot came right back out through the burlap, but something stayed inside to fill the sacks when he tied them shut, althought it had no weight. When the mess cook brought chow down to the firesiders Kinburn said he would wait until he finished filling sacks. He caught a glimpse of Roach and Rothrock eating at the workbench. They were absolutely black and exuberant as ever. Before Kinburn was ready to eat they had gone back in and he could hear the clink of their chipping hammers in the corrugations on either side of his own.

"Hand me the chow in," he told them outside. "I'll eat it in here."

Crouching awkwardly in there he wolfed the food, his black hands turning the bread black on its way to the blackness of his mouth. He wanted to save a few minutes on eating time.

He wire-brushed the combustion chamber in a driving fury, his ears sharp for the continuing hammer clinks of the other two. He brushed with his left hand when his right arm failed him, so that he would not lose time while resting it. When he started cleaning the corrugation at last, he could still hear the hammer clinks.

It was hard carbon rather than soot, and it was crusted rather loose and crumbly. A few strokes with his chipping hammer would break up a section and then his scraper could bite into it. He found a way both to press and to push with the heel of his left hand on the butt end of his file scraper, while he pulled with his right hand, and he could bring the carbon showering off in coarse flakes. Then a few vigorous strokes with the big wire brush would leave the surface a smooth, clean black. It was very awkward working in that cramped space, but the steady work noises from either side kept Kinburn feverishly at it. He was about three-quarters done with it when the noises stopped. Then he listened for the voices out there, gathering that Flangeface was inspecting the two wing furnaces. He heard a whoop from Roach.

"Okay, *Izz-rah!* Let's hit the beach!"

All the noises out there stopped. Kinburn tried to drive himself faster. When he had finished he swept the coarse stuff into a sack and dropped it outside without calling for someone to take it. He threw all his gear out clattering on the floor plates, all but his light, which he left gleaming on the clean, corrugated surface. Then he crawled out painfully himself and stood there panting. He was guessing it had been about twenty minutes since the others had gone up.

No one was in the fireroom except Skip Lea and the fireman on watch. Lea came up. He had a strange, quizzical look on his sharp features.

"Giving up, Kinburn?" he asked. "Had enough for today, have you?"

"I had enough, all right, but I ain't giving up," Kinburn said. "I'm through. It's clean in there."

"Make finish, hey?"

Lea sounded surprised and doubtful. He looked into the corrugation, then turned to face Kinburn with narrowed eyes. He was biting his upper lip.

"*Maskee,*" he said suddenly, after a moment. "I'll go get Flangeface."

Kinburn sat down wearily on the stacked planks from the dismantled scaffold. They were hard and splintery and black as the hand with which Kinburn caressed the top one. His mind wandered off to a thought of timbered hillsides and a sawmill he remembered, of moist white planks and the smell of fresh sawdust. Trees fell over and rotted back into the ground, he thought. But these planks were dry and black and hard and they could endure forever.

Skip Lea hit the floor plates with a bang and Flangeface Hogan came soberly behind him. He did not look at Kinburn and he scarcely more than glanced into the corrugation.

"It ain't clean," he told Lea.

That was all. He turned and walked ponderously away. Kinburn found himself standing with fists clenched and wanting to scream savagely at that broad back going away from him. But no words came and the back vanished and Kinburn rounded on Skip Lea, finding his voice at last.

"That son of a bitch!" he said. "Why ain't it clean? God damn it, you tell me why it ain't clean!"

Skip Lea looked uncomfortable. "You only got off the crusted stuff," he said. "That underneath is the real carbon, and all you done was polish it up with your wire brush." He could see that Kinburn did not believe him. "It's baked on there almost like paint," Lea said. "You got to chip and scrape it off like it was paint."

It was in his stomach and bowels that Kinburn could not believe it. He licked his lips, holding Lea's eye.

"It ain't going to end the world for nobody if you let the rest of it go till tomorrow," Skip Lea said. "If you had enough for today, just say so."

Kinburn was getting hold of it. Tight-lipped still, he pointed to the wing furnaces.

"Are them two all cleaned?" he asked tautly. "Is there more to do in them tomorrow?"

"No more cleaning."

"Then I'll finish mine."

"*Maskee*, if you want to." Skip Lea shrugged. "You can quit whenever you figure you had enough."

He had to fight for every square inch of dull gray metal cleaned of carbon. He had poured out his strength too lavishly too early and he had none left for this hardest part of it. It was too narrow in there to sit upright and he could not work his arms properly when he was flat. He had constantly to brace himself in some awkward position and to straighten his legs convulsively when a cramp took the muscles. His knees and elbows hurt him. He could see a score of places where on the first cleaning his hammer had broken through to true metal, and he could not understand why he had not seen it then.

Recurrently the conviction came that he could not go on and it always blurred over into hatred for Flangeface Hogan. There was no decency or feeling or fairness in Flangeface Hogan. He was some kind of mute, brute animal with arms like human thighs and a hump of muscle on the back of his neck.

The tube was like a steel bellows, successive hollows and humps ringing him round, with nowhere a flat surface. Each blow of his chipping hammer powdered carbon away only along the narrow line of impact. He beat out a narrow line from one hollow up the gentle slope and down into the next hollow. Four inches away he beat out a parallel line. Then he joined their ends with beaten gray lines like streams along the valleys and he had a four-inch square blocked out. It did not seem very big. He rough-chipped the square and cleaned it off with the scraper. The clean gray metal looked won and set apart and good to him. He started another line parallel to its edge and four inches away.

The squares end to end followed the gentle hill up the side of the corrugation and across the top, the most difficult portion. Each square in itself was not a hard job. Isolating a portion of the carbon weakened its power to discourage him. When Kinburn finished the first half of the hill the second half seemed to go easier, as if the clean gray surface wanted now to meet itself around the circle, to close the black gap separating its ends.

Twenty-four of the squares cleared one hill around the circuit. Twenty-four hills comprised the whole corrugation. It began to seem humanly possible. He broke new ground on the next hill. Then Skip Lea called in.

"Four o'clock, Kinburn. Time to knock off."

"I got a little patch to finish," Kinburn said.

He meant to finish only the square he was on, but a few more squares would finish the hill and he went on with it. When the hill was finished he thought for a moment and then began another one.

Homesteads, he discovered a part of his mind had been calling those squares for some time now. He encouraged the fantasy to emerge and he was people taking land. He was explorers blazing trails and mapping out townships. He was people moving in to cut down trees, get out stumps and boulders, fence and plow and plant and harvest the land won from wilderness. It was a pleasant fantasy and he was just getting it well begun when the fireman on watch called in.

"Kinburn, your chow's down here for you."

"Set it on the workbench," Kinburn told him. "I'll be out in a minute."

"Knock off, for God's sake!" Skip Lea's voice came in. "You done more'n a day's work now."

"In a minute. I got a little patch I want to finish."

He resented the interruption to his land clearing. He wished he knew more about that, how you drained a swamp and built a log house and a rail fence. He was not tired any more. He did not have to experiment to find a workable position. The steady pace took him round and round without cramps. He felt the pain in his knees and elbows, but it did not hurt him. It was like chopping the tree that last summer at home. Somewhere along the way, he half-remembered and half-experienced. Flangeface was calling, had called in. "Knock off, Kinburn." *I ain't finished.* "Come out now! That's an order!" *Go to hell.* He did not break for a moment the rhythm of his hammer.

The land clearing began to sink below the surface of his mind again, although it went right on and from time to time would break through. Memories of his hospital life began to play across the surface of his mind like movies on a screen. They were all whiteness, white surgical gowns, starched and rustling nurses, white tile and porcelain dressing rooms, white-enameled diet kitchens, white trash buckets, with white lids and a white trash of gauze inside them. The corpsman put in long hours but they did not really work, although they thought they did. They did not even have the idea of work. They could not imagine it. They were soft and fat and white like slugs and they thought that made them better than other people. What they did in the world was to mix themselves into and measure themselves against the pain and weakness and death of other men. Pain, weakness, and death were all of a whiteness. Reed Kinburn had said goodbye to all that. Health, strength, and work were all of a blackness. He knew himself black and proud and a man.

Almost with regret he saw that he was finishing. He squeezed out head first and stood up there, swaying slightly. The popeyed fireman named Dallas had the watch. He came hesitantly toward Kinburn.

"Flangeface is waiting up," he said. "I'll go tell him."

Kinburn nodded. He did not have to wait for Flangeface Hogan. A reaction was trying to flood him. He went slowly up the ladder holding to the thought that he was black and proud and done with that job. He was black and proud and weary almost to death.

The ship was asleep. He was alone in the brightly lighted wash-room. It was large and square and all white enamel paint and white tile deck with mirrors along one side above the white vitreous lavatories. On the other side the showers sprayed right out from the bulkhead, with no partitions or curtains to make a shadow from the white glare. Standing naked in the middle of the room Kinburn began feeling himself to be a shadow without anything to cast it.

He was absolutely black. Under his foreskin he was black. The skin was off his knees and elbows and the raw flesh there was more black than red. He felt almost reluctant and curiously un-certain about how to begin cleaning himself. A seaman, the quarter-deck messenger, came in and whistled.

"Sure glad I ain't a snipe," he said.

"Most of you deck apes ain't man enough to be a snipe," Kinburn told him, without anger.

The sluicing shower sent black water across the white tile. The soap lathered black on his arms and chest and when he rinsed it off he was as black as ever. The tide of reaction was flooding him. He lathered and scrubbed fiercely, until his cake of soap was worn thin, and his skin was still dark gray. Six times he lathered and scrubbed his left forearm, scraping with his fingernails until he drew blood, and his forearm remained dark gray.

The reaction became very strong and bad. His cake of soap was gone and he did not know how he could get another one. He began cursing softly to himself, almost in a whimper.

Flangeface Hogan came into the washroom.

He was smudged and streaked with soot from having been inside the furnace. He bulked in the doorway and his massive face was as expressionless as the face on a boiler front. Kinburn met his eyes.

"Cleanest corrugation I ever saw in my life," Flangeface rumbled.

"Loan me a bar of soap, until I can buy some tomorrow," Kinburn said.

Flangeface whirled and went out, moving fast. Very shortly he was back with a bucket and a new bar of Lifebuoy soap. He filled the bucket and bubbled steam through the water to heat it and set it in one of the lavatories. All the while he talked.

"Shower's no good for soot. You got to have a bucket. Bucket and soap and loofah sponge. Here, I'll show you. Turn around. I'll scrub your back."

The loofah sponge grated pleasantly across Kinburn's shoulders. Loofah sponges were some kind of dried vegetable skeleton used to filter grease out of the feed water in the hot well down below. Water made them swell up. While he scrubbed Flangeface kept talking in his grating rumble.

"Cleaning firesides . . . way to try out a new fireman, see how much he can take . . . you was cleaning the thousand-hour furnace, only you didn't know it."

Whenever a boiler had a thousand steaming hours, Kinburn gathered, they cleaned firesides. All the furnaces were lit off when the ship was under way but only the center furnace was used in port. When the middle furnace had a thousand hours the wing furnaces might have only two or three hundred hours. The center furnace was always by far the worst to clean.

"You done three men's work today . . . never seen a new man make it past five o'clock before," Flangeface rumbled on. "From the start I figured you was going to. You was outworking both them other dunnigans punching tubes and everybody down there knew it except you."

So Flangeface checked Kinburn's reaction and turned it back to pride. It was more than words or any expression in his face or voice. It was a strong, warm feeling that emanated from him without meditation. Kinburn looked at his back in the mirror and it was still a dingy gray.

The rest has just got to wear off," Flangeface said. He handed Kinburn the loofah sponge. "Use the same water," he said, pointing to the black suds. "They ain't wore out, just because they're black. The blacker the suds, the better they work."

Kinburn scrubbed himself. Flangeface stood there, talked out but radiating warmth and approval like a boiler front. Now and then he found a few more words.

"Your cot's set up on No. 3 hatch. Sleep as late as you want in the morning. I'll tell the sheriff . . . Take tomorrow off. Get them knees fixed up in the sick bay . . .

"Go ashore soon as you feel like it. Mama Lottie will know the beer is on me as soon as she sees your eyes."

When he knew for sure that Kinburn was all right, Flangeface said good night and went out. Kinburn finished scrubbing. He was not white. He had midnight rings around his eyes, knees, and elbows because he could not scrub right up into them. But he felt clean and he liked the clean, carbolic smell of himself. The last thing he did in there was to put his black uniform to soak in the bucket of strong black suds.

Stretched out on his cot, he felt the pleasure of rest to the very center of his bones. He thought it was the most voluptuous feeling he had ever experienced. No. 3 hatch was beneath the forward overhang of the prom deck, which the sailors called the *front porch,* and it was the most sheltered sleeping place on the main deck.

Hearing the reef, he drifted toward sleep and discovered that the underneath of his mind was still scraping carbon in the corrugation. Lazily he sought through his feeling for the familiar bitterness that usually attended upon his sleep. It was not there.

INDEX

Abstract terms (*see* Connotation)
Activate, speech to, 143–45
Advertising (*see* Propaganda)
Analysis, using comparison and contrast, 85–86
Arbitrary relationships, 37
Assumption, 47–51
Audience response, 127
Averages:
  arithmetical, 53
  mean, 53
  median, 53
  mode, 53

Bifurcation (*see* Propaganda)
Bodily action, 126–28

Carroll, Lewis, *quoted*, 35
Cause and effect, 93–94
Chronological order, 92–93
Coherence (*see* Rewriting and proofreading)
Comparison, in paragraph development, 84–87
Conclusions, in speeches, 124–26
Concrete words, 38–40
Confidence, in speaking, 113–14
Connotation, 38–42
Continuing action step (*see* Informative speech, conclusion)
Contrasts, in paragraph development, 84–87
Controlling idea, 75–79
  in limiting subject matter, 76–77

Deductive reasoning, 139–41
Definition, as paragraph development, 91–92
Denotation, 38–40
Details, in paragraph development, 81–84
Distortion, 52–61
  by graphs, 55–56
  by omission, 57–60

Distortion—*cont.*
  polls, 56–57
  statistics, 52–57
  by stereotyping, 61

Enthymeme, 140
Evaluation forms:
  informative speech, 136
  group discussion, 159
  persuasive speech, 146
Eye contact (*see* Bodily action)

Fact, 63–65
Favorable response, 38–39

Gestures (*see* Bodily action)
Generalities (*see* Propaganda)
Graphs, used in distortion, 55–56
Group discussions, 147–59
  elements of, 149–50
  leader, 150
  learning discussions, 147–48
  panel, 147, 148–49
  problem-solving, 148, 150–58

Illustration, used in paragraph development, 87–89
Impromptu speaking, 114–17
  defined, 116
  self starters, 117
Inductive reasoning, 138–39
Inference, 47–51
Informative speech, 131–35
  body of, 132–34
  conclusion of, 134–35
  defined, 131
  introduction to, 131–32
Introductions, speech, 122–24
  humorous, 123
  question, 123
  quotation, 124
  narrative, 123–24
Invectives (*see* Propaganda)

Judgment, 63–65

Leader, of discussion, 150
Learning discussions, 147–48
Lee, Irving J., *quoted,* 37
Lippmann, Walter, *quoted,* 45
Logic (*see* Persuasive speech)

Melville, Herman, *quoted,* 82–83

Negative response, 38–40
Neutralize, speech to, 144–45
Neutral words (*see* Connotation
    and denotation)
Nixon, Richard M., *quoted,* 142–43
Note cards, used in speeches,
    119–21

Observation, 43–47
    mental, 45
    visual, 45
Observed facts, verification of, 50
Omission, used in distortion, 57–61
Outlines, 95–101
    procedures, 100
    samples of, 98–100
    sentence outline, 99–100
    topic outline, 98–99

Panel discussions, 147, 148–49
Perception, 43–47
Persuasive speech, 137–46
    forms of, 143–45
    logical appeal, 138–41
    personal appeal, 141–43
    psychological appeal, 141
Positive response, 38–40
Posture (*see* Bodily action)
Premise, 140
Problem-solving discussion:
    actual discussion, 155–56
    case study, 150–58
    determining issues, 152–54
    examples of, 148
    participants, 151–52
    preparation, 154–55
    selection of problem, 150–51
    solution, 156–58
Pronoun, agreement (*see* Rewriting
    and proofreading)

Proofreading (*see* Rewriting and
    proofreading)
Propaganda, 66–72
    association, 67–68
    bandwagon, 69
    bifurcation, 69–70
    generalities, 71
    indentification, 68–69
    invectives (name-calling), 71–72
    testimonial, 70
    used in advertising, 66–72
Punctuation (*see* Rewriting and
    proofreading)

Reasons, use of in paragraph de-
    velopment, 89–91
Rehearsal, steps in, 121–22
Reinforce, speech to, 143–45
Rewriting and proofreading, 103–9
    coherence, 103–5
    pronoun agreement, 108–9
    punctuation, 106–7
    verb forms, 107–8
    wordiness, 105–6
Roosevelt, F. D., *quoted,* 138–39

Sentence outline, 99–100
Silone, Ignazio, *quoted,* 37
Statistics, used in distortion, 52–57
Stereotyping, 61
Substitution (*see* Connotation and
    denotation)
Summary (*see* Conclusion)
Supportive materials, 77–79
Syllogism, 140

Topic, narrowing and limiting of,
    77–79
Topic outline, 98–99
Topic sentence, 75–79

Unfavorable response, 38–39

Verb forms (*see* Rewriting and
    proofreading)

Wordiness (*see* Rewriting and
    proofreading)